D1252125

SILENT BATTLE

Silent Battle

Canadian Prisoners of War in Germany 1914–1919

Desmond Morton

Lester Publishing Limited

 Lester Publishing Limited acknowledges the financial assistance of the Canada Council and the Ontario Arts Council.

Canadian Cataloguing in Publication Data

Morton, Desmond, 1937–
Silent battle : Canadian prisoners of war in Germany, 1914–1919

ISBN 1-895555-17-5

1. World War, 1914–1919 - Prisoners and prisons, German. 2. Prisoners of war - Canada. 3. Prisoners of war - Germany. I. Title.

D627.G3M67 1992 940.4'7243 C92-094236-9

Text and jacket design: Counterpunch/David Vereschagin

Lester Publishing Limited
56 The Esplanade
Toronto, Ontario
M5E 1A7

Printed and bound in Canada

92 93 94 95 5 4 3 2 1

To the memory of Jan,
who would have made this a better book had she lived

Contents

Introduction

VETERANS WITH CLAIMS ON THE GOVERNMENT USUALLY INSIST that they are the "forgotten men" of Dieppe, Hong Kong, or the Korean War. Given the chronic historical amnesia of Canadians, chances are good that the claimants *have* been forgotten, though anyone with reasonable library skills could easily refresh his or her memory. That is not true of the 3,842 Canadians who languished in German prison camps in the First World War. Only fragments of their plight sometimes appear in first-person reminiscences of the war, and bibliophiles can discover occasional crumbling books by ex-prisoners, which can legitimately be dismissed as war propaganda.[1]

In 1931–32, former prisoners emerged to present claims of maltreatment to a royal commission distributing German reparations. But most Canadians, including the commissioner, Mr. Justice Errol M. McDougall, were more preoccupied by the ravages of the Great Depression. The gruesome catalogue of torture, beatings, starvation, and medical neglect, presented in drafty little hotel meeting rooms, made little impact on McDougall and none at all on other Canadians. The war was over. A few more unemployed veterans were simply taking another bite at the public purse.[2]

Canada's war prisoners posed a problem for those who took pride in this country's military achievements during the First World War and who wanted that pride to remain unadulterated. In their official histories of the Canadian Expeditionary Force, encyclopedic in their scope, neither Colonel A. F. Duguid nor Colonel G. W. L. Nicholson made any significant reference to prisoners of war.[3] Prisoners were a flaw in the heroic myth of men fighting to the death rather than surrendering. In her popular history of the overseas work of the Canadian Red Cross, Mary Macleod Moore insisted that no Canadian ever surrendered until he had been wounded.[4] That was, of course, nonsense, and no one with war experience would believe otherwise, but it was characteristic of patriotic expectations.

Other Canadians wanted hateful memories of the war buried. In an early manifestation of an almost quintessential Canadian response, victorious soldiers became villains and an enemy had to become a friend—in the ironic words of a contemporary comic song, "Let's Not Be Beastly to the Boche." Still other Canadians concluded that prisoners of war had nothing to be proud of and, if they had suffered for defying their captors, they had largely been the authors of their own misfortune or they had exaggerated their ordeal. However, a prisoner cited with apparent approval by the reparations commissioner confessed: "I did not look for trouble. I saw enough of it."[5]

Why not leave it there? For a start, there is a legitimate fascination with stubborn endurance in the face of terrible adversity. Writing of the British prisoners who shared the same grim experiences, Michael Moynihan recognized "a new concept of courage":

> Far from the spotlight of the fighting front, the silent battles being waged in these drab backwaters of war were against degradation and despair, physical collapse and mental stagnation. They were battles in which the chief enemy could be oneself, and with which we may more readily identify than with those much-documented battles long ago waged with bullet and bayonet.[6]

Secondly, Canadians are entitled to know their own history. People who bury their history for convenience or to avoid embarrassment pay a price. Because Canadians forgot their prisoners from the First World War, they could not recognize that the vast slave army that underpinned the Third Reich had its precedents in the "peatbog soldiers" at Vehnenmoor or the brutalized labourers of the K-47 coalmine. Canadians captured at Hong Kong and Dieppe had a harder time explaining the long-term consequences of their ordeal because no one cared to recall that thousands of earlier prisoners had also known starvation oedemas, "barbed-wire disease," and the fear of an unpredictable but imminent beating. The symptoms the reparations commissioner set aside as the routine effects of aging were those that prisoners of Japan and Germany would know in their turn between 1941 and 1945.

THIS STUDY OF CANADIAN PRISONERS IN THE 1914–18 WAR grew out of a fascination with the experiences of all the 610,000 men and women who enlisted in the Canadian Expeditionary Force. Other historians, thank goodness, have generously left intriguing gaps to be explored. My partner in this adventure, as so often before, has been Barbara Wilson of the National Archives of Canada. Her unrivalled knowledge of the CEF and its records is an unrecognized national treasure. Karen Woloshanski of the National Personnel Record Centre has been a patient guardian of the Privacy Act and has been as generously cooperative as the law allows. Stephen Brown, a young scholar with a brilliant knack of coaxing German archives to yield their secrets, has done his best to give this work a perspective from "the other side of the hill."[7] Gratitude is due for the assistance of the German Federal Archives at Stuttgart and the Bundeswehr's Historical Archives at Freiberg. Like others in the field, I was also the grateful guest of Mr. Roderick Suddaby, Keeper of Records at the Imperial War Museum in London.

As readers will soon discover, the human detail of this story would be missing without the wisdom of the dominion archivist, Sir

Arthur Doughty who, as historical recorder overseas, preserved the interviews with former prisoners and escapers, and Errol McDougall, whose systematic mind preserved details others might have ignored. There is always good reason to be sceptical of reminiscences compiled for potential material gain more than a decade after the event and all one can say in defence is that McDougall was as tough a judge as any academic critic would wish to face. I have also been dependent on the contemporary work of the American neutral observer, Dr. Daniel J. McCarthy of the Faculty of Medicine at the University of Pennsylvania. Critics will note, of course, that by the time his book appeared, neither the United States nor Dr. McCarthy was neutral.[8]

As usual, my students and colleagues have been patient guinea-pigs for my theories and discoveries. Their insights and criticism have improved the resulting book without, for a moment, relieving the author of responsibility for the errors and misjudgements that remain.

1

Prisoners and Covenants

As the throngs poured into Burlington House from London's mid-winter gloom, they found much to see. Lord Beaverbrook—still better known as Max Aitken, the gnome-like newspaper proprietor from New Brunswick—had hired the best artists he could find from Britain and Canada to work at his expense for the Canadian War Record Office. The work of Augustus Johns, C. R. Nevinson, C. Day Lewis, Maurice Cullen, and Alfred Bastien spread across the walls of the Royal Academy's gallery, an astonishing mixture of traditional battle art and of vorticist abstractions.

Yet no eye could avoid what Beaverbrook's own paper, the *Daily Express*, described as "the ghastliest thing in these rooms."[1] It was a bronze frieze depicting a soldier, arms outstretched on a great door and hands nailed to the wood by bayonets, left to hang. Beneath, a small cluster of German soldiers drank, threw dice, and mocked the soldier's agony.

Few visitors needed to be told the story. Some had read it four years earlier in the *London Times* on May 10, 1915. During the terrible Second Battle of Ypres in April of that year, counter-attacking troops had discovered the body of a Canadian soldier, crucified on a Belgian barn door. German bayonets, jabbed through his hands and into his neck, left no doubt about the culprits. The story spread, growing a little as it inevitably would. Some insisted that the man's eyes had been gouged out, others claimed that he wore a barbed-wire crown. On May 19, barely a week after the *Times* report, Private Frank Maheux of the Second Canadian Contingent, still stationed in England, reported to his wife that it was six Canadians who had been captured. When the ground was retaken, they found them all "nailed with a baynette in each hand to the barn and it was marked in English that show you Canadians to stop in Canada. . . ."[2] By 1917, Harold Peat insisted in his popular memoirs, no fewer than three sergeants had been crucified—and he had seen one of the bodies.[3]

It was a remarkably useful story. In a Christian age, a Hunnish enemy had proved capable of mocking Christ's own agony on the cross. Commanders welcomed this savage warning to soldiers who might, in terror or war-weariness, consider surrendering. Canadians, in particular, now had an appalling atrocity to avenge and if the report encouraged them to take no prisoners perhaps that was a valid means of transforming the casual colonials into ruthless fighters. Private William Gosford of the 5th Western Cavalry learned that, after a stretch of trench was recaptured, a comrade had been found with "large nails through the palms of his hands. . . . The next time we were in combat, our officer told us to take no prisoners, 'shoot the bastards or bayonet them.'"[4] A British sculptor decided to make his own powerful statement about the savage act. Derwent Wood, too old for the trenches, had volunteered to make face masks for soldiers whose features had been destroyed by wounds. Now his hands shaped a work he called *Canada's Golgotha.* Aitken accepted it with the delight of a true showman.[5]

There was only one niggling problem. Was the story of the crucifixion true? Had Canada's best-known prisoner of war ever existed? On November 11, 1918, after the Burlington House exhibition was scheduled and before it could open, the war in Europe had ended. The well-publicized contribution by Canadians to an unexpectedly early victory made Beaverbrook's show even more opportune. The horror of Wood's sculpture was timely too, as it fed the crusade by

Beaverbook's fellow publisher, Lord Northcliffe, to hang the kaiser and squeeze Germany "until the pips squeak."

Well aware of the bronze frieze and its likely impact, the German foreign office demanded evidence of the crucifixion.[6] Sir Edward Kemp, minister of the Overseas Military Forces of Canada, was eager to oblige. What everyone knew should have been easy to prove, but was a little harder than expected. Most survivors of Ypres in 1915 were dead, wounded, or long since back in Canada. Arthur Meighen, Kemp's cabinet colleague, had a letter outlining the story from a respected soldier from Manitoba, but, when pressed, he could not produce it. Eyewitnesses turned out, on inquiry, to have heard the story from unimpeachable sources who, on further inquiry, had also heard it second-hand. In March, however, Canadian efforts were finally rewarded by formal statements from a British soldier of highly respectable ancestry and a Canadian corporal who had earned the Victoria Cross. Each man agreed, independently, that he had seen a Canadian sergeant nailed to a barn door near Ypres. One had seen the horrifying atrocity on his way back from St. Julien, the other had been walking up the Ste. Jeanne road. Canadian honour was satisfied; German villainy was confirmed.[7]

Unfortunately, if the witnesses really remembered the location, they must have been three kilometres apart and on ground the Germans had never captured, significant facts that the Germans promptly divulged. This discrepancy would not have surprised the commander of the Canadian Corps, Lieutenant General Sir Arthur Currie. Throughout the war, Currie had done his best to track down every version of the crucifixion story. As commander of the 2nd Brigade at Ypres, Currie knew that the victim might well have been one of his own men, and, unlike Canadian officials in London, he knew the ground and the battle. Perhaps reluctantly, but with growing conviction, Currie concluded that the crucifixion story was a fraud.[8] Others might only have admitted, as Scottish courts sometimes do, that the case was "not proven," but when Canadian war art was later exhibited in New York, Wood's sculpture was not included.

A decade later, the curator of the National Gallery was persuaded to put it in storage and to allow no more photographs to be made available to the public.[9]

By then, of course, *Canada's Golgotha* was no longer a weapon against Germany but against the victorious Allies. The Nazis used Derwent Wood's artwork as proof of the bottomless British capacity for deceit.[10] The sculpture was a three-dimensional symbol of wartime propaganda, with all its pornographic fiction of bayoneted Belgian babies, violated women, and murdered priests. Within years of the armistice, the real war criminals were no longer German soldiers but were the bumbling politicians, incompetent generals, profiteering munitions contractors, and merchants of lies. From avid credulity, the public mind had swung to a resolute scepticism about "atrocity stories," which, for many, would last until the gates of Belsen were opened in 1945.

That was tough luck for Canadians who had survived captivity in Germany between 1915 and 1919. Because the best-known of their number had been the invention of fervid imaginations, the often dreadful experiences of real prisoners of war became embarrassing contradictions of a public eagerness to find virtue in old enemies and wickedness in former politicians and generals.

HUMAN BODIES CAN BE REMARKABLY HARD TO KILL IN THE heat of battle, and human minds prefer even the near-certainty of torture and enslavement to immediate death by sword or club. Such agonizing outcomes were, of course, the normal fate of captives, and captivity itself was almost as old a by-product of war as death, rape, and devastation. Long before contact with Europeans introduced them to the savagery of the Spanish Inquisition or judicial ordeals with burning coals or *la peine forte et dure*, for example, prolonged ritual torture was part of the warlike culture of the Hurons and, presumably, of other North American natives.[11]

Whatever their fate, prisoners of war were the helpless property of their captor. The slaughter of prisoners could demonstrate a ruler's power and terrify his enemies. Slaying unbelievers, helpless or not, seemed an acceptable act of devotion to gods or ancestors. The survival of captives often depended on their value as labour, their capacity to satisfy lust, or their potential for ransom. Prisoners of war—men, women, and children—restocked the slave pens of ancient Egypt, Greece, and Rome and made possible the tremendous architectural achievements of civilizations as disparate as the Mayans and the Khmers.

In European warfare, values and expectations changed over time. Among Christians, the slaughter and even the enslavement of wartime enemies who might also be fellow believers grew less acceptable. Greed, combined with the rules of chivalry, required different treatment for those of "gentle birth." The institution of ransom reflected the juridical notion that the value of bodies and even their parts could be reckoned in material terms. Part of the attraction of medieval battle was the prospect of sudden enrichment at the expense of a captive. When the French king was captured at Poitiers in 1356, his initial ransom of four million crowns was suggested as an elaborate compliment to his power and nobility. It was also vastly more than his war-ravaged and rebellious kingdom could afford.[12] At Agincourt in 1415, a later English king, Henry v, ordered the slaughter of his prisoners after his outnumbered army was attacked from the rear. More than just his enemies were shocked; his own soldiers lost a fortune in potential ransom money. In the Renaissance era, mercenaries brought an even more civilized spirit to the battlefield. Warriors sold themselves to the highest bidder and, since they might be victims of the next shift in the fortunes of war, they refused to indulge in the mindless slaughter or enslavement of fellow professionals.

An age which also renewed the classic search for the broader philosophical principles that govern human conduct found much to consider in the rules of war in general and the treatment of helpless prisoners in particular. In *De jure belli et pacis*, published in 1625, Hugo Grotius insisted: "It has long been a maxim, universally received among the powers of Christendom, that prisoners of war cannot be made slaves, so as to be sold or compelled to the hardships and labour attached to slavery."[13] Ransom, he explained, was the preferred alternative, and he even suggested an appropriate fee for the humblest soldier: a month's pay. Even Islam, he suggested, had accepted limits on its rights over prisoners. An exception, Grotius acknowledged, were "those rude or barbarous people, who without any declaration or cause of war, consider all mankind as enemies."[14] When the Treaty of Westphalia brought the unspeakably horrible Thirty Years' War to an end, exhausted belligerents agreed to release their prisoners without ransom or other conditions.

The endless dynastic wars of the eighteenth century, fought by expensive, highly trained armies, reflected a growing sense that the destruction of life and property, beyond the strict requirements of victory, was unwarranted. In *De l'esprit des lois*, written in mid-century, Montesquieu insisted that a captor's only right over a prisoner was to prevent him from causing further harm. A prisoner was no longer private property but a helpless person entitled to be removed to safety. Rights over prisoners should no longer be exercised by their immediate captor or even his general but by the state. Among the routine preliminaries to the outbreak of war in the Age of Enlightenment was the negotiation of cartels, stipulating scales of ransom and procedures for the exchange of prisoners of comparable ranks. Reciprocity was the rule, with reprisal the only sanction for misbehaviour. As gentlemen, officers were often released from captivity on their vow or promise to take no further part in the conflict until their exchange or ransom had been negotiated. Humbler prisoners, presumably immune from the high principles of honour, were crowded into dank, fetid fortresses to wait their turn for exchange. If they perished of cold, hunger, or disease, they only shared the fate of most common soldiers, even in victorious armies. Only gradually could the humanitarian theories of philosophers and jurists overcome the callousness of officials, the assumptions of class difference, and the limits of subsistence economies.

Even those awful realities were affected by the technological and productive advances of the nineteenth century. Horrors once accepted as inherent in the human condition were no longer necessary and, therefore, no longer tolerable. Conditions in the British military hospitals at Scutari or at the Confederate prison camp at Andersonville were hardly new in the annals of warfare, but never before had means existed to bring them rapidly to public attention and never before had they seemed so unnecessary. Equally intolerable were the barbarities suffered by prisoners on both sides of the Franco-Prussian war. Armies themselves changed to reflect nineteenth-century Europe. While the officers in most European armies clung to aristocratic status, privileges, and pretensions, conscripts in the ranks were no longer landless peasants or starving slum-dwellers, but young citizens whose good health and future labour were concerns of public policy. Nations now had a practical as well as a humanitarian reason to protect their own. Just as important was the notion that captives were entitled to their own allegiances, that it was improper to torture them for information and almost as wrong to coerce them to convert to a captor's beliefs. This, as American historian Richard Speed suggests, was "the liberal ideal of captivity" and, like liberalism itself, marked a short, imperfect interlude in human affairs.[15]

The great jurist Grotius had taught a Europe busy colonizing much of the rest of the world to distinguish between "civilized" and "uncivilized" warfare. The tortures that awaited British prisoners during the Opium Wars or the Italian survivors of General Baratieri's army after Adowa in 1896 contrasted with the behaviour expected of "civilized" powers when they waged war on each other.

Civilizing warfare was an idea even older than Grotius or Emmerich de Vattel, but its modern version was born when a Swiss, Henri Dunant, found himself among the forty thousand dead and wounded on the battlefield of Solferino in June 1859. His description of the suffering of the wounded led, in Geneva in 1864, to the "Convention for the Amelioration of the Condition of the Wounded in Armies of the Field."[16] This cause ultimately found an unlikely champion in Nicholas II, Tsar of All the Russias. Shocked and, unlike his generals, appalled by the grisly future of warfare as depicted in a widely read book by a Warsaw banker named Ivan Bloch,[17] the well-meaning Russian emperor invited several nations to a highly publicized peace conference at The Hague in 1899. It would be difficult even now to argue with the sentiments expressed there: "The maintenance of general peace and a possible reduction of the excessive armaments which weigh upon all nations present themselves . . . as the ideal towards which the endeavours of all Governments should be addressed."[18] Cynics noted that the tsar, with his backward, ill-equipped army, had good, practical reasons to restrict or outlaw such deadly innovations as poison gas or aerial bombardment. Still, it is always hard to favour horror, and most major powers were represented in 1899 and again, eight years later, when the conference was reconvened.

The Hague negotiations covered a vast array of subjects, from restrictions on technological innovations to the rights of merchant shipping. In most such areas of policy, national interests differed, and negotiations produced sharp subterranean and sometimes public disputes. That does not appear to have been true of discussions on prisoners of war. Both sides in war could expect to take prisoners and both sides could expect to lose them: interests were reciprocal. In 1899 and again in 1907, guidelines were arrived at which seemed to fulfil the tsar's highest humanitarian expectations without apparent impracticality.

The first point, seemingly anachronistic, was to insist that prisoners of war were the responsibility of the captor government, not of the individuals or units that had captured them. In fact, the point was crucial if governments were not to blame mistreatment of captives on distant commanders or individual soldiers. Prisoners, the signatories agreed, were entitled to humane treatment and, except for arms, horses, and military papers, they also retained their personal property.[19] As a governing principle, prisoners must receive the same standard of food, shelter, and clothing as their captor's soldiers.[20] By the same token, they would be subject to the same discipline as their captor's army. "Any act of insubordination justifies the adoption towards them of such measures of severity as may be considered necessary."[21] If they escaped and were recaptured before they got back to their own army, "they [were] liable to disciplinary punishment." If, however, they got away and were later recaptured, there would be no punishment unless their escape was due to breaking their *parole* (word of honour). In that case, they "forfeited their right to be treated as prisoners of war and could be brought before the courts."[22] Prisoners were also bound "if . . . questioned on the subject," to give their true name and rank, and anyone who failed to oblige was "liable to have the advantages given to prisoners of his class curtailed." The information was important if the captor nation was to fulfil its obligation to keep accurate and up-to-date records on the prisoners in its custody.

No one assumed that prisoners would be kept in idleness, but neither could they be considered slaves. "The state may utilize the labour of prisoners of war according to their rank and aptitude." The 1907 amendments specified that officers would be excepted.[23] The work must not be excessive "and shall have nothing to do with the military operations."[24] Prisoners might work for themselves, for the state, or for private employers. If they laboured for the state, they must be paid "at the rates in force for work of a similar kind done by soldiers of the national army. . . ." Private employers would meet pay scales agreed upon by the military authorities. Whatever the rate, "the wages of the prisoners shall go towards improving their position, and the balance shall be paid them on their release after deducting the cost of their maintenance."[25]

As gentlemen, officers could not possibly be put to work; instead, the detaining power would pay them at the rate for their own officers of corresponding rank, "the amount to be ultimately refunded by their own government."[26] Other rights and privileges were extended to all prisoners, from free postage to "complete liberty in the exercise of their religion, including attendance at the services of whatever church they belong to," subject, of course, to good order and police regulations. At the end of the war, prisoners must be repatriated "as quickly as possible." Meanwhile, "relief societies, properly constituted," would have "every facility to perform their humane work."[27]

While the 1907 meeting at The Hague was more wide-ranging and argumentative than its predecessor, Chapter II of the resulting convention, dealing with prisoners of war, was hardly altered. The major change was far greater detail in the information to be gathered by a "central bureau" and reported on behalf of prisoners: "the office must state . . . the regimental number, name and surname, age, place of origin, rank, unit, wounds, date and place of capture, internment, wounding and death, as well as any observations of a special character."[28] While the information would only be provided to the prisoner's government after the war, it would presumably be a safeguard that prisoners, once taken, would be properly accounted for.

No civilized nation could possibly disagree about prisoners, though other chapters of the convention were more controversial and ratification took time. After the 1899 meeting, Germany and Britain had ratified the Hague Convention within a year, on September 4, 1900. The Americans took a little longer, until April 9, 1902, but eventually all the future belligerents of 1914–18 had signed. Unfortunately, that was not the case for the 1907 document. On November 27, 1909, the revised convention was endorsed by only twenty-five countries, including Britain, Germany, and the United States. Among the absentees were Serbia, Bulgaria, and Turkey. Since the 1907 convention took effect only if all belligerents were signatories, prisoners in the First World War could only count on the 1899 convention. In practice, however, the major powers accepted the 1907 wording.

ANOTHER INTERNATIONAL CONFERENCE IN THE SUMMER OF 1906 at Geneva had elaborated the earlier 1864 agreement on the wartime protection of medical and hospital personnel, chaplains, and the sick and wounded. Under the protection of the red Geneva cross, suitably identified doctors, nurses, orderlies, and clergy would be considered non-combatants, protected from violence and promptly exchanged if captured. A special convention of the 1899 Hague Conference had already extended protection to suitably marked hospital ships.

Meanwhile, a private international organization had created a role for itself in the treatment of prisoners of war. The Red Cross had grown out of Henri Dunant's description of Solferino into an impressive network of national societies, which Dunant and the other Swiss founders had inspired at the 1864 conference. The movement then evolved into another purely Swiss and largely French-speaking society, the International Committee of the Red Cross (ICRC). In the Franco-Prussian War of 1870–71, the ICRC had created a bureau at Basel to convey information about French and German prisoners. The Balkan War of 1912 was a further opportunity to provide service and, unwittingly, to gain experience for a much greater conflict. Could the ICRC do more? Some national societies argued that prisoners of war were a special problem, requiring special national committees far broader than the Red Cross. At the Ninth International Red Cross Conference in Washington in 1912, the Swiss view prevailed. While national Red Cross societies would create "national commissions" to collect and forward relief for their prisoners in enemy hands, the ICRC would act as intermediary, transmitting relief and, where permitted, distributing it to individuals and depots, "taking into account the donors' wishes, the needs of the prisoners and the directions of the military authorities."[29]

On the eve of their greatest war, Europeans could take comfort in renewed evidence of their exceptional civilization. Whatever horrors their scientists and engineers might devise for the greater destruction of the enemy, captives of war could count on safety, security, and welfare. Indeed, at least one expert concluded, they would be "the spoilt children of the international law of war."[30]

On July 28, 1914, only months after the Balkan Wars had apparently ended and the International Committee of the Red Cross had closed its information bureau at Belgrade, Austrian guns opened fire on the Serbian capital. The Great War had begun. As Austria manoeuvred to attack Serbia, the tsar mobilized his armies in her defence. In Berlin, telegrams, prepared long in advance, set a huge military machine in motion. By August 3, France and Germany were at war. A day later, German artillery began shattering Belgian frontier fortresses and, that night, the British Empire joined the war. Two weeks later, near Mons on the Belgian border, the massive German flanking attack smashed into a tiny army of British regulars. After a few hours of murderous fighting, the British fell back. The German sweep continued, driven by a pre-war plan that envisaged surrounding and capturing the French army in a matter of weeks. Unknowingly, the French had helped the German plan by neglecting their flanks and plunging their army towards the lost province of Alsace. The war, it seemed, would be over long before Christmas. Berlin even had troops enough to beat back the Russian invasion of East Prussia.

Then, as ever in war, things went wrong. In Alsace, German defenders forgot their own war plan and hurled back the French, slaughtering thousands, capturing even more. The shattered French divisions fell back, regrouped, and then faced north against the real German threat. In East Prussia, reinforcements drawn from France helped destroy an invading Russian army. By August 30, the Germans were free to round up ninety thousand prisoners. It was a fatal triumph. With his troops close to exhaustion and now needing the divisions he had sent east, the German commander shortened his sweep. Instead of enveloping the French, he ran into their slowly building trap. The chance of a quick and easy German victory dissolved on the Marne in early September.

Too weary to move, both sides dug in. In October, the Germans tried to regain control, sending masses of fresh but inexperienced troops north in a bid to outflank the French at the Belgian border town of Ypres. There, on October 21, the Germans again ran into the little army of British regulars. Two weeks later, both armies had virtually been destroyed. The terrible stalement that Ivan Bloch had predicted a generation earlier was now a reality that stretched from the English Channel to the Swiss frontier. A war that should have been measured in weeks would last for fifty-one months.

REMOTE BEYOND THE ATLANTIC, CANADIANS HAD LITTLE idea of the war they had automatically entered when Britain's ultimatum to Berlin had expired at midnight on August 4, 1914. Patriotic speakers could talk of sacrifice, but their audiences and the holiday crowds that thronged the streets of Canadian towns and cities responded more to the excitement and glory of war. The young men who hurried to armouries to enlist feared mainly that the conflict would be over long before trains and ships could deliver them to the battlefields. If there were memories of war, they were coloured by the dusty South African veldt and galloping horsemen.

Colonel Sam Hughes, Canada's passionate minister of Militia, ripped up the country's formal mobilization plan and summoned all who would volunteer to Valcartier, a sandy plain outside Quebec City. From the thirty thousand men who appeared, most of them British-born, he fashioned a First Contingent. When it left in early October other contingents followed, until close to half a million Canadians had volunteered for war.

Canadians knew little of Europe or modern war. Pre-war politics had focused briefly on Britain's bitter naval rivalry with Germany and the Conservative government's preference for sending money to buy more British battleships at the expense of Canada's "tinpot navy." Canadians also knew that Hughes had preached the imminence of war with Germany, but, truth to tell, a growing number of his countrymen thought Hughes was a little crazy—at least until August 1914. If Germany was part of that "vortex of European militarism" Liberal leader Sir Wilfrid Laurier so often warned against, so were

France, Russia, Austria, and perhaps even a few imperialists in Great Britain. In Canada, after all, Germans ranked third in ethnic bulk after the French and British, and they were decent, hard-working, and loyal folk. In Winnipeg, the editor of the *Free Press*, John Wesley Dafoe, might thunder that Canada was at war with "kaiserism" and Prussian militarism, but most Canadians simply believed that they were marching shoulder to shoulder with the Empire against people misguided enough to be the king's enemies.[31]

That tolerance would shift slowly as the early days of excitement turned into weeks and then months of bewildering set-backs for the Allied cause. A century free of full-scale war had immunized people from an awareness of its horrors. It was easy—perhaps too easy—to believe that all the atrocities of this conflict were Germany's invention. Paranoia grew. It was thought that Germany's early victories—huge frontier fortresses crushed, French armies hurled back, the finest British army ever sent to the Continent in full retreat—could only be the outcome of spies and treachery. Canadian editors, politicians, and the general public demanded that Germans and all other "enemy aliens" be confined for the sake of safety. Conscious of the cost and the threat to post-war immigration if professionals and skilled workers felt ill-treated, and hopeful that the war would soon end, Ottawa temporized. Only in October, when the British urged action, did the government undertake a comprehensive policy of interning German and Austro-Hungarian subjects of military age.[32] Meanwhile, across Canada thousands pressed forward to enlist, drilled in civilian clothes, and believed confidently that, by the second year of the war, Canadians would be part of the triumphal Allied advance on Berlin.

In England, mired on Salisbury Plain in the wettest winter anyone could remember, the First Contingent evolved into the 1st Canadian Division. Raw recruits and imperial veterans became soldiers together, conscious of an identity that set them apart from and, in their own eyes, a little ahead of the British army. As Canadians, they felt entitled to ignore red tape and eyewash: the infinity of regulations, the saluting, the polishing, and the officious bellowing that made up military life. Even British-born Canadians felt themselves superior to the crude constraints of army discipline. Finally, in early February, a royal inspection marked the end of their training and the beginning of their big adventure. With officers hardly better trained than their men, the Canadians crossed to St. Nazaire, boarded French freight cars marked "Horses—8/Men—40," and wended their way across France to the British line near Neuve Chapelle. For a few exciting weeks, they were on the fringe of a gallant but futile British offensive. Then, officially "blooded" and battle worthy, the Canadian division marched up the line to Belgium and a town called Ypres. On April 17, they moved into position, replacing a French division. Their war was about to begin.

ALMOST EVERY MILITARY PREPARATION IN EVERY COUNTRY had been based on the expectation of a short war. Countries had mobilized every soldier and resource they thought necessary to win a quick decision. Casualties on both sides had been enormous. In the August battles of the frontier, the French had lost a quarter of their 1,250,000 men; more than half were prisoners. Much of the Belgian army had been captured, and between the retreat from Mons and the desperate struggle at Ypres, more than twenty thousand of Britain's best soldiers had become German prisoners.

In conventional terms, the German army had won tremendous victories in 1914, conquering Belgium and the industrial heartland of France. In the east in December, its armies had another huge triumph, over the Russians. By early 1915 Germany had close to a million Allied prisoners, and there would be many more to come. Long trains of cattle cars, crowded with ragged, unshaven enemy, were the visible evidence of military success, but what happened when the cars were emptied? Obviously a military plan that envisaged the capture of France's army and the subsequent destruction of Russia's should have anticipated masses of prisoners; however, it had also anticipated early victory. In a short war, prisoners would have been penned in fields, housed in tents, fed, watered, and guarded until an armistice recognized the German victory. That was not to happen in 1914. Instead, Germany faced a tremendous administrative problem. The obligations of the Hague Convention were clear. How could they be met?

The answer was that German military administrators would adapt as best they could. Pre-war plans called for the decentralized solution the German army had always preferred. In Berlin, the war ministry quickly established general guidelines for dealing with prisoners. The ill-assorted Allies, for example, would get to know each other better. British, French, and Russian prisoners would share the same camps, even the same huts. Other instructions added a little precision to the Hague Convention: prisoners must have two woollen blankets, a towel, and eating utensils; quarters must have artificial lighting, heat, and plenty of ventilation; each officer-prisoner was entitled to fifteen cubic metres of breathing space, while other ranks had to be satisfied with five.[33] The rest was up to the twenty-four highly autonomous army corps districts into which the German Empire was divided. Army corps commanders would select the camps, tender contracts for food and building materials, make the rules, and assign commandants and guards. They, in turn, would erect the fences, the guard towers, and the huts and, as the Hague Convention clearly insisted, exercise proper military discipline over their new charges.

Like the empire it served, the German army was still an administrative federation of Prussians, Bavarians, Württembergers, Saxons, and other national armies. The imperial war ministry in Berlin had to work patiently and respectfully through war ministries in each of Germany's kingdoms. Army corps districts often reported more faithfully to their immediate political superiors than to Berlin. In wartime, the corps commanders exercised, and obviously enjoyed, an impressive autonomy. Far from the rigid military machine its critics often depicted, the German army favoured independent thinking within the broadest of guidelines. Military traditionalists were fond of the principle *Alles hängt vom Kommandeur ab* (all depends on the commander). Some army corps allowed captured enemy non-commissioned officers to exercise extensive authority in the camps; in others the German guards were in full control and the camps resembled overgrown prisons.

Camp commandants varied too. Almost all had been judged unfit for active service; some were kindly, a few were vindictive or sadistic; all had been bred in a tradition which expected instant obedience and mental conformity from subordinates.[34] As ever, it was easier to give orders than to execute them. War is not a humanitarian exercise, and the civilized restraints of the Hague Convention were easily forgotten when soldiers far from battle discovered any flicker of resistance among an otherwise hangdog and dispirited crowd of prisoners.

By late 1914, the prisoner-of-war problem was particularly acute. Compared to the challenge of mobilizing fresh divisions and reinforcing old ones, the prisoners' situation was a second priority. Aged captains, colonels, and generals, pulled from retirement to command the camps, and the elderly *Landstürmer* (reservists) conscripted as guards, were ill-fitted by nature or experience to tackle the administrative crisis. Food supplies were insufficient; adequate clothing was almost non-existent. Prisoners captured in August and September were not dressed for cold weather, and the winter of 1914–15 was particularly brutal. Some of them, desperate from hunger, had sold their clothing for food, while others insisted that their military greatcoats had been stolen by their captors.[35]

The most notorious administrative failure in the first year of the war occurred outside the historic town of Wittenberg. Some 12,000 to 15,000 Russian, French, and British prisoners had been crowded into pens on a four-hectare site beside a main railway line. A shortage of mattresses meant that three prisoners had to share a single straw-filled palliasse. Ever obedient to Berlin's orders, the commandant insisted that each mattress be shared by a French, Russian, and British prisoner. Unfortunately, the Russians had brought typhus to the camp and by December an epidemic raged. After opening the internal gates so that the sick and healthy mingled freely, the German guards, administrators, and medical staff abandoned the camp, guarding the perimeter with machine guns and fierce dogs. Supplies were pushed down a chute into the camp, orders were shouted from a safe distance, little was offered in the way of medicine. A handful of French and Russian medical personnel, detained in spite of the Geneva Convention, did what they could. It was not much. A few British doctors volunteered their help; all but one of them died. Thousands were stricken, hundreds perished. Only in August, when the disease had run its course and neutral criticism had grown audible, did the Germans return. The authorities soon replaced the commandant, but the memory of Wittenberg was much harder to eliminate.[36]

A similar situation developed at Gardelagen, a much larger camp, although, perhaps because there were fewer British prisoners, it was less publicized. Once again, the camp was dirty and badly managed, no parcels got through, and prisoners of all nationalities spent their days in cramped, freezing barracks, sitting or lying on palliasses. The sick mingled with the healthy. When typhus struck, the German staff also fled. A senior French doctor was left in charge of a handful of Russian, British, and French medical officers to cope with the crisis. Of 11,000 inmates, 2,000 were affected and 300 died.[37]

One result of the genuine suffering in the first months of the war was the dissemination of horrifying tales of misery, some of them gross exaggerations, others, like Wittenberg, too true. All of them were based on a belief in the same deliberate policy of *Schrecklichkeit* (frightfulness) that the Germans had applied to Belgium in the first weeks of the war. A more beneficial outcome was the introduction of neutral inspection. The idea grew from James Gerard, U.S. ambassador to Germany, who had nobly taken it on himself, as "protecting power" for Britain's interests, to distribute relief supplies to British prisoners at Döberitz, near Berlin. Faced with German claims of cruelty and neglect in Britain's internment camps, Gerard had a sensible, if unprecedented, idea: why not send an American official to examine the British camps and report back? John Jackson, a former ambassador in the Balkans and official at the U.S. legation in Berlin, was available. The American embassy in London soon made the arrangements, if only to cool some of the talk of atrocities, maltreatment, and reprisals. Neutral inspection also showed that the Americans were doing their job and observing the rule of reciprocity. The biggest stumbling block was getting the German war ministry in Berlin to reply. In his memoirs, Gerard recalled telling Gottfried Von Jagow, the under-secretary at the German foreign office: "If I cannot get an answer to my proposition about prisoners, I will take a chair and sit in front of your palace in the street until I receive an answer."[38]

Gerard and the Americans deserved credit for a valuable idea though, inevitably, others insisted they were responsible. The British, for example, claimed they had taken the initiative by inviting the American ambassador to send representatives to their internment camps. The French were equally obliging, undoubtedly to encourage neutral reciprocal visits to their numerous soldiers in German hands. By early 1915, the major belligerents had conceded the principle of inspection. Appropriately accredited representatives of neutral "protecting powers"—Americans on behalf of the British and Spanish for the French—began visiting the camps.

After a little experience of Germany's military system, visitors learned to seek an escort from the local army corps headquarters. They met with the camp commandant, viewed prisoners on parade, with special attention to the state of their clothing and footwear, tasted the soup in the prison kitchens, and solemnly measured the huts for the appropriate cubic capacity.[39] Gerard insisted that commandants have an opportunity to remedy problems before higher authorities were notified. However, publication of his reports in Britain so annoyed the Germans that Washington directed him to desist.[40] Predictably, given local conditions and German belief in decentralization, observers found that prison camps varied widely in their comfort, discipline, and administrative efficiency. By the same token, authorities in some camps welcomed visits, allowed confidential communication with prisoners, and found the resulting reports to be fair and even sympathetic; other commandants did their best to restrict contact with prisoners and punished those who complained. Prisoners themselves insisted that the Germans knew when neutral observers were coming and made appropriate preparations. Seldom did observers penetrate the thousands of work sites where many prisoners would spend the most arduous years of their captivity.[41]

Still, there were rules to protect prisoners of war, and in 1914 there was enough world opinion to influence their enforcement. The war, after all, was more than a conflict over territory; it had become a test of rival cultures and societies. Even the Germans, utterly convinced that they were surrounded by backward, venal, or treacherous neighbours, had their own proud *Kultur* to uphold. They also had their own captive citizens to protect. Like their enemies, they were easily persuaded that German prisoners had been victims of atrocities, and, like their enemies, they would use the weapon of reprisal to protect them.

2

Captured

THE FIRST CANADIAN PRISONERS IN GERMANY WERE HARDLY soldiers at all. International law was vague about the status of civilians in what, suddenly, had become an enemy country. Among the Canadians travelling in Germany at the outset of the war was the noted *nationaliste* and editor of *Le Devoir*, Henri Bourassa. German frontier guards wisely allowed him to slip across the border. A twenty-one-year-old from Toronto, Arnold Chadwick, managed to get from Leipzig to the Dutch border when German guards assumed he was too young to enlist and let him pass.[1] Other Canadians were less fortunate.

On both sides military authorities insisted, with little dissent, that enemy aliens of military age and training must be prevented from joining their own forces. When the British intercepted a ferry-load of German reservists at Harwich, the Germans reciprocated. Lieutenant Colonel Percival Anderson, retired after a long career in the Canadian Ordnance Corps, had visited Germany to put his children in school there. He was arrested, but Mrs. Anderson persuaded German police to release her husband by arguing that he was Canadian, not British. By the end of September, German officials understood the Empire better and the hapless Anderson, arrested a second time, was on his way to spend the war at Schlosse Celle, a dank and elderly castle in Hannover.[2]

A lot of other Canadians shared his fate, if not his destination. By September, Germany had imitated Britain, and its dominions, by rounding up enemy males of military age. Six to seven thousand British tourists, migrant workers, businessmen, and professionals were eventually interned at Ruhleben, a race track outside Berlin. Among them were two young Canadian music students, Ernest Macmillan and J. Davidson Ketchum.[3] Hugh Young was representing the Canadian publishers Copp Clark at Nuremberg when war broke out and was also interned at Ruhleben. So was Allan Lochead, a McGill graduate who had been working on his Ph.D. in agricultural bacteriology at Leipzig. Russian-born Canadians Joseph and Moses Gelin were passing through Berlin with Moses's two children on their way home from Odessa when they were arrested in early August 1914. George Purdy, master of the 3,300 ton *Pandosia*, was held up at Hamburg when the German naval authorities closed the Elbe. Arthur Chambers, who was born in the Magdalene Islands where his father had served briefly as a missionary, had been raised in Holland, but had lived all his adult life in Germany with his wife and child. Unfortunately for him, he was still an *Engländer* of Canadian origin. He would spend the next fifty-one months at Ruhleben.[4]

It promised to be a grim experience. In the stables at the track, prisoners were crowded six to a stall. Still, they were better off than others who were crammed into unlit, unventilated haylofts. In the early months, many had only the clothes they stood in, and the toilet and washing facilities were exiguous. One British prisoner recalled breaking into tears when he saw the dank, foul-smelling hole where he was expected to spend the rest of the war. Jewish prisoners, like the Gelins, were initially segregated and crowded together with Russian Jews in the waiting room of an old railway station, and later in the oldest and dirtiest of the stables. When the Russians were transferred to Holzminden, non-Jews took their place until the oldest stable was also the most crowded.[5]

Matters eventually improved at Ruhleben. Because the internees were civilians, some of them with influential friends, no camp attracted more international attention during the war. Huts were built, prisoners grew some of their own food and increasingly managed their own affairs.[6] As for the morality of confining civilians in wartime, the British couldn't claim the high ground. By seizing the German reservists at Harwich, they had, for once, taken the first step in adding to the horrors of war.[7] Their dominions, of course, conformed. After such a hesitant start that any keen German or Austrian reservist had long since slipped over the border, Canada ultimately interned six thousand "enemy aliens," most of them disaffected subjects of the Hapsburg monarchy.[8]

The most prominent Canadian internee in Germany was Dr. Henri Béland, Liberal MP for Beauce and a former postmaster general in Sir Wilfrid Laurier's cabinet. Béland's recent marriage to a Belgian woman had trapped him near Antwerp when the German armies swept across his wife's homeland. Béland's appeals for the British to get him to the Netherlands were met with the advice that he, himself, should apply to the German authorities. It was a poor idea. Impressed that they had found someone of at least colonial significance, the Germans clapped Béland in prison and soon transferred him to the Stadtvogtei, a reasonably modern jail in Berlin where he joined a handful of British internees and unemployed Polish labourers.[9]

Ottawa's best efforts to help the former cabinet minister proved futile. The U.S. State Department was helpless, the British refused to offer up a senior German officer as an exchange, and Berlin scornfully rejected the ingenious claim by the minister of Militia that Béland, as a peacetime officer in the Canadian Army Medical Corps, should benefit from the protection the Geneva Convention afforded to medical officers. Sustained by parcels and occasional drafts of money from the Canadian High Commission in London, Béland stayed put. His captors treated him, a fellow prisoner claimed, "with a refined cruelty," refusing to tell him that his wife was dying until she had already passed away. After a period of profound and understandable depression, Béland pulled himself together and, by common consent, did all he could for his fellow internees.[10] As for getting him out, Laurier admitted to Sir Robert Borden, "I commence to believe that the more efforts made on his behalf the worse it was for him."[11]

It had taken Canadian politicians a little while to realize that a Europe at war had rapidly forgotten the niceties of civilized diplomatic intercourse, to say nothing of the humane spirit of 1899 and 1907. Almost four thousand other Canadians would soon be privy to this change as well.

UNLIKE CIVILIAN INTERNEES, SOLDIERS WHO SURRENDERED could look to well-established precedents and the promised protection of the Hague Convention.

Canadians became prisoners of war in many ways, from mass surrenders to flyers who survived the crash of their frail aircraft behind enemy lines. Some 377 Canadians with the British flying services became German prisoners. One was captured by the Bulgarians, another by the Austrians, and two officers survived Turkish prisons.[12] In trench warfare, both sides staged quick raids to seize a few dazed prisoners for the information they could reveal. Individual soldiers blundered over enemy lines when they were lost at night in "No Man's Land." Patrols stumbled into each other, leaving dead, wounded, and prisoners. Major offensives almost inevitably swept over the first or second line of defences, leaving confused, shell-shocked, and wounded defenders to give themselves up. Attackers, in turn, fell victim to determined counter-attacks. At least one Canadian soldier who became a prisoner was charged with desertion to the enemy; others were suspected of the same.[13]

Almost two-thirds of Canada's prisoners surrendered during two German attacks: at the Second Battle of Ypres in late April 1915, and at Sanctuary Wood on June 2, 1916. Prisoners were also captured during the confused and unsuccessful fighting at the St. Eloi craters in early April 1916 and during the Somme, when failed attacks left wounded and sometimes unwounded Canadians behind the German lines. Even Canada's triumph at Vimy Ridge on April 9, 1917 included the 75th Battalion's set-back at Hill 145. A month later, Fresnoy, a village in front of the ridge, was taken and then lost by units of the 1st Canadian Division, who suffered heavy casualties. At Lens, during August, Sir Arthur Currie's plan of holding Hill 70 so that wave after wave of German attackers could be destroyed on its approaches was a brilliant success, but many Canadians were also killed and taken prisoner. This was the result once again during the vain attempt by the 44th Battalion to seize the Green Crassier at Lens on August 23, 1917. The Manitoba-raised unit lost 258 men in a hopeless attack; 87 of them were taken prisoner.[14] The Canadian Cavalry Brigade lost prisoners during mounted charges in the Battle of Cambrai in 1917, and again in March 1918, when it and the Canadian Motor Machine Gun Brigade were part of British efforts to stem the German spring offensive. The triumphal Canadian advances of the last hundred days of the war helped bring about the end in 1918, but they also saw the heaviest Canadian casualties. Among the losses were over 300 prisoners of war.[15]

Though not part of the Canadian contingent, 176 members of the Newfoundland Regiment were captured at Monchy-le-Preux on April 14, 1917 during the initial Arras offensive. A German counter-attack then overran the battalion and virtually destroyed it as a unit for the second time. About 150 Newfoundlanders survived captivity.[16]

Most Canadians have been taught to regard the performance of the Canadian Contingent at the Second Battle of Ypres as a military triumph. The pride is warranted. During three terrible days, the 1st Canadian Division endured its baptism by fire in trenches that consisted mainly of sandbagged walls and shallow ditches. They survived the second poison gas attack in human history. This was accompanied by a storm of artillery fire that shattered the makeshift trenches, deafened and terrified their defenders, and caused many more casualties than the gas. As massed German infantry approached, the Canadians learned that their Ross rifles frequently jammed after only a few rounds. Desperate men had to hammer back the bolt with boots or shovels to reload. It was a brutal initiation to war. Troops with better training, weapons, and leaders might easily have fled, but most of the Canadians stayed and fought. For fifteen hundred of them, the cost of that decision was their three-year ordeal in German prison camps.

THE SECOND BATTLE OF YPRES BEGAN LATE ON THE AFTERnoon of April 22, 1915. From their trenches, Canadians could see a mysterious greenish cloud rise and roll towards the two divisions of Algerians, Senegalese, and French reservists on their left. Suddenly, the frightened soldiers began to flee. Some of them, half-choking, ran through the battalions holding the Canadian left flank in front of St. Julien. The Germans advanced, but cautiously, conscious that they too had little protection against the new horror weapon. The Canadians swung round to protect their open flank. That night, two of the Canadian battalions kept in reserve, the 10th and 16th, launched a counter-attack against Kitchener's Wood. After confused but bitter fighting, barely five hundred Canadians remained. Most were dead—or had been taken prisoner. Worse followed. On April 23, there were more costly and unsuccessful counter-attacks. Companies of the 1st, 2nd, and 4th Battalion attacked Germans on Mauser Ridge in broad daylight—in mass formation. They were shot to pieces. British troops brought up in support fared no better.

At 4 a.m. on Saturday, April 24, the greenish cloud emerged again from cylinders in the German lines, a dense wall of gas three or four metres high. A gentle breeze pushed it up the slight slope towards the Canadian battalions on Gravenstafel Ridge. A German bombardment, begun the day before, again unleashed its devastating fury on the Canadians. At the apex of the Canadian position on the ridge was the 15th Battalion, almost wholly formed by Toronto's 48th Highlanders.[17] With supporting artillery out of range and no flanking battalions to help, the 15th dissolved. One company was wiped out in a trench the Germans described as a mass grave. The other front-line company was destroyed as badly gassed men dropped their useless Ross rifles and kits and tore open their jackets and shirts in a desperate bid for breath. Four of the 15th Battalion's officers and 216 of the men were killed; 10 officers and 247 other ranks surrendered.[18] Massed German battalions swarmed forward into the gap. Others assaulted the village of St. Julien, farther along the line, attacking repeatedly and at enormous cost until the handful of Canadian survivors surrendered or made narrow escapes. Caught between the two prongs, under devastating artillery fire, was the 7th Battalion, which preferred to call itself the 1st British Columbia Regiment. With the 15th wiped out, its left flank open, its trenches pulverized, and its colonel and two company commanders dead, the 7th pulled back, leaving the survivors of its two forward companies to surrender. Lieutenant J. C. Thorn, who had been captured earlier that morning and had managed to get away, suffered the humiliation of surrendering a second time. Only a handful of men escaped, their retreat covered by two Colt machine guns commanded by a quiet-spoken mining engineer, Lieutenant Edward Bellew.[19] The unit suffered the second-heaviest casualties of the day: 5 officers and 171 others killed, 7 officers and 260 other ranks were captured. Across the front, when nothing stopped the ranks of advancing Germans, the few remaining Canadians fell back to positions in the rear, gradually abandoning the ridge. Those who stayed died or, if the Germans allowed it, they surrendered.[20]

If the Canadian line held at all, the credit belonged to Winnipeg's 8th Battalion and its commander, Lieutenant Colonel Louis Lipsett, a cool British regular. Protected by urine-soaked handkerchiefs and towels, the battalion somehow held its ground against the same suffocating cloud that had overwhelmed its neighbours on the left. Its artillery was close enough to help and it got powerful support from the 5th Battalion on its right. Still, the unit paid a price: 114 dead and 5 officers and 167 other ranks taken prisoner.

On the left of the shattered 15th was the 13th Battalion—formed from Montreal's elegant 5th Royal Highlanders, also known as the Black Watch. On April 22, the 13th had held the shoulder of the German attack; now it had to stage the hardest operation in war, a fighting retreat. It succeeded, but at heavy cost: 4 officers and 120 men dead, 2 officers and 167 men taken prisoner, most of them wounded. Farther down the slope, the Germans had isolated the village of St. Julien and its garrison, most of them from two companies of another Toronto unit, the 3rd Battalion.[21] The Toronto men were confident that British reinforcements would soon break through to relieve them. They were wrong. By early afternoon, it was too late. Exhausted, decimated, and out of ammunition, the Canadians began to surrender. The British counter-attack came an hour too late to save them. Next day, the remnants of the western brigade withdrew, leaving many casualties and prisoners. Bill Alldritt was presumed dead behind his machine gun; he somehow survived.[22]

For the Canadian division, the worst of the fighting and dying ended on the night of April 24. The battle had cost the raw division 6,036 men, half its infantry strength. The Germans had captured 1,410 Canadian prisoners, 627 of them wounded and 87 of them soon to die from their wounds. The British commander-in-chief shrewdly praised the shaken Canadians, claiming they had "saved the situation."[23] But they had also lost many of their men and most of their illusions. For the British, the struggle at Ypres continued well into May, at an ultimate cost of 59,275 casualties. Meanwhile, the final German assault fell on another Canadian unit, Princess Patricia's Canadian Light Infantry, formed largely from British reservists in Canada at the outset of the war. In a single day, the unit lost 392 men, some of them becoming prisoners of war.

A LITTLE MORE THAN A YEAR LATER, ON JUNE 2, 1916, THE untried 3rd Canadian Division faced its own baptism by fire at Mont Sorrel, not far south of the earlier battle of Gravenstafel Ridge. The 8th Brigade was composed of units of the Canadian Mounted Rifles originally raised to fight in Egypt. Now they had taken over trenches on virtually the only high ground left to the British in the Ypres sector. More experienced troops might have noticed some of the warning signs. For weeks, two divisions of the 13th Württemberg Corps had pushed their digging steadily closer to the Canadian lines. British flyers had spotted trenches far behind the German line that strongly resembled the Canadian positions—a hint of rehearsals for a coming attack. Other pilots reported guns, mortars, and stacks of ammunition concentrated in front of the Canadians. Perhaps the divisional commander, Major General M. S. Mercer, and Brigadier General Victor Williams of the 8th Brigade wanted to see for themselves. Certainly both generals were in the forward trenches that morning when the Germans suddenly unleashed a four-hour bombardment. Never before had any Canadians experienced such a deluge of shells. In his history of the battle, G. W. L. Nicholson cites a German description: "The whole enemy position was a cloud of dust and dirt, into which timber, tree trunks, weapons and equipment were continuously hurled, and occasionally human bodies."[24]

General Mercer's body was found in Armagh Wood, just behind the front line. Two commanders of adjacent CMR battalions, one of them an MP, were also killed. Troops dragged a badly wounded General Williams into "The Tube," a tunnel that Canadian engineers had been building. His host, Lieutenant Colonel John Ussher of the 4th Canadian Mounted Rifles, soon followed him there and found 118 wounded, 40 engineers from the 2nd Canadian Tunnelling Company, and a couple of platoons of his own unit. German shells closed one end of the tunnel and then the other. On the surface, dazed survivors offered little resistance as ranks of Württembergers walked up the gentle slope and used primitive flame-throwers to wipe out the few defenders who were not willing to give up.[25] After two hours of near-asphyxiation and growing panic, sappers in "The Tube" managed to dig their way to the surface. Ussher faced an unpleasant surprise:

> We were entirely surrounded by the enemy, who had reached a position ¼ mile at least to the rear of us. Gen. Williams was not fit to consult and a decision devolved on me. There was nothing for it but to surrender. We were like rats in a trap: one German with a bomb could have finished the lot of us.[26]

In the day's operations, the Germans captured 30 Canadian officers and 506 other ranks, including Ussher and a by-now unconscious Brigadier General Williams, 2 medical officers, and the brigade chaplain, Captain Gillies Wilken. Much later, Wilken was the hero of a lurid account of the battle. "Having . . . done all he could for the dead and dying," he had allegedly seized a rifle and, when the ammunition was gone and his bayonet broken, "this astounding parson, baring his arms, flew at one brawny Boche with his fists." If true, such behaviour might be heroic but it was certainly in contravention of the Geneva and Hague conventions. The official historian, Colonel A. F. Duguid, offered militant Christians a more discreet version: Wilken had been captured at the headquarters of the 1st Canadian Mounted Rifles with other survivors of the battle.[27]

In his study of front-line experience in the Second World War, *The Sharp End*, John Ellis warns that being taken prisoner in battle is always a matter of luck. Blinded by blood-lust or bent on avenging a comrade, soldiers may not always accept surrender. Raw and undisciplined troops often boast that they do not take prisoners—as some Canadians claimed in their diaries and letters home.[28] The enemy was not the only threat: shell fire from both sides swept the battlefield, killing and maiming both sides indiscriminately.[29] Captured near Ypres in 1915, Corporal Edward Edwards of

Princess Patricia's Canadian Light Infantry (PPCLI) later claimed that the Germans shot or bayoneted some of his helpless comrades.[30] Some of those appealing for reparations after the war presented evidence that they had been stabbed by German guards during the march to the Belgian railway town of Roulers.[31] After his capture at Mont Sorrel, Captain Wilken claimed that Germans, advancing as reinforcements, casually shot down two of his fellow prisoners.[32] Captured near Courcelette in 1916, Sapper Sidney Meakin deflected the rifle of a German intent on shooting him. The bullet passed through his private parts.[33] John Trevenna, captured with five others after the Fort Garry Horse attack at Cambrai, claimed that angry Germans killed one comrade, wounded another, and shot him through the thigh.[34] Captured during the Canadian assault on the Canal du Nord in 1918, Private F. J. Hamilton was struck by a German colonel and threatened with death: "I don't care for the English, Scotch, French, Australians or Belgians," shouted the colonel, "but damn you Canadians, you take no prisoners and you kill our wounded."[35] Such claims, common on both sides, made the moment of capture very dangerous.

Apart from the Hong Kong disaster on Christmas Day, 1941, and Dieppe eight months later, more Canadians surrendered on April 24, 1915 than in any other battle in the century. Everyone's experience was different; all would be remembered through a haze of time and self-justification. Captain Tom Scudamore, a peacetime militia officer and real estate agent, commanded one of the two lost companies of the 7th Battalion. The adjutant, his "oldest friend," had asked him to hang on as long as possible. A head wound convinced him that he had done all he could and he led the remnant of his company back down the road to St. Julien only to run into the Germans. After a brief delay while he argued that he could only surrender to a German officer, he and eight of his men gave themselves up. A German grabbed Scudamore's useless Ross rifle as a souvenir. "I told him he was welcome to it," he later recalled.[36] Private George Scott was with Scudamore's group, waiting for a stretcher-bearer to help him with a wound in his side and grieving the death of his best friend only minutes earlier. "The next thing I heard was Capt. Scudamore saying 'Everybody stand up,' and a bandage was lifted as a white flag."[37] As his captors hurried Scudamore back to their lines, he passed advancing German infantry: "Men in the successive waves either lunged at me with their bayonets, clubbed their rifles or threatened me with a bomb, but my captors cursed them and we reached their cottage which was their acting headquarters."[38]

A member of Scudamore's company, Private M. C. Simmons, had been sent back for ammunition when the Germans attacked. He was badly hit in the shoulder and passed out. His next memory was of peering from the bottom of a trench as the Germans passed and hearing another 7th Battalion company commander, Major Peter Byng-Hall, tell his men to surrender.[39] One of those men, Harry Howland, felt terrified. He lost his cap in an effort to haul the strap for his cased wire-cutters over his head. He did not dare pick it up. As he wrote later in a third-person account of his experiences: "Weaving to avoid blows aimed by advancing troops, the prisoners cross the field to the road, continuing to run after reaching it. Guards as well as a few comrades keel over, hit by shrapnel bursting in the leafless trees lining the road." Howland considered playing dead but he noticed Highlanders, probably from the 15th Battalion, bayoneted in the back and thighs.[40] Harry James of the 13th Battalion, shot in the legs, later claimed that he broke his arm protecting himself from being clubbed or bayoneted. Another soldier of the 7th Battalion, Lawrence Walker, insisted that he had been deliberately bayoneted after his capture.[41]

South of St. Julien, Major Peter Anderson, a Dane from Edmonton, commanded the 3rd Battalion's scouts. He was unwounded but dazed when the Germans overran his position, and his watch had been shot away. For a while, the Germans left their prisoners where they were, under fire. Then they marched them back along a road to Staden, with British shells falling all around them.[42] Another member of the 3rd Battalion, Arthur Gibbons, was immobilized with a wound in his right thigh. A German officer stopped one of his men from bayoneting the Canadian, but kicked Gibbons when he was impertinent. Then Gibbons was ignored for four agonizing days while German stretcher parties cleared their own wounded.[43] He was not alone: many Canadians, at Ypres and later, waited for days to be rescued; many others obviously succumbed to their wounds after suffering the horrors of thirst and pain.

Evacuating wounded on a battlefield still being torn by shot and shell was not easy or safe. If Canadian wounded suffered further injuries during evacuation, so did their German rescuers. In the midst of bloodshed and passion, some prisoners recalled acts of kindness and sympathy from their German captors. Corporal J. E. Finnemore, painfully wounded in the leg, was saved by a German soldier who evacuated him in a wheelbarrow while under fire.[44] Edwards of the PPCLI, whose life was threatened by a furious German officer, was saved by "a stalwart, bearded Prussian officer" with a cooler understanding of the rules of civilized war.[45] Once out of artillery range, Howland recalled, German guards lighted prisoners' pipes and cigarettes, and traded their own cigars for Canadian brass buttons. Captain Lyman Gooderham, Major General Mercer's aide-de-camp, was unconscious for the first two days after his capture at Mont Sorrel. To reassure parents and friends, perhaps to please his captors, or maybe because it was true, he and his friend Lieutenant W. E. Massey-Cooke of the Canadian Engineers praised the Germans in their letters home.[46]

BARRING SLAUGHTER IN THE HEAT OF BATTLE AND "SOUVENIR-hunting" by front-line troops—an offence Canadians notoriously reciprocated[47]—Germans generally did their duty by the prisoners at Ypres and Mont Sorrel. The Hague Convention required that prisoners be promptly removed from danger. This was no easy task while both sides mercilessly bombarded the battlefield, and its approaches and roads were clogged by the conflicting streams of advancing reinforcements and supplies and retreating wounded. Some Canadians at Ypres and Sanctuary Wood charged that they were kept in danger too long; others complained that they had been force-marched to the rear, despite wounds, exhaustion, and hunger. "They cuffed us, they buffeted us, they pricked us cruelly with their saw bayonets," complained Edwards in a book directed at wartime readers, "and then they laughed as we dodged awkwardly aside."[48] Corporal Peter Thornton of the 4th Canadian Mounted Rifles, wounded in the chest and right leg and with a smashed jaw, could go no farther. An impatient German officer shot him in the back and shoulder. German stretcher-bearers collected him later and he survived.[49]

Private Stephen O'Brien, sixteen years old when captured on June 2, 1916, claimed that he and two hundred fellow prisoners were kicked, beaten with rifle butts, and robbed by their German escorts as they were force-marched to the rear.[50] Uhlans, German lancers, were used, like French and British cavalry, to escort prisoners beyond the range of machine guns. Several Canadians complained that the uhlans' lances were used to stab at prisoners and to wound sympathetic Belgians.[51] Prisoners from Ypres, many of them bleeding from wounds, most of them affected by chlorine, and all of them exhausted and hungry after the day's battle, marched eleven or twelve kilometres to Roulers where they were herded into St. Michael's Catholic church.

Although prisoners were a valuable source of information for both sides, few Canadians described brutal or systematic interrogation. Major Anderson of the 3rd Battalion claimed that he told his men to say nothing: "Pretty soon a German officer came along and said in good English: 'Where are the rest of the men around here?' I replied 'These are all the men we have here including the dead ones. But we have thousands a few yards to the rear. You had better go and get them also.' 'No thanks,' he replied, 'We don't want any more at this price. It is too expensive.'"[52] A few weeks later, Corporal Edwards also exaggerated the growing strength of the British armies and was later a little chagrined to hear a German staff officer give an accurate briefing to a visiting general on recent changes of command in his own battalion, the PPCLI.

Prisoners soon learned that misunderstanding their captor's English could bring painful consequences. William Quinton, a Newfoundlander, provoked the wrath of his German interrogator by assuming that the correct answer to his question "What is your Reegaumeen (regiment)?" was "Church of England."[53] Captured at Mont Sorrel, Private O'Brien of the 4th CMR seems to have been an exceptional case. He insisted that he was kicked and beaten with rifle butts when he refused to answer questions. Later that same evening, two of the Canadian prisoners were shot for refusing to give up personal belongings. "Some of this may seem far fetched," he later wrote, "but every word is true."[54]

This was certainly not everyone's experience. After Mont Sorrel, two German officers, both of them Cambridge graduates, interrogated Captain Wilken, taunted him for being an Oxford man, and demonstrated that they knew more about the Canadian dispositions than he did. They also treated him to the last good dinner he would experience in captivity.[55]

Captured flyers often recalled the welcome by German aviators as the deceptively cordial beginning of their ordeal. Whether or not comradeship existed in the air, Germans realized that they would get more information by kindness than kicks. Some pilots were invited to inspect German aircraft in the hope that they would unwittingly reveal technical developments. Once they were deposited in a cell of the local jail or in the foul casemates of former French fortresses at Cambrai or Douai, cordiality ceased. For the first eleven days of his captivity Lieutenant Cecil Blain, who had come down behind the German lines during the Somme offensive, found himself in a little two-bed cell in an old French fortress at Cambrai:

> The heat was intense and the smells almost unbearable, which entices flies and other vile insects by the million. The place was fairly full. Dysentery raged among the men, and as far as I

> could judge no attempt to check it was made. The wounded were practically uncared for, and it was not an uncommon sight to see an English soldier looking like death holding up an arm which was a mass of blood, straw, dirt and raw flesh.[56]

At least one Canadian officer had an even more unpleasant post-capture experience. Lieutenant Edward Bellew, the machine-gun officer of the 7th Battalion, had been awarded the Victoria Cross for his gallantry in fighting to the last. The Germans, however, charged him as a war criminal for continuing to fire his machine-gun after a white flag had been raised in surrender. Convicted and sentenced to be shot by a hurried German battlefield tribunal, Bellew had his case heard again by a more formal court martial and he was acquitted. The experience, he later claimed, had left him emotionally scarred. His gallantry award was not announced until his release.[57]

Brigadier General Williams, still adjutant general of the Canadian militia as well as commander of the CEF's 8th Infantry Brigade, was Canada's highest-ranking prisoner of war. Since he lay unconscious for several days after his capture, recovering painfully from severe head injuries and broken ribs, Williams obviously held limited intelligence value for his captors. They did, however, find comfort from his interrogation. Even on June 26, he was still seething at the fate of his brigade. The British artillery supporting the 3rd Division had been incompetent and left his men to their fate, he claimed. British staff officers, he declared, were military amateurs, clinging to an Ypres salient that made no military sense. A major attack was coming but it was not likely to be at the Somme. "If the Germans want to punish me," he told his interrogator, "all they have to do is to put me together with English officers." In contrast to the British, Williams insisted, Canadians had no hatred of Germans and would eagerly seek them as immigrants when the war was over.[58]

Usually, the Germans seemed to have more to tell their new prisoners than to learn from them. The German conviction that the world had misunderstood their need to go to war led to primitive attempts to win the minds, if not the hearts, of their captives. At the same time, Germans felt entitled to vent the special animus they felt against Great Britain, the one-time ally turned bitter imperial rival.[59]

A common feature of reminiscences by Ypres prisoners was reports of abusive harangues by German officers, accusing their Canadian captives of killing wounded, using "dum-dum" bullets, and of being *Geldsoldaten* (mercenaries). The Canadian soldier's basic pay of $1.10 a day translated into four marks, a huge sum by the standard of European conscript armies or even the British army. Prisoners later recalled that Germans contrasted French and Russian conscripts who had to fight with their British and Canadian captives who had deliberately chosen their fate, presumably out of personal hatred for an encircled and endangered Germany. "We did not declare war on Canada," insisted the officer who interrogated Scudamore. "What right have you to come over here and kill our good Germans?" Scudamore's answer, that they had come for fun, provoked rage and blows from the officer's riding crop, most of which, he claimed, fell on the sentry.[60] Private Scott of the 7th Battalion described his arrival at Roulers in terms fellow prisoners echoed less eloquently:

> We were lined up and a German officer of high rank walked up and down in front of us brandishing his sword near our faces, cursing and shouting. Literally foaming at the mouth, his face swollen and red, he presented a terrifying and disgusting sight and one I was often to see again in Germany.[61]

In contrast, the normally resentful Corporal Edwards of the PPCLI recalled the visit of an elderly German general, intrigued to find Canadians in a regiment named for Queen Victoria's granddaughter. The old general, himself related to British royalty, gave orders that the prisoners were to be well treated.[62] Private Mervyn Simmons, another British Columbian, met a German cavalry officer whose brother was an engineer at the Dunsmuir collieries on Vancouver Island.[63] Captain Scudamore persuaded a Württemberg *Jäger* to fetch coffee, proving to his own satisfaction "that all good riflemen of whatever nationality are good fellows."[64]

At Roulers, the German railhead eleven kilometres east of Ypres, prisoners were collected in the big Catholic church, still foul-smelling and covered with straw and manure from the cavalry horses earlier stabled there. Officers were belatedly segregated from the men and lodged in the nave. Other ranks lay on the floor of the transept. Anderson recalled a fellow major who, alone, had kept his warm greatcoat. The senior officer had also managed to find a couple of mattresses and he curled up "to sleep the sleep of the unjust" while the other prisoners shivered through the night.[65] Canadians also had their first experience of the thin soup and sour black bread that would be dietary staples during their long years of captivity. The Germans issued two regulation postcards for prisoners to notify their family and friends of their whereabouts and some of the guards offered to buy chocolate. A few trusting prisoners gave them money and, to the surprise of doubting Thomases like Howland, were vindicated when the chocolate appeared.[66] Seriously wounded Canadian prisoners were collected behind the German lines and brought to a nearby school where Belgian nuns did much of the nursing.[67]

A year later, after Mont Sorrel, prisoners seemed to have had fewer memories of verbal and physical abuse by their captors, though capture, for Canadians as for other prisoners, was a brutal and frightening experience. Private O'Brien, who seems to have seen more than his fair share of atrocities, reported that a German officer cold-bloodedly shot a wounded man from Toronto who was too weak from loss of blood to keep up. "As we went along the men were becoming weaker and we were kicked, pushed and spit on by the German troops stationed along the road. One more man dropped but we kept on so I do not know if he was killed." Near their destination, a railway yard, according to O'Brien:

> Some Belgian women were by the roadside with water and bread they wanted to give us but the guards forbade them to do

> so. One of the Belgian women threw a loaf of bread to us, the guard immediately rushed at her and drove a lance into her stomach, killing her almost instantly.[68]

Canadians captured at Ypres, the St. Eloi Craters, and Mont Sorrel were evacuated to hospitals or to camps in Germany as rapidly as could reasonably be expected. Prisoners taken at the Somme and later in the war often had a different experience. To perform the massive labour needed to create the defensive system the Allies would christen the Hindenberg Line, the Germans drafted huge contingents of Russian prisoners and supplemented them with French and British troops when they caught them. Such prisoners were either not registered with the information bureaux or their address was given as Limburg, the main depot for prisoner-of-war parcels and mail. In 1917, German authorities insisted that such work was no more than a reprisal against the British and French who had contravened the Hague Convention in the same way. By the summer of 1917, however, the British and French insisted that they had moved all their prisoners at least thirty kilometres behind the line while the Germans continued to employ prisoners in military work the Hague Convention certainly had not condoned.

Newfoundlanders, captured at Monchy-le-Preux when their battalion was overrun in a German counter-attack, became victims of the reprisal policy. Prisoners were crowded into Fort McDonald, an old French fortress at Lille: a hundred men in a dank, dark, nine-by-three-metre cell, with burnt-bean coffee for breakfast, a slice of bread and watery soup for lunch, and nothing for supper. Only writing paper was in ample supply, and the men were instructed to remind their family, friends, and British politicians of their plight as "prisoners of respite." When the Newfoundlanders were finally released from their cold, damp cell, many were too weak to walk and at least two had died.[69] Most Canadians taken during the battles of Vimy Ridge, Fresnoy, and Lens in 1917 spent their first weeks and sometimes months of captivity in the same appalling conditions at

Fort McDonald, emerging only to construct trenches, load ammunition, and perform other warlike chores within range of their own guns.[70]

THE HAGUE CONVENTION HAD CONFIRMED THE TRADITIONAL social distinction between officers and other ranks. Few of the Canadian troops ever met their officers again in captivity. Anderson, Scudamore, and the others were taken to the Roulers station and loaded in fourth-class passenger carriages. They were dirty and overcrowded—"a nightmare" insisted Captain Wilken a year later—but distinctly superior to the manure-strewn cattle cars provided for ordinary soldiers. Thorn recalled that officers taken at Ypres were loaded six to a compartment "with a black private from one of the French Zouave regiments. This private was pushed into our carriage and the officer, in very good English, told us he was sending with us one of our black friends to keep us company." German officers, according to Major Anderson, "seemed to think it was a great joke."[71]

Including the wounded, who seem to have joined the German casualty stream, no Canadians of any rank recalled their journey into captivity with any pleasure. Prisoners complained that they were loaded "like cordwood," fifty to sixty men to the small European freight cars, and left for as much as three days with little food or water. W. F. Chambers, a signalman in the 13th Battalion who was captured on April 22 when he strayed into the gap left by the departed Algerians, recalled:

> Each man was assisted into his Pullman by a friendly German boot and for four days and nights we were forced to travel in these luxurious staterooms where it was impossible to sit or lie down without a boot in your mouth. A piece of bread and some coffee were our daily ration combined with unlimited abuse which happily we did not fully understand.[72]

Overcrowded, thirsty, and hungry, with minor wounds becoming infected, the journey to captivity was a bitter memory all Ypres prisoners shared. The Canadians also felt the passions of patriotic or bereaved German civilians. Instead of distributing refreshments at German railway stations, according to Edwards, guards rolled back the wagon doors to display their prisoners. Canadians were introduced as men who had cut the throats of German wounded. Civilian crowds roared their anger and surged against the guards to seek revenge. At Dresden, Lieutenant Thorn remembered, a German woman spat in a Canadian officer's face. But for their guards, claimed Anderson, "we should have been torn to pieces."[73] At Giessen, a mob of angry German civilians besieged the train and threatened the column of prisoners on their way to the camps. "One man was hit full in the face by all the spit a well-dressed woman could collect."[74]

Not everyone was hostile. Simmons remembered a sympathetic blond-haired youngster at Cologne who voluntarily filled the prisoners' water bottles.[75] Private John Vaughan, a Haligonian captured in 1916, was fed potato soup during his journey and allowed to visit a station lavatory.[76] When other-rank prisoners had been shunted off to their camp at Giessen, Scudamore found that the guards would let officers buy whatever they could afford from railway station restaurants. More normally, prisoners arrived late at night, exhausted and hungry after two or three days cooped up in boxcars. Few, by that stage, had much impression of where they were or what the future promised.

3

Barbed-Wire Disease

BY THE TIME CANADIAN PRISONERS BEGAN ARRIVING IN 1915, the worst problems of food, clothing, and overcrowding in the German camps had been overcome. As the neutral "protecting power" for British interests, the United States had increased the staff of its Berlin embassy and begun systematic inspections. German prisoner-of-war policy, published to a highly critical world in February 1915, was as civilized as any humanitarian could desire: "Prisoners of war are protected against unjustified severities, ill treatment and unworthy handling; they do, indeed, lose their freedom, but not their rights; even captivity is, in other words, no longer an act of grace on the part of the victor but a right of the defenceless."[1] As Europe's most sophisticated military power, the Germans had recovered rapidly from the largely unavoidable misery of the first winter of the war.

Most of the Canadians taken at Ypres were sent to the famous university town of Göttingen or to Giessen in Hesse, home of a less famous university where the nutritionist Julius von Liebig had established his reputation. An American neutral observer, Dr. Daniel J. McCarthy, described Giessen as an average camp. His colleague, Dr. Karl Ohnesorg, an assistant American naval attaché, was more flattering. Giessen was, he reported, one of the best-organized and most contented camps, especially after the Russians had been removed.[2] Göttingen was approved by Gerard, especially when a few professors at the famous local university braved public opinion to help establish a library in the camp and its commandant, Colonel Bogen, permitted the YMCA to erect a hut.[3] Most of the Sanctuary Wood prisoners were sent to Dülmen in Westphalia, which figured as one of McCarthy's show-places. Food and quarters were satisfactory, medical and sanitary requirements had been addressed, and prisoner NCOs were left to exercise authority.[4]

Camp regulations in the xth Army Corps required all prisoners to be segregated, fumigated, deloused, inoculated, and then quarantined for a couple of weeks before joining the main body of inmates. Many prisoners recalled four and as many as eight needles jabbed, in German military fashion, into their bare chests. Some, well indoctrinated in Hunnish *Schrecklichkeit*, later insisted that they had been infected with tuberculosis or some other nameless but dread disease.[5]

In quarantine, prisoners became familiar with the slow starvation of the German camp diet. An anonymous diarist described how he and other half-starved Ypres survivors bartered boots, shirts, overcoats, and valuables with French prisoners in exchange for bread or a helping of soup.[6] Some of the wounded who had been compelled to accompany the able-bodied finally found treatment at the camp *Lazarett* (hospital); others were told, with occasional blows and kicks, that they were malingerers. Gas casualties had particular difficulty establishing their claims.

At Dülmen in 1916, Vaughan recalled waiting naked for an hour before joining a hundred British sailors whose ships had been lost in the inconclusive naval battle at Jutland. Vaughan's inoculation and vaccination were performed by a French doctor who had been held as a prisoner of war. Next, he and other Canadians were harangued by the elderly commandant. Through an interpreter, the German promised that he would teach them to be soldiers. He also notified the Canadians that they had no business being in the war since they did not know whether their forefathers were German or English.

Canada, he claimed, belonged to Germany as much as England. However, if they behaved themselves, no harm would come to them.[7]

The quarantine period was a time of depression and disorientation. After the desperate post-capture struggle to survive, the days of idle waiting allowed the harsh fact of being a prisoner to sink in. "Without freedom of movement throughout the camp, forced to subsist on the camp ration foreign to their taste, and huddled together in barracks with other strange nationalities whose languages they do not understand," claimed McCarthy, "the depression and resentment once thus begun rarely completely leaves the prisoner of war."[8] For Vaughan and other prisoners taken at Mont Sorrel, their own defeat was aggravated by the suspicion that Jutland had been a disaster for the seemingly invincible British fleet. Gloom deepened with news that Lord Kitchener, the seemingly masterly British secretary of state for War, had drowned in the sinking of HMS *Hampshire* on his way to Russia.[9]

Once released to the main camp, many prisoners could find a little to cheer them up. Vaughan recalled being issued with a couple of blankets, a spoon, and a bowl. That was better than using his newly issued steel helmet as a receptacle for his soup or coffee. No knives were issued; prisoners had yet to discover how seldom there would be meat to cut. For the most part, prisoners were housed in hurriedly constructed wooden huts. Since the majority of British prisoners had been confined since 1914, newcomers were both welcome as fresh faces with recent news and resented as interlopers. Since survival often depended on food parcels, some British prisoners shared their hoard with newcomers until the Red Cross had been notified of their capture; others left newcomers to fend for themselves.[10]

Many German camps were worse than Giessen. Embarrassed by the relative comfort of an officers' prison, Chaplain Wilken asked permission to minister to prisoners at Minden, a camp of 20,000, a thousand of them British. According to McCarthy, Minden was a punishment camp with a sordid reputation. Leaky wooden huts sat in a vast expanse of yellow clay. Prisoners shivered in dirty, worn-out bedding amidst the odour of open-trench latrines. Many of the British inmates were non-commissioned officers who had refused to work. They paid for their defiance by being drilled, endlessly, by German privates.[11] Wilken endured three months at Minden before his complaints led to charges of insubordination, a fine of three hundred marks or thirty days in the punishment cells, a successful appeal, and transfer to Holzminden. As a non-combatant under the 1899 convention, he should have been repatriated long before, as was the Canadian medical officer taken at Ypres, Captain William Hart, captured with the wounded of the 5th Western Cavalry.[12]

Non-commissioned officers shared captivity with the rank and file. In British and French camps, German NCOs insisted that they *were* officers as defined in the Hague Convention and could not be compelled to work; for British and Canadian sergeants and corporals, it was all a matter of local option. Some of them were left with considerable authority, while others were subordinated to German privates and harshly punished if they defied the orders to work. At Dülmen, Private Howland was introduced to the system of using British sergeants as barracks chiefs or *Dolmetscher.* Prisoners rechristened them "dumb-majors" and presented them with a tough and thankless job.[13] Still, the American observer McCarthy believed that camps operated better when the Germans left matters to imprisoned non-commissioned officers, and he praised British NCOs for cooperating whenever the German authorities were "half reasonable." As for the typical Canadian sergeant, ". . . too much cannot be said in praise of him."[14]

While some prison camps were based on existing German barracks or fortresses, most were dreary enclosures set in open fields and scrub. At Giessen, double fences of barbed wire were patrolled by sentries and guard dogs. At the corners stood wooden watch-towers, often equipped with machine guns. A board fence, three to four metres high, set the horizons of a prisoner's life. An individual camp like Parchim held as many as forty thousand prisoners; others might be half that size, but all were normally subdivided into enclosures for two thousand men. By the time the Canadians arrived in April 1915, most prisoners were housed in ten or a dozen low wooden huts per enclosure, with a few lean-tos housing latrines, a wash-house, and a kitchen where the prison staples of coffee and soup were boiled.[15] Bucket latrines and open-channel cement latrines regularly overflowed, and cleaning them up was a punishment no prisoner wanted. McCarthy, who visited many of the camps, described "the average prison barrack":

> Low long rows of double-tier bunks take up the central floor space of the barrack. Long tables for serving food are placed next to the walls. Bags filled with straw, sea grass or paper serve as mattresses. Each prisoner is supplied with two blankets and these are thrown over the mattresses. Every available space is used for food packages and clothes. The place has a dim, confused, unkempt appearance on account of the crowding of men, the arrangement of the bunks, food packages, clothes, etc. At one end of the barrack a small room is usually walled off for the non-commissioned officers. This is furnished with cots instead of the usual bunk arrangement.[16]

Each hut was designed for two hundred prisoners. Most were heated by stoves and lit electrically, and the prisoners usually fared better than their comrades in the field, with a weekly shower and a dry-heat sterilizer to control the ever-present lice. Whatever was theoretically possible, McCarthy found the huts dirty, untidy, and a reflection of their demoralized occupants. As the Germans expected, a self-segregating mixture of British, French, and Russians was bound to quarrel about housekeeping, ventilation, and much else. The British preferred fresh air; the Russians a warmer but odorous fug; the French detested bad smells but feared a *courant d'air.* Prisoner memoirs reflected those national tensions. Canadians accepted the general British conviction that the Germans favoured the French and Russians, assigned *Engländer* the most miserable work, and took special pleasure in flaunting the wartime slogan *Gott straft England.*[17] The *Continental Times*, a propaganda sheet written largely by German-Americans and issued from Berlin, insisted that the war would last only until England had bled her allies to death.[18] German guards echoed the message.

There were exceptions to the German policy of integration. Russians, as Dr. Ohnesorg reported, were removed from Giessen, perhaps because of the typhus problem. Despite their dismissal of formal British protests against mixing nationalities, integrating black and white prisoners exceeded the Germans' own racial sensibilities. All Moslem, African, and Indian prisoners were sent to Zossen where a large mosque was built at the kaiser's command, doubtless as a timely gesture to his Turkish allies. It became a prominent feature in the illustrated booklets published by the Germans to celebrate their humanitarian treatment of their prisoners of war. The Germans also concentrated Irish prisoners, including a number of Canadians, at Limburg to help encourage them to join Sir Roger Casement's Irish Brigade. The unit, they were promised, would serve on the Russian front and its veterans would be sent to the United States at the end of the war, with a thousand-dollar gratuity. Private James Sullivan of the 3rd Battalion, captured at Ypres, had already suffered a painful beating by guards at Giessen for failing to understand orders in German when he was transferred to Limburg. He was not in a mood to switch sides. When only a handful of prisoners accepted the offer, German treatment changed.[19] Sullivan recalled that he was beaten and condemned to twenty-eight days' solitary confinement for "insubordination."[20]

Until they were worn out, prisoners wore their own uniforms, with identifying strips of bright red or yellow paint on the sleeves, up the back, and down the trouser leg. Troublemakers were identified by a bright red or brown circle painted on the back of their uniforms. Harry Howland, an Ypres prisoner, annoyed his captors by painting a realistic replica of the Iron Cross on a prisoner's uniform and drawing a sword hilt at the top of his trouser-stripe.[21] German policy was to issue uniforms from "war booty" and, when that was exhausted, to authorize camp commanders to provide replacements. "The clothing generally consists of a suit, necktie and cap, besides shirts, socks, warm underwear and good shoes as well as overcoats and woolen blankets to protect against the cold," claimed the prisoner-of-war regulations.[22] In practice, few Canadians ever saw more than thin German blankets and wooden clogs. Germany suffered an acute wartime shortage of most kinds of cloth and of leather, and prisoners were not a high priority. By 1915, when British prisoners' uniforms had been reduced to rags, the Red Cross had shipped large quantities of dark blue serge coats, trousers, and overcoats, as well as shirts, underwear, and socks. In well-managed camps there was no shortage. Since the Red Cross clothes lent themselves to conversion to civilian clothing for escapers, sleeves and trouser legs were ripped open by the Germans and brightly coloured cloth was sewn into the new seams. Still, clothing seems to have been a real problem for the Canadians. In 1916, Ohnesorg reported that Canadian prisoners were in particular need of uniforms.[23]

At the end of April 1915, the German war ministry also defined its promise of "a plentiful diet." Prisoners of medium weight doing light work would receive twenty-seven hundred calories a day; those doing heavy work would get 10 per cent more; those doing nothing—hospital patients, for example—would get 10 per cent less. The morning meal would include soup with 100 grams of solid substance. Stew at lunch would include 90 to 120 grams of meat (or corresponding quantities of fish, soya, or horse beans), 500 to 600 grams of potato, and 500 grams of other vegetables. At night, prisoners would be fed 500 grams of potatoes in their skins and a combination of herring, cheese, rice, butter, and sugar. In October, Berlin announced further improvements. "Despite numerous modifications of the quantities of individual items," claims Speed, "the overall amount of food remained roughly equivalent. In short, the calories provided by the basic menu remained much the same through the war."[24] That was not what the prisoners remembered. Chambers, who began his captivity at Meschede, left a detailed description of his weekly rations, which was generally echoed by his fellow prisoners:

> Our rations consisted of a bowl of synthetic coffee (burnt ground barley) for breakfast, nothing else. At noon we had soup of which there were five varieties—sauerkraut and water, boiled pot barley, chestnut, bean, and an extra special abomination of fried fruits stewed up with potatoes. Each soup had a few potatoes boiled in it for flavour. They rang the changes of these occasionally with some boiled fish. At night we got two potatoes and a piece of bread. I think the bread was supposed to be held over for breakfast but once we got it we ate it. Sometimes with the potatoes we got a raw herring or a piece of cheese, sometimes a sausage, but the cheese and sausage were such vile smelling things that it required a great deal of effort to devour.[25]

At Giessen, Howland recalled acorn coffee for breakfast, watery soup at noon, and a thin gruel and sometimes a herring or sausage at 5 p.m. when the daily bread ration, 100 grams, was issued. The bread, as Chambers noted, was expected to last until breakfast, but it seldom did. Except for the bread, everything in the German diet could be eaten with a spoon, hence the absence of knives and forks. The predominantly liquid diet, claimed Howland, sapped the prisoners' physical strength and left most of them with a lifetime legacy of stomach disorders. According to the nutritional knowledge of the time, German rations lacked the fats and protein needed for cold weather and for the manual labour prisoners were soon called upon to perform.[26] Admittedly, few Canadian prisoners ever acknowledged that the basic rations of the German army—black bread and soup and the occasional sausage or herring—were fit for human consumption. Private Bertram Ashbourne of the 3rd Battalion remembered the bean soup: "There was no body in it. Nothing to help nourish us."[27] Arrivals at Dülmen in 1916 were treated to "Sand Storm," a porridge, Stephen O'Brien reported, that "looked like sand, and did not taste much better." The noon meal was soup made from mangels and the odd potato. "The boys were all very hungry and the thought of food almost drove us mad."[28]

Even if prison food had been adequate, it would still have been a preoccupation. Lacking other outlets, some prisoners fought and conspired against each other, and food was the most frequent focus. Canadians were almost unanimous in believing that food was one way their guards favoured the French and encouraged the traditional enmity for the British. The prisoner chosen to dish out the soup could play favourites, doling out greasy flavoured water from the top of the pot to enemies or, for friends, digging deep with his ladle to bring up whatever solid meat or vegetable there might be. Edwards recalled German amusement that hungry British prisoners volunteered for kitchen work in order to get enough to eat. It was French prisoners, according to Vaughan and Simmons, who usually got the job of cooking and serving the food and, accordingly, could favour their friends.

FROM THE FIRST MONTHS OF THE WAR, THERE WAS ONE CLEAR alternative to starvation in the camps: food parcels from friends and relatives. Even in wartime, the mails passed through neutral Switzerland, Denmark, and the Netherlands to reach Britain and Germany. The German horror of theft helped keep even enemy parcels sacrosanct. The problem for senders was to identify and locate the recipient. This was the task the International Committee of the Red Cross had performed in 1870 and which, at Washington in 1912, it had prepared itself to perform again. Within days of the outbreak of war in 1914, the Swiss body had opened an information bureau in Geneva to help transmit information about prisoners and other casualties from one side to the other. Counterpart offices soon opened in Berlin, London, Paris, and Petrograd, the Russian capital.[29] The Germans promptly began passing thousands of names through their

Red Cross Society to Geneva while their enemies fussed that the Hague Convention required an "official" information bureau and wondered whether they should respond. The Allies eventually had no choice. In London, a prisoner-of-war information bureau near Covent Garden ultimately employed three hundred people to keep track of prisoner-of-war and internment camps throughout the British Empire (including Canada) and to keep a record of the constantly shifting location of British prisoners in Germany.[29]

From the first, French and British prisoners depended on parcels from families and friends to supplement their meagre and unpleasant German rations. A painful memory was that of waiting for the first parcel to arrive. Chambers remembered his frustration when, after months, his first mail from home arrived—a letter asking whether he would like food parcels. An English relative, empathetic if impractical, mailed him a package of sandwiches and cake "which, in spite of being a trifle mouldy, was cleaned up in short order."[31] Lieutenant Sandy Baird, a Newfoundlander, urged friends to send butter, milk, jam, sugar, tea, tinned meat, and good St. John's hard tack. "It would keep well and, soaked overnight, the next morning fried with a little bacon fat or dripping, would make an excellent breakfast."[32]

Those without such supplements suffered grievously. Russians, with no more than German rations, "looked when undressed like the India famine victims," Private Simmons recalled, "with their washboard ribs and protruding stomachs, dull eyes and parched skin."[33] Chambers remembered: "Two or three fellows would pool their parcels and mess together and adopt a Russian prisoner." In return for washing up, mending clothes, and other small services, the Russian got whatever his "messmates" disliked.[34]

Transmitting private parcels to prisoners soon turned into a nightmare. Many people had no practical idea of what prisoners needed. String and wrapping paper broke, and mail bags arrived with their contents smeared with melted butter, broken eggs, and shattered bottles. A few prisoners boasted that they had managed to smuggle in maps, compasses, and other tools of escape, but censors were generally condemned for opening parcels and allowing the contents to spoil. Shrewd and well-connected prisoners accumulated generous donors while friendless prisoners got nothing. Poor families could often spare a son or husband pathetically little. To supply the hapless Henri Béland, the Canadian High Commissioner simply ordered the well-known Army & Navy Stores to oblige with its standard packages. Others looked to the famous London provisioners, Fortnum & Mason. Still, some prisoners were lucky to get an occasional package of biscuits, corned beef, or a severely flattened birthday cake.

Because so many British prisoners were army regulars, captured in 1914, the depots of British regiments got involved, often with practical assistance from the Church Army, an Anglican relief agency. In the honoured British tradition, a Prisoners of War Help Committee was launched to tackle the problem and, like most other wartime patriotic charities, found the task entirely beyond its strength. In 1915, the Red Cross took over, establishing a depot in South Kensington that eventually kept 750 people busy. The goal was to provide a 4.5 kilogram parcel to each prisoner every two weeks. A formidable woman, Lady Evelyn Grant Duff, took charge of providing British prisoners with white bread. She arranged to ship flour from Marseilles to Geneva, contracted with bakeries, and organized to have loaves delivered by road and rail to Frankfurt. Ideally, bread reached the camps within a week, but prisoners welcomed Lady Duff's "Swiss dodgers" even if they were rock hard or mouldy. Later, she moved the bakery to Berne, opened up routes through Holland and Denmark, and provided biscuits or rusks in the summer when the problem of bread mould was at its worst.[35]

By the time Canadians became interested in prisoners, the dominant role of the Red Cross had been established. The Toronto-based Canadian Red Cross had already appointed an overseas commissioner, Colonel H. W. Blaylock, primarily to address the needs of the sick and wounded. After Ypres, Evelyn Rivers Bulkeley took charge of a new Prisoners of War Depot. She began with two helpers and 180 prisoners' names taken from a list supplied through Geneva by the German Red Cross. Within a few weeks she had learned of more Canadians in twenty different locations. The lists grew to include Canadian civilians and merchant seamen interned in German camps and, by the end of the year, fourteen hundred prisoners of war. In Canada, friends and relatives were as generous and eager to help as anywhere else. Patriots were easily persuaded to adopt a prisoner and keep him supplied. However, by the fall of 1916, the British had had enough of the flood of private parcels—which they also felt obliged to inspect as a potential channel of intelligence and contraband to Germany—and insisted that, from February 1, 1917, only official parcels would be permitted. With characteristic insensitivity, the order exempted parcels to officers.[36]

The new policy caused an uproar in England, Canada, and, when they heard of it, in the camps. "Are we mothers not suffering enough without being cut off from sending our dear sons something from 'Home' to cheer and brighten them," wrote a Montreal woman whose son was at Cellelager.[37] Sergeant-Major A. E. Thompson, a Giessen captive, protested that prisoners had been picked on as easy victims in a campaign of food conservation: "They pick out the one helpless body of men there is, men who cannot move a finger to help themselves, nor express themselves freely in writing. . . . We have all too little to keep us in touch with the home folks when they cut off the home parcels we have."[38] As recipient of so much anguish, the Canadian prime minister, Sir Robert Borden, added his own protest, only to be informed from London that the War Office had made its ruling and the complaints would have to be swallowed for the greater good of the war effort.[39]

Over time, the War Office reluctantly modified its policies. By the summer of 1917, officers too had to get along without private parcels, though the head of the Canadian Red Cross assured Borden they would still get two extra parcels a month. "There should be as little as possible said publicly that the officers' parcels will be selected with special regard for their requirements." By 1918, the War

Office had even relented on private parcels provided they were limited to one every three months and restricted to an austere range of items that included pipes, tooth powder, shaving soap, and such soldiers' favourites as buttons, rank badges, dubbin, and hobnails.[40]

The Red Cross emerged from the controversy with added power and responsibility. The Canadian organization undertook that it would send three 4.5 kilogram parcels every fortnight to each prisoner—a thousand boxes or three tons of parcels a day—as well as Lady Duff's loaves. Each month, prisoners would be sent 225 grams of tobacco and 250 cigarettes. Each prisoner would receive a supply of warm clothing twice a year and a new overcoat once a year. Because packages were officially packed, with strictly specified contents, border inspections could be cursory and lengthy delays could be avoided. To ensure parcels reached their destination, comprehensive records were kept. The prisoner to whom a parcel was addressed was expected to return a card showing he had received it. If there was no response after three months, the Red Cross asked the Germans for information.[41]

To pay the cost, an estimated $40 per prisoner per year, the Red Cross urged families and "adopters" to contribute. When the minister of Militia, Sir Sam Hughes, discovered how much prisoners depended on the Red Cross for food, he promptly ordered a $1.10 monthly deduction from their pay—and then made it voluntary. A notice in each soldier's paybook suggested: "If you are taken prisoner and wish to assign a small portion of your pay, say 10s[hillings] a month to the Canadian Red Cross Society for the purpose of purchasing comforts, write to the Chief Paymaster. . . ."[42] Whatever soldiers in the field might feel about such a precaution, at least some prisoners were furious. Doubtless reflecting his son's view, R. L. Thompson was indignant that the Red Cross would dun "these poor fellows as prisoners" to pay for a few extra luxuries. Through her office, Mrs. Bulkeley became the intermediary for correspondence about prisoners' pay, family problems, and official policy. When Ottawa proposed sending its prisoners spending money to help alleviate their misery, Mrs. Bulkeley was the expert who advised against it. The cash, she sensibly explained, would be useless in most German camps and it would also be unfair to send men their pay when they had not asked for it. If prisoners needed money, she had been able to arrange international money orders. American Express, she pointed out, was more efficient than the post office.[43]

While officers occasionally grumbled about the monotony of a steady diet of tinned food, and nutritionists noticed that fats were almost as lacking in the parcels as they were in the official German ration, there were no complaints from the lower ranks.[44] While members of the CEF in England and France often condemned the Red Cross for giving its highest priority to the welfare of officers, prisoners of war were unstinting in their praise of Red Cross packages. While German censors in regular camps forbade letters that were too explicit about hunger, escapers and repatriated prisoners offered Mrs. Bulkeley's co-workers genuine testimonials. "No one but a prisoner of war can appreciate what all the good things sent by the Canadian Red Cross meant to us." Without the parcels, another claimed, "I believe firmly all the boys would have been on the departed list by now, myself included."[45] Not only did parcels feed prisoners, cakes of soap could be bartered as luxuries virtually unknown in much of Germany by the later years of the war. Indeed, if they received parcels, prisoners were better fed than most Germans. "What do you think of a country where even women and children and soldiers in uniform come begging for food from English prisoners," wondered Corporal G. B. Edie in 1918. "I am sorry for the women and children but, for the soldiers, never."[46] It may not have occurred to Edie that a less disciplined people might have found it impossible to tolerate being worse fed than some of their prisoners of war.

The vast and well-publicized effort of the Red Cross to deliver parcels to prisoners of war left an impression that its beneficiaries lived in comfort. While some did, many were both hungry and malnourished. Packages were usually cut off from prisoners in reprisal camps, as well as those working behind the German lines or imprisoned in local cells or in the penal fortresses at Cologne or Butzbach, and denying parcels was among the commonest forms of mass punishment. Parcels were often slow to follow prisoners as they moved from worksite to worksite and at each stage the risk grew that some of them would be stolen or destroyed. For many prisoners, they meant the difference between constant hunger and the acute starvation that Russian prisoners faced, but they were seldom the basis for a comfortable life. Private A. J. Cleeton, released after three years at Sennelager, weighed 40 kilograms, not his normal 64.[47]

Both the Geneva and Hague conventions required combatants to treat sick and wounded as they would soldiers on their own side. Like German military patients, prisoners received special hospital flannel clothing, a quilt, and a palliasse. Sometimes they shared wards with the Germans, less often they were put in separate and inferior accommodation. A country that probably led the world in medical science in 1914 nonetheless provided frugally for the medical needs of its soldiers—and its prisoners.

Treating enemies on the same footing as fellow soldiers is a moral challenge even devoted professionals might find hard to meet completely, and emotions ran high, even in 1915. Atrocity stories of enemy maltreatment of wounded prisoners abounded on both sides. A popular British propaganda poster recorded the legend of the German nurse coldly pouring water on the ground in front of a thirsty but helpless British officer. Because wounded prisoners were repatriated as early as 1915, accounts of their experiences may have been shaded by wartime prejudices. An anonymous sergeant of the 2nd Battalion, writing in a London magazine, claimed that he had suffered agonies during his evacuation. There was hot food and coffee for German wounded but nothing for *Engländer Schweine* (English pigs). A surgeon at a German naval hospital in Bruges set his leg without anaesthetic, and it was only days later that his dirty clothes were removed and a German sailor gave him a bath. When a clumsy orderly removed his cast, his bone was broken again. A month later, attempting crutches, he fell on the polished floor, to the jeers of German patients. After a spell in the Bruges jail among "the German scum, who were doing two to three and five years for refusing to fight," he was finally transferred to Germany and to highly professional treatment at Cologne.[48]

While the sergeant's account portrays both light and shadows, all wartime writing about the prisoner experience served a propaganda function. Certainly that was true of *A Guest of the Kaiser*, a wartime book by Private Arthur Gibbons, who became a recruiting sergeant after his repatriation. According to Gibbons, when he awoke from surgery—preceded by a *Gott straft England* lecture—he discovered that his injured leg was 14 centimetres shorter than its mate and his foot had been turned so that he could now see his heel. Everyone, from nurses to the hospital chaplain, joined in tormenting him. It wasn't until he got back to Toronto that his leg was rebroken and fixed.[49]

Prisoners were not easy or comfortable patients. While British and Canadian soldiers welcomed a "Blighty"—a wound bad enough to remove them from the battlefield to the comfort and cleanliness of a hospital in England—a wounded prisoner faced very different but simultaneous adjustments: to disability and to captivity. Helpless in an alien and uncomprehending environment, they could easily assume cruel maltreatment when damaged legs were amputated.[50] Like Germans, Canadian prisoners suffered from shortages of drugs and cotton bandages. Private Percy Wakefield, captured at the Somme with shrapnel in his legs, complained that fragments were removed without anaesthetic and the wounds were covered by paper bandages.[51] German rations were as unpleasant a discovery in hospital as in the camps. At Cologne, Lieutenant Norman Wells found that there were two food classes and "all the stuff for the second class was put in a kind of bucket and then stirred around till it looked like a pig's trough. The bread was awful stuff, very dark brown and sour and hard." He was luckier: first-class food was "quite eatable, though

I expect our hospitals would have shuddered at it."[52] Officer-prisoners often complained that they were expected to pay for their hospital and medical treatment.

Private A. M. Allan of Princess Patricia's Canadian Light Infantry was picked up by Germans two days after the Mont Sorrel offensive. A surgeon operated on his shattered jaw, Belgian nuns fed him through a glass pipe, and, after he had been evacuated to an improvised hospital in Stuttgart, he believed that he was fed and cared for as well as German wounded.[53] Private C. W. Baker, gassed and shot in the hip at Ypres, had little treatment until he reached a hospital at Paderborn, but then German orderlies did what they could. His German surgeon was "rough but efficient," operating four times without anaesthetic.[54] Corporal F. W. Newberry of the 7th Battalion, wounded twice at Ypres, reported fair treatment during his long pilgrimage to a hospital at Hofgeismar. Once there, he participated in the funeral of a Canadian private and of Captain M. V. Harvey of his own battalion. On both occasions, the Germans provided military honours, including a band and firing party.[55]

WARTIME CONDITIONS AND THE IMPOSSIBILITY OF FOLLOW-UP made proper treatment difficult. William Gray, whose jaw was shattered at Lens, praised a German surgeon for a delicate wiring operation, but the wires had to be removed weeks later by a Russian prisoner.[56] Ambrose Zapfe of the PPCLI, captured at Hooge after five days in the open, complained that he was sent for treatment to a venereal disease hospital, where he had no protection from infection. He survived intact.[57] Lieutenant Alvin Ferguson, taken prisoner in March 1918 after his plane crashed, noted the overcrowding and shortages in German hospitals, but found that his German doctor was "very gentle" and his nurses "very nice." His greatest misery came as infection spread through his leg during a lengthy journey across Germany to a camp at Kalmerschlitz. A Russian doctor saved the limb, however, and by June he was taking his first steps.[58]

Many Canadian prisoners suffered from battlefield wounds or poison gas. Most of the seriously wounded from Ypres found themselves at a former Catholic monastery at Paderborn, but a majority were classed among the "walking wounded," capable of making their own way out of battle and even as far as a camp in Germany before receiving treatment. This was a painful and demoralizing experience. On the whole, wounded prisoners were treated promptly at the camp *Lazarett*, but, as in their own army, sickness was more likely to be challenged as malingering. Language, cultural differences, and the undoubted fact that many prisoners were intent on "dodging the column"—avoiding work for the enemy—meant that many who were genuinely sick were denied treatment. A Canadian doctor at Minden, Captain F. S. Park, complained that his German superiors were "in the main what might be called student probationers" who "vaunted their superiority" by changing his diagnoses.[59] Like other prisoners, the sick and wounded found the food unsatisfactory and a few encountered brutality, incompetence, and grossly inadequate facilities. So did some German soldiers.

Except at the moment of capture, officer-prisoners shared a very different experience from their men. The Hague Convention reflected the values of a class-based society. Brigadier General Williams' plea that he would prefer to be imprisoned with men in the ranks rather than with British officers reflected strong feelings, not a demand he or the Germans could take seriously. When the cattle cars filled with their men were shunted off to Giessen, officer-prisoners from Ypres continued down the line to Bischofswerda, a new cavalry barracks south-east of Dresden on the edge of the Bohemian hills. Scudamore, for one, remembered the beautiful countryside. While officers were crowded several to a room and had to put up with the moods of the German commandant, a peacetime bottle manufacturer, they were free to play tennis, baseball, and football, read, organize theatricals, and to do whatever self-discipline and ingenuity could devise to overcome idleness and despair.[60] Men from their own armies acted as orderlies, preparing meals, cleaning quarters, and polishing their officers' boots. German regulations called for the provision of "a sufficient and nutritious fare."[61] At Bischofswerda in 1915, Major Anderson reported that breakfast was a small white roll and "dishwater coffee"; dinner included soup, meat, sausage, fish, bread, and potatoes; tea could include a pickled herring. "A person could live on it quite alright, but it was by no means what we would eat at home."[62] For men at Giessen, it would have seemed a feast.

All but a few prisons for officers, claimed McCarthy, were satisfactory. Most were in fortresses, barracks, high schools, and sanataria. Many Mont Sorrel prisoners were sent to Clausthal, a camp in the Harz Mountains that a British investigative committee would condemn as one of the least satisfactory in the system. To a cheaply built peacetime hotel, the Germans had added three sleeping huts, a substantial set of fences, and a few outhouses for the officers' orderlies. The British insisted that the dining room was grossly overcrowded, sanitary facilities were inadequate, and mass punishments such as closing the exercise yard or shutting off electricity in the bedrooms were common. Lieutenant Wells, taken at Mont Sorrel with the 4th Canadian Mounted Rifles, would have agreed. "The overcrowding was scandalous," he complained, "and at least twice as many men as there should be were in each room. No curtains were allowed; one or two rooms purchased them and they were torn down. . . ."[63] Wells also found, however, that officers were left alone with their sports, food parcels, and cooking facilities. In winter he had an opportunity to flood a small skating rink. Officers who promised to return could wander in the country or shop and visit doctors and dentists in the nearby town. Wells's chief complaint was about the loud-mouthed, abusive camp commandant named Heinrich Niemeyer, and the unfairness of periodic searches. Niemeyer's brother Karl ran an even more repressive regime at Holzminden.[64] Neither Niemeyer was running a hotel.

The 1907 Hague Convention required that officer-prisoners receive the same pay as officers of the captor nation, subject to a postwar reconciliation. In return, officers were expected to pay for their own food, clothing, and other needs. Since German rates were roughly half those of the British army, and the British had relatively few officer-prisoners, this created immediate difficulties. After some delay, the Germans announced that they would pay subalterns 60 marks and more senior officers 100 marks, the equivalent of $15 a month for a lieutenant and $25 for a captain. Most of the money was promptly deducted for the cost of rations.[65] Operating in their own bureaucratic world, army pay officials in London promptly saw savings to be made. British authorities decided that staff officers lost their extra allowances after sixty-one days and those with acting rank dropped to the pay of the substantive rank. Early in 1916, Canadian officials notified their captive officers that, since the Germans were now providing their food, their dollar-a-day messing allowance had been cancelled and Ypres prisoners would have to pay back as much as $221 each. Furious protests from Major Peter Byng-Hall and a redeeming common sense soon cancelled the cut, but not without leaving a powerful sense of grievance.[66]

British officers often judged camps on their facilities for games and amateur theatricals—though they admitted that the French were usually more skilful at such pastimes. Captain Douglas Lyall Grant devoted himself at a succession of camps to the study of Spanish—a somewhat quixotic pursuit in a setting where French or Russian instructors would have been easier to find. He also recalled that Canadians introduced their camps to baseball. At Holzminden, a British side called the "Mugs" and experienced chiefly in cricket took on the Canadian team and beat it.[67] Grant summoned a set of bagpipes from home, hid his illegal diary in the waistband of his kilt, and ensured that in any camp that held him hogmanay and St. Andrew's Day were properly observed. At Stralsund on the Baltic, Lieutenant Alvin Ferguson, a Canadian in the Royal Flying Corps with medical ambitions, planned to use his prison days to study chemistry and botany. Courses in physiology and anatomy fell through.[68] Free of the need to work, better provided with food parcels than men in the ranks, and sometimes even able to draw on their own funds, officer-prisoners could govern their own lives. Enforced idleness became a tremendous test of character, in some ways tougher than the forced labour that faced men in the ranks. Sadly, many vegetated, taking to their beds in cold weather and stirring from them only for the obligatory inspection. Orderlies could be obliged to bring them their meals. Others, like Grant and Ferguson, struggled to fill their days with sports and organized study; a few plotted and worked to escape.

Prison was still prison, however. Officers were required to report for two daily roll-calls and an angry commandant could keep them standing for hours. Regulations for a typical camp warned that guards had orders to shoot to kill if any prisoner attempted to escape. All German officers must be saluted and the occupants of a bedroom must spring to attention if an officer entered. Uniforms must be worn during the day. Officers must be out of bed by 9 a.m. and the canteen would close off sales at 8 p.m. The junior officer in each room must oversee the orderlies in clean-up and bed-making. Meals at 8 a.m, 12 p.m., and 6 p.m. would be announced by a single sound of the bell. Prisoners could write two letters a week, but they must be in pencil and "the writing must be done in large and plain characters."[69]

Offenders against the innumerable rules were summoned to the commandant for a tongue-lashing and, all too frequently, for a spell of bread and water in the camp cells. At Clausthal, Niemeyer was no respecter of rank and dignity. Wells reported that the Senior British Officer (SBO) at his camp, Major General H. S. L. Ravenshaw, was harshly disciplined after telling Niemeyer that he thought collective punishment for individual offences was unfair. Fortunately for the general, the single punishment cell beside the camp pigsty had by then been replaced by a sixteen-cell building. The camp commander kept it filled with victims of his wrath.[70] Serious troublemakers, persistent escapers, and those for whom their captors had conceived a special animus were transferred to camps like Strohen and Holzminden. Ingolstadt, a ring of brick fortresses that were notoriously damp, ill-lit, and cheerless, was a destination for regular escapers.[71] At Magdeburg, the prison was a warehouse where officers, some of them elderly, were housed without any pretence of privacy or much hope of cleanliness.[72]

When Winston Churchill, Britain's First Lord of the Admiralty, announced that U-boat crews would be treated as criminals and jailed in naval prisons, the Germans reciprocated by consigning an equivalent number of British officers—preferably those with titles or double-barrelled names—to a regime of solitary confinement in civilian prisons. With Churchill's departure and his successor's announcement of a change in policy, the specific reprisal ceased.[73] Still, others followed. When the Allies began bombing German cities within range of their aircraft, the Germans located reprisal camps for officers in the centre of such frequent targets as Freiberg. The British retaliated by placing their more senior prisoners in coastal resorts, where they were subject to bomber and Zeppelin raids.

As the war continued conditions in the officers' camps deteriorated, particularly in 1918 when German food shortages brought the country close to starvation and when German military successes brought hordes of new prisoners and a corresponding slump in morale.

CAMP ROUTINE, AS DESCRIBED BY MCCARTHY AND IN PRISONER memoirs, was as deadening as the surroundings. Life centred on the overcrowded, ill-lit hut, jammed with double-decker bunks and all the occupants' possessions. According to Simmons, the day began at 6 a.m. with prison coffee and any bread that had survived the hunger of the night. Bedding was folded and inmates waited listlessly until *Appell* or roll-call at 10 a.m. when the camp was counted. The noon meal was soup, supplemented by whatever was left from the latest food parcel. An afternoon of football, languid gossip, or camp chores included another roll-call. At 5 p.m., guards issued the day's ration of black bread—a two-kilogram loaf for eleven men, according to Vaughan.[74] An evening meal promised more soup, with perhaps a pickled fish or corn mush. Prisoners, crowded into their huts, might join a game of cards until lights-out. Then, as McCarthy described it, "the tired, loathsome day had gone the way of ever so many tired, loathsome, never-ending days, to be followed by the beginning of another such day on the morrow."[75]

McCarthy found French prisoners taken at Verdun, who sat day after day, motionless and brooding, and he described their condition with appropriate clinical detachment. "There they sat, woe personified, apparently looking through the barbed wire, but with that vacant look which could only mean a refusal to accept as real the things they saw and to look through it and beyond it to what might have been."[76] Gilbert Taylor, confined in Dülmen with a badly wounded arm, described days that consisted mainly of hunting for the lice and fleas that infested his body and bedding. Corporal Edwards of the PPCLI reported: "We became sick of the sight of one another, as even the best of friends do under such abnormal circumstances." Since he had nothing to talk about, he took to walking with a Russian: since neither understood the other, there could be nothing to discuss. "We knew nothing and could only speculate on the outcome of the commonest events which came to us on the tongue or rumour or arose out of our own sad thoughts."[77]

"It was a situation where a man had to have a very strong mind," recalled a young British Columbian, "and he had to have a determination built in that he was only there for a short time, that it couldn't last."[78] Officers suffered the same misery. Captain Walter Haight, a Canadian medical officer with brilliant professional prospects, returned from his years at Bischofswerda, Crefeld, and, ultimately, Niemeyer's psychological hell at Holzminden with acne, bad teeth, and a mind too mentally disoriented to manage in private practice.[79] His fellow doctor, Captain F. S. Park, was more fortunate in having worked at Minden where, despite poor conditions and German perversity, he was busy and needed.[80] Another Holzminden prisoner, Lieutenant Frederick Walthew, described much the same conditions as Corporal Edwards:

> With nothing to do except cook our meals—most of which came out of tins from our parcels and only required heating up—I think it was extraordinary that we managed to exist—I won't say live—in such harmony as we did. Trifles which in ordinary life one would absolutely ignore, assumed mammoth proportions when one was herded up in a small space for an indefinite period with three hundred men drawn from every walk of life. It was incredible the intensity of dislike one could work up in a very short time for a man's face, the way he did his hair, and his habits and hobbies generally.[81]

Observers soon had a name for the neurotic symptoms of prolonged captivity: "barbed-wire disease."[82] At least for their lower-rank prisoners, the Germans had a cure.

4

Labour and Pain

THE UNEXPECTED LENGTH OF THE WAR WAS A CRUEL BLOW for its prisoners. It also presented each belligerent with huge problems. Apart from the perceptive Ivan Bloch, experts of all kinds had predicted that wars between major powers could last only a few months, for the obvious reason that national economies and international finance simply could not stand the strain. The experts had a point, though their estimates were off by up to four years. In the meantime, governments had to wrestle with seemingly insoluble problems, and no government did so with more clarity of mind and ruthlessness of purpose than Germany's.

In the first year of the war, Germany had mobilized an army of 4.3 million troops. The price of the series of victories in Belgium, France, and Poland was that close to eight hundred thousand Germans had been killed, captured, or wounded seriously enough to be returned to Germany.[1] If a war effort designed for a few months of total commitment had to be sustained for a further year and perhaps longer, labour would become a crucial component. The British were intent on a naval blockade, cutting Germany's access to many natural resources. The Ukraine, Europe's granary in 1914, lay behind the Russian lines. Food must be grown and harvested, and additional acreage must be cleared, drained, and fertilized. A host of imported necessities, from lumber to chemicals, must be produced at home. Germany had been the first to realize the enormous quantities of material required for the siege warfare in the trenches. At every stage, from mining iron ore to loading finished artillery shells, extensive labour was needed to rebuild Germany's huge stockpiles of munitions.[2]

The idleness of a million and a half Russian, French, Belgian, and British prisoners was both a problem and an opportunity. While employers and workers in Britain resisted using prisoners as forced labour, and their German counterparts may have been no more enthusiastic, the need was too great to be ignored. Moreover, Germany had plenty of recent experience in turning reluctant, unskilled peasants into a disciplined, hard-working labour force, and their prisoners would now be the recipients of that brutal but effective process. There was also a small, added benefit: thanks to the French and British belief that their men would starve without regular food parcels, the burden of nourishing at least part of this massive workforce would be shared with the enemy.[3]

Putting prisoners to work was certainly legal. The Hague Convention's Article VI had been explicit: "The State may employ the labour of prisoners of war, other than officers, according to their rank and capacity. The work shall not be excessive, and shall have no connection with the operations of the war." Other sections provided for prisoners to work on their own account or for civilian contractors. Slave labour, of course, was banned: prisoners had to be paid whatever rate the captors would have given their own men. "The wages of the prisoners shall go towards improving their position, and the balance shall be paid them on their release after deducting the cost of their maintenance." On this subject, at least, Germany's *War Book*, published early in 1915, was not lacking in good sense or humanity: "Prisoners of war can be put to moderate work proportionate to their position in life; work is a safeguard against excesses. Also on grounds of health this is desirable. But these tasks should not be prejudicial to health nor in any way dishonourable or such as contribute directly or indirectly to the military operations against the Fatherland of the captives."[4]

Beginning early in 1915, the camps for other-rank prisoners became *Stammlager* (depot-prisons) for dozens and ultimately hundreds of *Arbeitskommandos* (working parties). The arrangements, as usual, were left to the army corps districts. Contracts were devised between local commanders and potential employers, covering wages, payment for military guards, accommodation and food for prisoners and escorts, and such minor details as medical attention and hours of work. Would-be employers ranged from Krupp, the huge munitions maker, to individual farmers in need of a few hands. Once arrangements had been completed for payment, accommodation, and safe custody for the prisoners, a handful of elderly *Landstürmer* marched them out to the scene of their future labour and handed them over to civilian overseers to put them to work. The guard remained, and its commander was armed with the virtual power of life and death over his charges—and the fear that he might face the front lines if he failed in his responsibilities.

Working and living conditions varied enormously. Prisoners sent as agricultural workers were usually housed in the local community hall or made themselves at home in a hayloft, where their guards could keep track of them more securely. Chambers, sent to a farm in the spring and summer of 1917, occupied a small bedroom where he was solemnly locked at bedtime each night.[5] German industry had long been accustomed to using ill-paid migrant labourers from poorer regions of the Empire and its Slav neighbours; prisoners of war simply took their place. Many work sites included wooden huts or barracks for civilian single workers. In some factories, disused buildings were walled off to accommodate prisoners. In others, huts were erected in the factory yard, and then walled off with barbed wire and sentry posts. The prisoners were supplied with mattresses and a pair of blankets. The larger factories usually provided adequate bathing facilities, latrines, and medical services. In conformity with the Hague rules, employers paid their workers 16 to 40 pfennigs a day for farm labour, 30 to 50 pfennigs a day in small industries, and as much as a mark a day in large factories. Prisoners were paid a quarter of the amount—invariably in prison scrip—and the rest was deducted for the cost of their food, shelter, and guards.[6] By the end of 1916, the Germans reported that 1.1 million of their military and civilian prisoners were happily at work. Most of them, 640,000 men, were engaged in agriculture, while another 340,000 were employed in "industry and trade."

Prisoners chopped weeds, dug ditches, harvested potatoes and turnips. At Bohmte, gangs of prisoners with shovels and wheelbarrows excavated a canal. At Vehnenmoor, they worked up to their knees in brown, foul-smelling water, cutting peat and draining bogs. On the moors around Sennelager, prisoners felled trees and cleared bush. Many prisoners worked in Germany's huge steel mills and chemical factories, loading and hauling carts; even more worked in the coal and salt mines that fed vital raw materials into the munitions factories. Large landed estates had work for parties of hundreds of men, and they also had foremen who had plenty of experience extracting a full measure of labour from reluctant workers. In German cities, prisoners swept streets and collected garbage. Outside Bonn, they worked on a bridge. On the Rhine, they loaded and unloaded barges. On islands along Germany's North Sea coast, prisoners built dikes and embankments. At Baltic ports, they stevedored. Wherever heavy, unskilled manual labour was required and could be organized, prisoners of war were drafted. They were, of course, given no choice in the matter. The Hague Convention clearly stated that prisoners could be put to work and few German officers felt obliged to win the cheerful consent of their charges. The convention was equally clear about discipline: the captors were in charge and disobedience of orders was among the most serious of military offences. Prompt and stern measures would check any rebellious tendency.

There was much to be said for giving prisoners work, not least as an antidote for "barbed-wire disease." In retrospect, captured officers sometimes envied humbler fellow-prisoners who at least had something to do all day. However, release from the deadening monotony of the camps was a blessing many British prisoners, in particular, were reluctant to accept. It is not hard to understand why. Most of them, taken during the retreat from Mons or at the desperate First Battle of Ypres in 1914, were professional soldiers, with a traditional distaste for manual labour and a strong feeling that they had no business helping their enemies. Furthermore, their own government had given the resisters a somewhat ambiguous message. When British prisoners at Döberitz had asked the British Foreign Office whether they should volunteer for work as their captors wished, Sir Edward Grey's reply had, at best, been obscure: "His Majesty's Government did not wish them to work in the manner referred to."[7] As transmitted by the surprisingly rapid rumour network that ran between camps, did that mean no volunteering or that British prisoners were honour-bound to resist all efforts to make them work? As in any group, some British prisoners preferred the quiet life, particularly after their misery in the winter of 1914–15. Others, by nature, were more resolute in their resistance, and Whitehall's ambiguous message gave them a pretext for their defiance.

On the issue of work, the American ambassador refused to argue the British case. Like McCarthy, Gerard may well have worried about the demoralizing consequences of idleness on men he and his observers could see and the British Foreign Office could not. Nor was Gerard particularly concerned if the Germans chose to use prisoners for work in industries closely associated with the war effort, such as steel mills, railways, and munitions factories. Theoretically, most work aided the German war effort, including harvesting crops.

When the Canadians from Ypres reached Giessen, the German labour program was in full swing. Seldom briefed on their role and responsibilities as prisoners—who could have imagined that their first battle would end in surrender?—the Canadians had to resolve the issue of work for themselves.[8] It was a tough call. Work, the Germans insisted, was their duty, and Ambassador Gerard's views were given ample publicity. Also, by the time they reached the camp, the Canadians knew that their guards could be brutal and easily provoked. Some bore wounds and bruises from beatings and stabbings inflicted since their surrender. Many more felt the after-effects of their own last battle: untreated wounds, eyes that still watered, and lungs that left them gasping for breath. They were hungry too, and weeks, even months, would pass before appeals for food parcels were answered by friends, relatives, and the Red Cross. But there was another side. Most of the Canadians taken at Ypres were British-born. Some were old soldiers, veterans of the South African War and sometimes of British regiments. It was natural to make common cause with fellow "imperials." The simple patriotism that told others to enlist in August and September of 1914 now told them to defy their captors. For still others, resistance was a test of manhood and a chance to wipe away the humiliation of surrender.

Their captors were not in a sympathetic mood. The special resentment Canadians had experienced at Ypres and Roulers continued at Giessen and other camps. French, Russian, even Belgian conscripts had not asked for their fate; it was not even clear that they were enemies of Germany. As volunteers or *Geldsoldaten*, Canadians, like the British, had chosen to fight. If people in distant Winnipeg or Victoria could be venomous in their anti-German passion, Germans were no different, and prisoners arrogant enough to be defiant could expect no mercy. Within a few weeks of their arrival at Giessen, Canadians were ordered to join work commandos. Some went willingly; others refused. The oft-repeated process of coercion soon became familiar. Charles Taylor, a thirty-one-year-old Torontonian, was among the first to experience it. When he stood his ground when his squad was ordered to work, guards promptly made an example of him. "He was taken out of the line before the squad and beaten with rifle butts." Fifteen years later Taylor could still feel the pain.[9] Another prisoner, Horace Pickering, endured his beating and then was sentenced to thirty days in Giessen's *Strafbaracke* (punishment camp), where inmates spent their nights in tiny cells and their days sitting in silence on low stools.[10] Eric Seaman, also from Toronto's 3rd Battalion, was willing to work on a farm but his placement turned out to be at the Holtzappel silver mines. By the end of his beating, he was sufficiently unconscious that he had no memory of being taken down the shaft.[11] At Meschede, after a few days of farm labour, Chambers and his fellow prisoners decided that they had done enough for Germany's war effort. Instead of resorting to violence, an officer and an interpreter spent three days arguing with them and then selected three "ringleaders" for the *Strafbaracke*. When that failed, the whole group was transferred to Giessen "where they had the reputation of being lion-tamers."[12]

One of the commonest German punishments was *stillgestanden*, two or more hours of standing rigidly at attention, preferably facing the rays of the sun. For an able-bodied soldier, it could be an ordeal; for men suffering from partially healed leg wounds or weakened by poor food or dysentery, it could be agony. Spencer Symonds, a former McGill University student captured with the PPCLI at Hooge, endured *stillgestanden* for as long as eight hours in wet, cold weather. Exasperated guards threatened to shoot him. Instead, he almost died from bronchial pneumonia.[13]

Private A. J. Cleeton of the 7th Battalion survived a similar experience. He may have realized that the promise of farm work in December was a ruse, but he wanted to escape too badly to think. Instead, on December 13 he and other prisoners found themselves at a shell factory near Dortmund. Half-remembered lectures on Salisbury Plain reminded him that, in principle, he was not obliged to do munitions work. The principle proved painful. As "nix arbeiters," he and a group of prisoners were beaten with rifle butts and prodded with bayonets. Finally, the guards turned to their version of *stillgestanden:*

> . . . you were stood there and they told you in German to stand

> erect, toes at an angle of forty-five degrees, thumbs in line with the seams on your pants. The pants were prison garb, a black material with a big three-inch stripe down the pants and the sleeves of the coat and down the back of the jacket. They stood us up there from five o'clock in the morning until ten o'clock at night, fifteen of us. . . . On one occasion one of our number, MacArthur, who was wearing a British Warm, felt his nose running. Of course he couldn't do anything about it. Even if you wanted to go to the bathroom there was no moving, you performed your business right there and that was that. So he hinted; he just turned his head, that was all. A German struck him across the back of the neck. MacArthur jumped and of course there were a dozen there, but he did have time to open his British Warm and say "Here, you bastards, stick it there." That was the last I heard of Jack MacArthur, the last I saw. We all went down eventually. Finally I collapsed too. I don't know how many were left, I think there were two or three when they put me in hospital. . . .[14]

Cleeton went back to Sennelager with double pneumonia. Somehow he survived, but the ordeal left him unfit for further work. A friend used cigarettes to buy an old typewriter and Cleeton spent the rest of his captivity typing out a German-approved religious paper, the *Münster Church Times*, on scrap paper.[15]

THE GENEVA CONVENTION EXEMPTED OFFICERS FROM WORK, but did the exemption extend to non-commissioned officers? In British and French prison camps, German NCOs insisted on the privileges of their rank. Would the Germans reciprocate? They found it difficult. German and even French NCOs were a class apart, professional soldiers who trained the members of large conscript armies. Their reward was guaranteed employment, pensions, and the status of dutiful and essential members of a vital national institution. In

German eyes, British sergeants and corporals were hardly different in class or status from their men. As for the Canadians, their NCOs ranged from middle-aged British veterans to boys barely out of their teens. Corporal J. G. Baker of the 15th Battalion was seventeen when he was taken at Ypres. Acting Sergeant Hilton Howe of the 4th CMR, captured at Mont Sorrel, was only eighteen; Lance-Sergeant Elmo Watt of the 75th Battalion, taken at Vimy Ridge, was nineteen.

As usual, the principle of local autonomy prevailed: in the xth Army Corps area, where most Canadians were held, NCOs were asked, sometimes even compelled, to work, with the promise that if they agreed, they would be treated "according to their station." In January 1916, the issue was apparently resolved when Britain and Germany agreed that "all non-commissioned officer prisoners of war without exception, shall be privileged to the extent that they will not be required to work, either inside of the camp or outside except in the capacity of overseer."[16] That changed rather less than the negotiators imagined. Duty-bound to furnish labour, commandants had no patience with barrack-room pettifogging. The Hague Convention said nothing against providing prisoners with military training and exercise, and so, if NCOs refused a request to work, they would be drilled and exercised until they changed their minds. After the usual angry threats and occasional beatings, sergeants and corporals who insisted on their status were dispatched to Grossenweidenmoor and other special camps for the remainder of their ordeal.

At Minden, Captain Wilken, the Canadian chaplain, was shocked to find British NCOs being drilled, abused, and humiliated by German privates. His interventions made him enough of a nuisance to German authorities that he was court-martialled and transferred to the tender mercy of Captain Niemeyer at Holzminden.[17] After a beating and a bayonet wound for refusing to work, Sergeant Albert Cross of the 2nd Battalion, a South African War veteran, was transferred with other Canadian NCOs from Giessen to Grossenweidenmoor. Despite further beatings and hours of *stillgestanden* facing the sun, he stuck it out.[18] Corporal Cecil Bullock of the 15th Battalion broke down when his leg wound started discharging after too much running around a 335-pace track. He was given a wooden yoke and two buckets and ordered to haul milk.[19] Henry Ralph, another 15th Battalion NCO who had been badly gassed at Ypres, agreed to work until he discovered that the work was associated with munitions. He was beaten badly enough to lose several teeth and was lined up for a firing squad before being dispatched to Grossenweidenmoor for ten-hour days of marching, running, and *stillgestanden.*[20] For many, the punishment was aggravated by the awkward wooden clogs the Germans issued to most of their prisoners.[21]

Faced with the monotony and futility of endless drills and the continuing encouragement to volunteer for work, some NCOs changed their minds. Others were denied the dubious privilege of rank because the Germans refused to recognize their stripes. Walker Kilby and Harvey Wallace, promoted to corporal in the 2nd Tunnelling Company but not confirmed before their capture, were both punished for claiming a rank the Germans did not believe. Corporal Joseph Bruce of the 16th Battalion claimed that his rank certificate was torn up and he was punished by long hours of *stillgestanden* in the freezing rain without his tunic.[22] When a parcel for Lance-Sergeant Watt of the 75th Battalion arrived at Dülmen, addressed to him as private, he was promptly set to cleaning latrines, the foulest work available. Eventually his rank was accepted.[23]

GIESSEN'S LABOUR CONTRACTS EXTENDED TO FARMS, MINES, factories, the Huesten Gewerkschaft stone quarry, and the Geisweid iron foundry. Prisoners who could be pushed into working in agriculture or at a cement factory drew the line at an industry clearly producing an essential raw material for German artillery shells. Fred Whittaker and Alfred Todd, with other members of British Columbia's 7th Battalion, refused to work at so obvious a munitions factory. Todd was promptly hit in the stomach, threatened with a firing squad for disobeying orders, and taken back to Giessen to be court-martialled. He, Whittaker, and four of the others were sentenced by court martial to two years' imprisonment. They spent twenty-one months at Butzbach prison and the remainder of their sentence at Cologne.[24] Colin Earle, a nineteen-year-old former student, captured with the 2nd Battalion, suffered a more immediate punishment. When a thorough beating "with rifle butts, swords and even . . . the point of the bayonet" failed to change his mind, he was "thrown into a box-like cell and steam from the exhaust of a boiler forced into the room." Though he was not burned by the steam, "his power of resistance was seemingly broken and he consented to go to work."[25] Harold Kenyon, captured at St. Eloi with Vancouver's 29th Battalion, was locked in the same steam room. He managed to breathe by lying flat on the floor and gasping at the air that seeped under the door.[26] One redoubtable prisoner boasted of surviving five days in the "steam room."[27]

Gradually, Geisweid became the destination for Giessen's recalcitrant inmates. Prisoners lived in damp cellars and worked twenty-four-hour shifts every other Sunday to feed the huge blast furnaces. Carl McCarthy was one of the prisoners who injured themselves just to get a break from endless work on empty stomachs. He got blood poisoning after he cut his finger, but his guards refused him medical attention.

Given a choice, most prisoners would have preferred farm work. It seemed healthy, familiar, and neutral. It also offered a chance at extra food and a better hope of escape. It was not a complete release from casual brutality, however—nor were prisoners necessarily dutiful workers. Sent to a farm near Giessen with six other prisoners, Frank Coburn believed that the farmer had promised them a bonus if they worked especially hard. When it was not forthcoming at the end of the week, the men decided to strike. Within hours a squad of German soldiers arrived and proceeded to beat the prisoners into submission. Then they were taken back to Giessen and put in the punishment cells.[28] Even if the "fannigans," as prisoners called themselves, did not make their own trouble, they sometimes encountered it anyway. An angry farmer impaled Robert King with a hay fork; Frank Boreham was permanently injured when a youth hit him on the leg with an axe.[29] Another prisoner told how a German officer home on leave summoned prisoners from neighbouring farms and beat them for his own amusement and public entertainment.[30] Tom Smith was convinced that a farmer had deliberately unloaded a cart-load of potatoes on him, injuring his back.[31]

While some Canadians spent the rest of the war at Giessen and its outlying work camps, other prisoners, and especially those who made trouble for their captors, were surprisingly mobile. When Coburn was put to work building a dam, the chief engineer was accidentally killed. Once again, he faced two weeks of punishment cells—and then a further two weeks when he was accused of being lazy. In December 1915, Coburn was sent to a stone quarry where prisoners lifted and loaded snow-covered rocks with their bare hands.[32] Alan Kingscott, a twenty-year-old Toronto tile setter, began at Giessen and then worked at a mine near Lauienburg until his health broke down and he refused to continue. That brought him a term in the prison at Butzbach. He spent a year in a silver mine at Lichtenhorst and then, like many Canadians, helped dig canals at Bohmte. When months of working in freezing water again left him gasping with bronchitis, he was sent to a farm where at last he could report he was "fairly treated." Hazelton Moore, painfully wounded and captured at Mont Sorrel, spent months in hospital before he was released to Cellelager. He worked at a nearby farm and then a cement factory before being sent to the Rosenberg salt mines. After four unhappy months, he was sent to a cement factory at Merseburg where he was employed at breaking and loading rock. After his health and strength gave out, Moore's final work was at a sugar beet factory near Brunswick. He found it an improvement.[33]

Ernest Comins, a nineteen-year-old former bread salesman, was less fortunate. As one of the Giessen "nix arbeiters," he spent six weeks in hospital after a German rifle butt smashed his elbow. When he continued to refuse work, he was tied to a post with his arms over his head and his toes barely touching the ground. Two weeks of this ordeal, four hours a day, persuaded him to change his mind. He was then sent to *Arbeitskommandos* at Soltau, Lichtenhorst, Bohmte, and Grossenweidenmoor, where he was assigned to fire the boilers at a sugar factory. Soon, he recalled, his hands were so blistered he could not carry on. When he collapsed, guards got him working again with rifle butts and a pail of water. After nine brutal months in a salt mine at Soltau as a punishment for shirking, Comins ended the war on a German farm.[34]

Many Canadians from Giessen spent months at Vehnenmoor, located in a vast peatbog where prisoners were employed cutting turf and digging ditches. Transferred to Cellelager, a peacetime German training camp, Mervyn Simmons of the 7th Battalion soon regretted leaving Giessen. The German staff, he claimed, took little interest in their work, the camp food reflected it, and his parcels, of course, would take months to catch up. A move to the labour camp at Vehnenmoor seemed an improvement until he got there. The site was a dreary, treeless plain, the barracks were filthy and jammed with three-decker bunks. Mervyn Simmons recalled a January day:

> Two smoking stoves burning their peat made all the heat there was. The double row of berths lined the walls. Outside, the rain and sleet fell dismally. Bert had a bowl of prison soup before him and a hunk of bread, dark and heavy. He was hungry, wet, tired and dirty. . . .[35]

Corporal Edwards, also sent to Vehnenmoor, found that seven hundred French, British, and Russian prisoners were expected to cook all their meals in a few syrup tins on two small stoves. The water supply was dark with peat fragments. Prisoners worked through the winter of 1915–16 in water up to their knees, with no place to dry their clothes.[36] George Spademan was twenty-four when he was injured in the back at Ypres. His wound was untreated for three days until he reached Giessen. He was sent to Vehnenmoor in

January 1916 and, after a brief spell in the camp cells "for not doing what was required," he spent the rest of the winter standing in water-filled ditches, cutting peat. William Langford, an Ypres prisoner, endured three years of digging ditches. One of them caved in, breaking his leg. When the Germans refused to help, he recalled, friends set his leg for him. For refusing to work with a fracture, Langford got fourteen days' solitary and twenty-eight more days of sitting with his leg wired to a stool.[37] British and Canadian prisoners at Vehnenmoor also shared bitter memories of a British regimental sergeant-major whom they accused of ingratiating himself with his captors and selling prisoners' boots and food. "He excelled in all the arts of the sycophant," recalled Edwards:

> The pleasure of the guards was his delight, their displeasure his poignant grief. He assumed the authority of his rank with us, he reported the slightest of misdemeanours amongst us to the guards and was instrumental in having many punished.[38]

Another punishment camp was Mettingen, where prisoners slept in dugouts and dug ditches to drain swampy land. William Adair, sent to Mettingen after an escape attempt, remembered the brutality of the officers in charge. The commandant often found the prisoners at breakfast and ordered them on parade. When they moved too slowly, he dumped their table. A prisoner who attempted to protest was given two years in prison and his witnesses thirty days each. The second-in-command enjoyed beating the last man out on parade. Having suffered two beatings, one man struck back, only to be sentenced to prison for nineteen years for striking an officer. Severe asthma eventually rescued Adair from Mettingen, but at the cost of a year in hospital at Munster and a life-long health problem.[39]

Bohmte, Mettingen, Vehnenmoor, and other mass labour projects involved exposure to the elements in both the dry, hot summers and the long, cold winters of the north German plain. The work was dreary, monotonous, and, in the minds of most Canadian prisoners, degrading. Prisoners soon learned one German word, *langsam* (slow). Those with a resister mentality schemed at ways to reduce their labour or, if possible, to avoid it altogether. Guards and overseers, with their own quotas of work to satisfy, had the power to beat obvious shirkers with rifle butts, bayonet scabbards, and rubber hoses. Given the harsh working conditions, crowded, unsanitary barracks, and chronic malnutrition, sickness and accidents were inevitable. German supervisors dismissed illnesses as malingering and injuries as self-inflicted. Both were offences to be punished by verbal abuse, beatings, or solitary confinement on bread and water. At Sennelager, "some of the men were treated very brutal," recalled Gunner W. Hand, a Mont Sorrel prisoner.[40] Like soldiers in all armies, they could also be helpless victims of a superior's whims and vices. Sergeant Alvin Dunbar of the 15th Battalion recalled a night at Bohmte when a drunken officer called out the guard and amused himself by ordering prisoners in and out of their quarters. Guards stood by and beat laggards as they struggled to get through the narrow door. He bore the effects of one of their blows for the rest of his life.[41]

PRISONERS' ACCOUNTS RECORD AN ALMOST ROUTINE BRUTALITY in many *Arbeitskommandos*. Did they exaggerate? Since most accounts were devised as claims for compensation as a result of maltreatment, authors had to recall, elaborate, and perhaps even invent such episodes. Twelve or fifteen years later, the specific physical evidence had often vanished or mingled with the scars of any working life. While prisoners sometimes corroborated memorable beatings or torture, the unending monotony of prisoner existence left most men with little precise memory of dates or hours. Though some men secreted notes in the linings of their uniforms, the prohibition of personal diaries was highly effective in eliminating documented evidence of maltreatment. Nor were former prisoners often frank about their own contribution to any ensuing violence. Among themselves, prisoner stories almost always featured the outwitting of guards and overseers, with few references to the brutal consequences for men caught malingering, sleeping out of sight, or other numerous forms of "dodging the column." As in the universal myth of the rabbit and the fox, the only point of the story is the triumph of the weak over the strong.[42]

What *was* consistent was the German belief that physical coercion was the chief effective means of extorting work. As ever, there were exceptions, though. Whenever they encountered commanders and employers who behaved with fairness and generosity, almost all prisoners cheerfully did their best. Lichtenhorst, a peatbog camp where prisoners dug ditches and cut heather, could have been another Vehnenmoor. Chambers remembered it as the best ten months of his captivity. "The Commandant was a man of his word and when he gave an order and it was obeyed, that was the end of it." When prisoners had dug their three metres of ditch a day, they were free for recreation that ranged from music and amateur theatricals to an "international" soccer league. When a sergeant won permission for Irish prisoners to celebrate St. Patrick's Day, every prisoner suddenly became Irish. "This commandant was a real sport and gave us all a holiday. . . . If only we had had the same treatment at other camps, there would not have been half the trouble and we would have been more willing to work. It was the continual "Schweinhund" business which put our back up."[43] Transferred to Bohmte in November 1916, Chambers encountered a commandant who was, he claimed, "a temperamental tyrant" who terrorized guards and prisoners alike. Since the British fought on Sundays, he reasoned, they must work on Sundays too. At *Appell* (roll-call), prisoners were commanded to bring all their possessions so the commandant could dispose of anything he considered superfluous. At the work site, he "would come storming down to the river and devil us around, waving his sword frantically, declaring we were loafing and must keep on until dark."[44]

Though most Canadian prisoners had urban work experience and some were skilled tradesmen, the Germans made little use of their expertise.[45] The veteran miners of the 2nd Canadian Tunnelling Company joined the same labour gangs as other prisoners, even when employed in coal and salt mines. According to Howland, this was in part because prisoners themselves claimed to be "magicians," "paint-watchers," and other fanciful trades, and in part because of policy. Germany had no intention of sharing industrial secrets with her unwelcome wartime guests.[46] One luckless exception was Sergeant James Wink, a Toronto watchmaker. When he refused to pursue his trade on Germany's behalf, he was knocked out with rifle butts. When he recovered, his optic nerve had been sufficiently affected that watchmaking was now impossible. Instead, as an NCO, he wasted his time drilling at Grossenweidenmoor.[47]

Prisoners sometimes seem to have been treated as almost expendable. Private W. H. Johnston of the 47th Battalion was captured during the Somme offensive. During the winter of 1916–17, a year of record cold, he was sent with 119 British prisoners to build a sea wall on Norderney Island on Germany's North Sea coast. They were issued only a linen shirt, trousers, and wooden clogs. Within a few weeks, a quarter of the group had been hospitalized for frostbite or dysentery. When prisoners collapsed during the bitter cold, comrades hauled them behind big rocks for shelter and then were forced back to their work.[48]

Conditions were usually easier for men sent to factories, but the long-term effects might be worse. Percy Goseltine, sent to a chemical factory at Mannheim, spent most of the war carrying heavy trays of burnt copper ore. When he fell and injured his spine, he was forced back to work. Barely able to walk, he was put in a basement cell without food or sanitary facilities. The fumes left him permanently disabled.[49] Working in a fertilizer plant left Walter Hayes with continuing eczema on his thighs and legs.[50] Daniel Merry blamed fumes and chemicals at the creosote plant where he worked for peeling the skin from his neck and face. At an oil sands refinery at Wietze, Andrew Fernie worked with fellow prisoners and civilian convicts shovelling oil sand through a grate into a hot furnace. The fumes were overpowering and he fainted often. At the end of the war, he was evacuated as a stretcher case.[51] Goggles, protective clothing, and other rudimentary safety equipment were available for civilian workers, but they were seldom provided for prisoners. During sixteen months at a foundry in Osnabrück, Frank Tilley, a twenty-year-old Torontonian, worked twelve-hour days. German workers had goggles, but he was given a piece of iron mesh to protect his face. By the end of his time as a prisoner, Tilley was "a mass of small burns on his body, feet and face," and his eyesight was permanently affected.[52] James Hutchison, a pre-war foreman at the Canadian Canoe Company, found that civilian workers at the Duisburg gas works had respirators but he had no protection. He struggled on despite the overpowering fumes, only to collapse in the end.[53]

By common consent the worst fate for a prisoner was to be sent to German coal and salt mines. A British wartime report described work in mining as "a singularly cruel and dangerous form of slavery."[54] The British also believed that it was no accident that, as Germany's most-hated prisoners, they were singled out for work in the mines. At Soltau, Mr. Justice Robert Younger was told, French and Belgian prisoners were threatened with the mines as a punishment, but "the British [were] sent there in the ordinary course."[55] In practice, the misery seems to have been shared among all nationalities. Wartime Germany needed all the labour she could mobilize for her mines and German workers were not eager to volunteer.

In almost any setting, mining is hard, dirty, dangerous work in a dark, enclosed environment that many people find terrifying. In most societies, miners are tough, clannish workers. Foreign prisoners were not part of the clan. German miners had an added reason to keep a hostile distance: their exemption from front-line military service depended on their employers, and fraternization with prisoners could signal an end to their special status. While civilian miners worked at cutting the ore, unskilled labour filled and emptied the ore cars and often dragged them along the underground galleries. It would have been heavy work for fit, well-fed men; for malnourished prisoners who had been "harshed about," it was hard and sometimes impossible. Because of the contract system, control of the prisoners was divided between the non-commissioned officer in charge of the guards and the civilian *Steiger* (foreman) who ran the operation underground. Prisoners alleged that their guards were openly bribed to keep the maximum number of prisoners working and the *Steiger* was armed for his underground custodial role and to enhance his authority. Output was easily measured by the number of cars loaded in a shift and shirking was harshly punished. John O'Brien, captured at St. Eloi with the 28th Battalion, spent a year at the notorious Auguste Victoria mine. After a long day in the pit, he recalled, the prisoners were forced to run a gauntlet of German miners if they had not met their quota.[56] Below ground, prisoners suffered beatings by shovels, pick handles, and miners' lamps.

Worse than the pits was work in the coke ovens, sprinkling water on the red-hot coke as it emerged and loading it on trucks. As at Geisweid, guards took a sadistic pleasure in forcing prisoners to stand close enough to the red-hot furnaces that their skin blistered and peeled. After a savage beating on his body and legs at the K-47 coalmine, George Draper spent eight weeks in hospital. He was still so weak when he was discharged that he could hardly walk. "He was made to stand to attention and placed in front of the coke ovens as a punishment for not completing the work assigned to him."[57] The routine work was bad enough. John O'Brien could have echoed a British prisoner's description of the "coke-oven punishment":

> The men had to do shifts of from half-an-hour to an hour unless they dropped out before, which they frequently did. The heat was intense and I have seen men with their feet and faces scorched and blistered. Most of the Englishmen working on this mine had been placed to work on these coke ovens at some time or other. The work was shifting 32 tons of coke in twelve

Canada's Golgotha, Derwent Wood's frieze, depicted one of the best-known German atrocities, a captured Canadian sergeant crucified on a barn door. Undoubtedly "the ghastliest thing" in a 1918 exhibit of Canadian war art, it was also based on a self-perpetuating myth.

TOP LEFT: In this German photograph of an unidentified prison camp, the wooden huts were each home to a couple of hundred men. The monotony of life in a dreary, overcrowded camp led to a form of depression described as "barbed-wire disease."

BOTTOM LEFT: A group of prisoners collected by a German photographer pose in their camp as evidence of humane treatment and living conditions that respected the Hague Convention. Canadian prisoners discovered that brutality and suffering often coexisted with a general observance of the rules. (PA182548)

ABOVE: One of the yards at Ruhleben. The racetrack stables were used to house the prisoners and they congregated in the yards between the buildings. Despite the fuss raised about it, Ruhleben was as good as internment camps got in wartime Germany. (PA182553)

ABOVE: A German photograph of a typical camp *Lazarett* or sickbay. At Minden a captured Canadian medical officer found himself supervised by German medical students. His staff consisted of a few overworked prisoners. (PA182543)

TOP RIGHT: Typical shower baths at a German prison camp, with guards and prisoners waiting for the photographer to shoot or the water to flow. Few prisoners complained about problems in keeping clean, but soldiers, whether free or captive, had little opportunity for personal privacy.

BOTTOM RIGHT: Civilian overseers, German guards, and an *Arbeitskommando* of Allied prisoners smile for the photographer. On a warm, sunny day, with a chance to work at their own speed, not many prisoners would have protested against ditch-digging. Photographers would not have recorded similar work in winter. (PA182546)

1402

TOP LEFT: Scientists at Ruhleben managed to improvise a small laboratory. The Canadian, Allan Lochhead, is seated on the ground on the left. (PA182554)

BOTTOM LEFT: Lieutenant Bellew and two of his fellow prisoners in their somewhat crowded room. The evidence of regular parcels is on the wall. (PA182551)

ABOVE: British and Canadian officers busy themselves with their handicrafts at Bischofswerda while a Russian officer looks on. On the right, Lieutenant Edward Bellew; next to him, the persistent but unsuccessful escaper, John Thorn; behind them both, Captain Scudamore. (PA182550)

"Brother! Don't shoot!" says the sign as demonstrators occupy a cavalry barracks at the end of the war. Prisoners of war were caught in the middle as the kaiser's power collapsed and deputies of the Soldiers and Workers' Councils nervously filled the vacuum. (PA182552)

> hours; sometimes it was quite impossible to do this in the time, and the men simply had to work until it was done.[58]

Frequently miserable living conditions added to the strain of long hours at the coke ovens or the pit. A British soldier, Ernest Evanson, described the quarters at Westerholt: "The beds in our barracks were arranged from end to end, one above the other, in eight rows with hardly room for two men to pass in the passages between the rows. The beds consisted of coconut matting stretched between wooden uprights. With our meagre issue of blankets they were very cold indeed in the winter time."[59] Evanson shared that hut for a year and a half with 222 men, among them William May, a former miner captured with 2nd Tunnelling Company at Mont Sorrel. May found something more disgusting than the hut: not only were the latrines right beside the barracks but they were "piled high with filth, the stench being terrible."[60] Guards routinely called midnight *Appelle* and forced partially dressed prisoners to stand for hours, sometimes in the rain. Parcels, letters, even smoking were forbidden for weeks after escape attempts and offenders were confined in cells that could be heated to unbearable temperatures. "Twenty-four hours of this were enough to make anybody do anything," claimed an escapee.[61] Hilton Howe, another Mont Sorrel prisoner who was sent to a Ruhr valley coalmine near Essen, recalled a sadistic German corporal who opened prisoners' parcels and mixed the contents into an inedible mess in front of the hungry prisoners.[62] Still, food parcels kept their recipients alive. Private Albert Martin, a Newfoundlander, survived almost two years in a Westphalian coalmine because he had food parcels. "The Russians around him died like flies."[63]

While Auguste Victoria or K-47 achieved widespread notoriety, most prisoners agreed that the salt mines were even worse. Sergeant W. H. Alldritt of the 8th Battalion, captured at Ypres, had been a fitness and outdoors specialist for the Winnipeg YMCA. He spent months at the salt mines at Frieden, near Hannover "under the most appalling conditions, under labor driven by the most inhuman of task-masters." He found that the conditions at Schende, where he was sent for punishment from April to November 1917, were even worse. Overseers were as brutal and there were no parcels. The food was inadequate. For an attempted escape, Alldritt was beaten unconscious by rifle butts. Rather than send him to prison and lose his labour, his guards forced him to work on Sundays. Emaciated, rheumatic, and going blind, Alldritt was a physical wreck by May 1918 when he was exchanged to Holland.[64]

Many of the Ypres prisoners sent to Göttingen—most of them members of the 15th Battalion (Toronto's 48th Highlanders)—were transferred to Cellelager and from there to the salt mine at Beienrode. One of them, Lance-Corporal Andrew Haley Jones, described the routine: wake-up at 4 a.m. for ersatz coffee, *Appell* at 4:45 a.m., and down the shaft by 5:30 to work from 6 a.m. to 1:45 p.m. with a breakfast break for cold soup. The afternoon shift worked from 2 p.m. to 9:30 at night, seven days a week. Salt was blasted into large heaps of sharp, jagged crystals, which prisoners loaded into carts with their bare hands. The ten men in a shift first had fifteen cars to load, and, from September 1917, thirty. If they failed, they stayed down until the work was done. As at Westerholt, Canadians found the sanitary conditions repulsive. At one end of the hut, Haley Jones remembered a two-bucket latrine for six hundred prisoners and a brick-channel urinal that drained outside. "The smell both from the wash house and latrine is unbearable in the building and even if you stand at the far end of the building the smell is perfectly disgusting. The cook house is also in the same building but partitioned off and the smell of the sour cabbage and turnips is perfectly revolting."[65]

In addition to chronic hunger and almost daily beatings, prisoners discovered some of the nastier features of salt mining, particularly the boil-like salt sores which developed whenever fragments of salt lodged in the skin or entered wounds or open sores. At Schende, Alldritt had suffered from as many as a hundred of them at once. Guards at Beienrode routinely refused medical attention and even when the camp medical officer, Dr. Tobius, finally appeared, he proved to be a harsh and brutal man, lancing the boils and leaving them open to bleed and absorb fresh salt. Some guards took on this duty for themselves. One found pleasure in breaking boils with a blow from a special club.[66] Gordon Foster, a carpenter, was forced to work on the wooden casing of the mine shaft. He was lowered on a plank, with a 180 metre fall beneath him. Fragments of salt fell in his eyes as he worked; there were no goggles for prisoners.[67] Sidney James of the 28th Battalion was barely out of his teens when he got to Beienrode. After beatings by guards, spitting blood and aching with salt sores, he finally poured boiling water on his foot to escape the mine.[68]

Brutality fed on itself. John Bailey of the 15th Battalion was condemned to go barefoot for six months because he had complained of the rough wooden clogs the Germans provided in lieu of boots. Thomas Jackson, a "nix arbeiter," was threatened with a firing squad and then beaten. Unwisely, a guard smashed his ankle with a rifle butt, giving him five weeks in bed unable to walk. Before he fully recovered, Jackson was forced down the pit where civilian miners thrashed him with belts, rubber hoses, and pick handles. In his post-war repatriation report, Haley Jones described a fellow salt-mine worker who was beaten so badly he was "one mass of weals and blood was coming through the skin."[69] Among the most brutalized victims of Beienrode was Bill Lickers, a former shipper and receiver from Saskatoon who also happened to be a full-blooded Mohawk. From the moment of his capture, he seems to have been picked out for special vindictiveness by Germans who may have read too many of Karl May's popular cowboy-and-Indian stories. At Cellelager, he had been tied to a post and beaten by an officer, allegedly for refusing to change his allegiance. At Beienerode, there were more beatings. When he was placed in punishment cells, bored guards visited him to administer extra "discipline." Finally, a blow with a heavy lump of salt left Lickers unable to move his head.[70]

Such abuses, the Germans insisted, were prevented by regular inspections. Prisoners, of course, could communicate their complaints to the proper authorities. In reality, claimed a Canadian escaper, officers visited the camp, inspected the guard, and left.[71] When a prisoner sent a complaint to the army corps headquarters in Hameln, it was returned through the guards with instructions that it be written in German. The complainer promptly suffered for his temerity.[72] So did Archibald McBride: "At the time of the visit of a high German official, the quality of the soup being particularly good that day, [he] ventured to comment that, while the food was better that day, it would probably be worse on the following and succeeding days. As a result of volunteering this information, he was later kicked out of bed and all the way to the mine, placed in the deepest cave in the mine—about a mile and a half from the shaft—and put at the heaviest work and kept there for two or three hours after the other prisoners had been taken up."[73]

The second check should have been the neutral visitations that had helped encourage a rapid improvement of the conditions in the winter of 1914–15. One problem was Ambassador Gerard himself. Having giving his approval to the work program, he would have found it difficult to pay heed to complaints which, for all he knew, came from idlers and malingerers. After a tour of the Westphalian work sites where most Canadians were employed, Dr. McCarthy reported a general German dissatisfaction with the typical British prisoner: "He gave much trouble and was generally disliked." Overseers preferred using the French to operate machinery and the Russians for hard, repetitive labour.[74] With thousands of locations to visit, the handful of American observers could see only a fraction of the *Arbeitskommandos* in action. Indeed, factory owners forbade visits on the claim that the foreign diplomats might discover Germany's industrial secrets. Gillies Wilken, the Canadian chaplain at Minden, had his own bitter perspective on neutral observers: "One supercilious young man to whom I had exposed (and he admitted) shocking hospital treatment and neglect of prisoners at a hospital in

Minden town, answered in so many words, 'There is a big war on and what can you expect?'"[75]

At Libau (now Liepāja in Estonia), Gerard's senior camp inspector, John Jackson, found five hundred British and Canadian prisoners unloading merchant ships and carrying sacks to warehouses and trains. The workers, he reported, spent their nights in a "well-aired," large room, sleeping on mattresses filled with wood shavings. The meals, he was told, were "good" though the British preferred their parcels. In off hours, the British played soccer with a ball supplied by the American embassy or swam in a nearby arm of the Baltic.[76] Given Gerard's policy, Jackson found no reason to observe that prisoners at Libau, a captured Russian naval station, were transferring supplies for shipment to the German army. Nor, in the autumn of 1916, had Libau yet been adopted as a reprisal camp for British prisoners, chosen for suffering because of a German belief that their own men had been forced to work close behind the British lines. Canadian prisoners at Libau, like Minard Hill and Percy Ogilvy of Vancouver's 29th Battalion, captured at the St. Eloi craters, faced the Russian winter without proper clothing or the food parcels they would have received in a regular camp. When Ogilvy and Hill (who had dislocated his back when he was captured) fell under the heavy log they were carrying, both men were beaten unconscious and left in the snow. Weary comrades dragged them back to camp. Peter Robinson, an Ypres prisoner at Libau, was tied to some trees for two hours in the morning and two more at night after starvation left him too weak to work. Of three hundred British and Canadian reprisal prisoners sent to Libau in January 1917, barely a third were still working when the camp was closed at the end of six months.[77]

Neutral observers took no responsibility for the condition of prisoners held behind the German lines in France and Belgium for the obvious reason that they were never allowed to visit the battle zone. Increasingly, from late 1916, the German army held onto its prisoners, worked them to the point of exhaustion and starvation, and only then transferred them to camps in Germany. The amount of work required behind the lines was enormous. Labour was needed to build the massive defences of the Hindenburg Line, to repair roads and railways, and to heft the masses of munitions and supplies the German field armies needed daily. Unlike the British and French, Germany could not recruit labour from her colonies or China. While French and Belgian civilians were conscripted and Russian prisoners were transferred from the Eastern Front, the needs were insatiable. From at least November 1916, British or French prisoners who could be put to work were kept on the Western Front. Through the coldest winter most Europeans could remember, they worked in whatever clothes they were captured in and were fed the basic German prison ration: acorn coffee and a slice of bread in the morning, thin soup in the middle of a nine-hour working day. An Australian who managed to escape through the German lines found that he had dropped from eighty-three to fifty-one kilograms in only three months of captivity.[78] Since the Hague Convention could hardly justify such treatment of prisoners, on January 12, 1917 Berlin claimed that their enemies had forced German prisoners to work within artillery range. They would have to take reprisals. (At least one Canadian reported Germans behind the lines loading amunition during the preparations for the Vimy Ridge attack.) On April 18, the British ordered that no prisoner was to work within thirty kilometres of the firing line. Nothing much changed.

Caputured at Fresnoy, Lance Corporal William Mann of the 19th Battalion was crowded with 160 to 175 prisoners in a 20 by 12 metre casemate of Fort McDonald and was fed sour turnip soup and 125 grams of black bread per day. Robbed of their mess tins, men drank from their boots or helmets, if they had them. The latrine was a barrel in the middle of the floor, emptied just twice in Mann's nine days there. William Dane of the 75th Battalion, taken at Vimy, spent twelve days at Fort McDonald and the same conditions followed him to Marchiennes. When he was too far gone to work, he was sent to a hospital at Valenciennes.[79] Like the Newfoundlanders captured at Monchy-le-Preux, some Canadian internees were notified that they were "prisoners of respite." A German NCO read them a written notice urging them to report their circumstances to relatives, friends, and "persons of influence in England" so that Germany "would be able to treat them properly." Eight of the Canadian prisoners dutifully addressed themselves to the High Commissioner in London, Sir George Perley: "We have been advised to write and state the conditions under which we are living." They were grim: 150 men sleeping in an old barn, without coats or blankets, forced to do eight hours' heavy work a day on a starvation diet.[80]

Unless they were officers or wounded, Canadians captured at Vimy, Fresnoy, Lens, Passchendaele, and the battles of 1918 usually spent their first months of captivity behind the German lines in conditions far worse than those experienced by most of the Canadians in Germany. As in all armies, ferocity to the enemy increased with distance from the front line, and the guards and overseers assigned to prisoner-of-war companies were no exception. Guards controlled prisoners with dog whips and clubs and their rifles. Alex Green, a twenty-one-year-old captured at the end of the battle of the Somme, was beaten for trying to steal a pumpkin.[81] Hugo Colver of the 14th Battalion remembered being thrashed for starting a fire to keep warm and clubbed for his reluctance to drag railcars loaded with artillery when British shells were falling nearby.[82] A twenty-one-year-old machine-gunner captured during the German offensive of 1918, Walter Peagram, was scarred for life with a wire whip when he hesitated over unloading German armaments.

Mostly, Peagram remembered the hunger pangs as he became a "living skeleton."[83] The food parcels that kept other prisoners alive in Germany could not reach prisoners behind the lines because, officially, they were not there. The Canadians who wrote to the High Commissioner had to pretend they were at Wahn in Germany. Later, Limburg, the main depot for Red Cross parcels, became the address used. Many names were simply not reported at all, and armies assumed that those unreported belonged in the "missing" category of their casualty reports.[84] Of the Newfoundlanders taken at Monchy-le-Preux in April 1917, only seventy-seven were reported to the Red Cross in July. Though parcels were sent immediately, by October the Red Cross had received only fourteen postcards, all dated September 10 and all pleading for food.[85] Names of members of the Canadian Cavalry Brigade taken during the battle of Cambrai in November 1917 were not released until the following spring, after they had served as behind-the-lines labour.[86]

The long-anticipated German assault on March 21, 1918 virtually dissolved the front-line divisions of the British Fifth Army. In the following days, German storm troops drove a huge dent in the British and French line. German attackers, so hungry that their own advance was slowed by the pillaging of British ration dumps, were in no position to provide adequately for over fifty thousand British prisoners. Scattered among them were a few Canadians, ranging from seven men of a railway construction unit which suddenly found itself in the front lines, to members of regiments of the Canadian Cavalry Brigade who had been sent to plug gaps. Some found themselves at Flavy-le-Martel, a former British prisoner-of-war cage. Instead of the couple of hundred Germans normally housed for a few days in three leaky prefabricated huts, over a thousand British soldiers were shoved into the buildings until there was barely room to sit. It had been a disgrace for the British; it became a death trap under the Germans. Dysentery spread among the hungry, verminous men, but still the work parties marched out daily. Guards ordered sick and dying men to get the camp cleaned up, and, when they failed, beat them. When the working parties returned, Captain Emil Müller amused himself by drilling them to make them better soldiers. He enjoyed riding into them on horseback, flailing them with his riding crop. Fortunately for them, his heart gave him trouble and he left on May 5. Nevertheless, the deaths continued into the summer.[87]

Since few behind-the-lines prisoners escaped, their condition was known chiefly to their fellow captives in Germany. At Minden on a bitter February day in 1917, Chaplain Wilken met "living skeletons, frozen hollow-cheeked human wrecks. None had overcoats or underwear. They claimed to be survivors of a group of several hundred who had been captured on the Somme and put to work at Cambrai."[88] Private Adair, in hospital at Münster, recalled a party of three hundred starving prisoners who arrived on May 1, 1917. A former divinity student, Claude Beesley of the 15th Battalion, described a party of 346 emaciated, exhausted prisoners who arrived at his camp on October 8, 1918. Within two months, 127 of them were dead.[89]

Of the thirty-eight hundred Canadian prisoners in German camps, most left no description of their experiences. The seven hundred or more who did may have had an exceptionally brutal and miserable time. Many Canadians had been clerks, high school students, and skilled tradesmen, with no experience of heavy manual labour in mines, quarries, and factories. Yet a majority of the Canadian prisoners came from the factories, workshops, and construction sites in Toronto, Vancouver, Montreal, and from the mines of Cape Breton and Vancouver Island. They should have adapted. Instead, industrial workers were as likely as former clerks and students to succumb to the hunger and brutality which were a prisoner's lot.[90]

Some prisoners found comfortable places to work—in a parcel room or sorting mail at Limburg, or even sketching the guards, as Allan Beddoes did at Giessen. Alex Yetman, a shipping clerk in peacetime, spent his captivity playing in the prisoners' orchestra at Mannheim until his tuberculosis earned him a transfer to Switzerland.[91] Other prisoners, at Geisweid or Libau or Bohmte, had long since learned to forget the Hague provision that their tasks "shall not be excessive and shall have no connection with the operations of the war." Writing after the United States had entered the war, McCarthy acknowledged that much of the work done by prisoners was slave labour, performed at the point of a bayonet and the threat of beatings; the barracks were dirty, with only bucket latrines at night; overseers controlled mail and parcels, forced the sick to work, and denied them medical attention.[92] Critics might claim that McCarthy was satisfying a fresh market for anti-German propaganda. He was also describing the experience some Canadians were compelled to live for three and a half years.

5

Resistance and Escape

AT THE END OF APRIL 1915, MAJOR PETER ANDERSON FOUND himself looking through barbed wire from the newly built German cavalry barracks at Bischofswerda. More than his fellow captives, he had a very clear idea of his next move. From the moment of capture, he had avoided being photographed or even being noticed. He had found a British officer, Lord James Murray of the Cameron Highlanders, willing to teach him German. In his youth, he had been a keen outdoorsman and hunter; now he exercised and discreetly rehoned forgotten skills. A reserved man, he occasionally let it slip that he had good friends in Switzerland. Patiently, he collected what he would need—well-soled boots, paper money, a German pipe and knapsack, extra socks, and even a rubber cushion in case he had to swim a river. As an officer-prisoner, allowed on his word of honour to roam free for short periods, he got permission to shop in the near-by village. Two well-intentioned ladies sold him a black oilskin rain-coat, a pair of woollen gloves, and a checked cap of a type popular with tourists.

Anderson had planned to take three months to prepare himself; he took five, though he was determined to leave before the harvest stripped the fields bare. On September 28, 1915, with the help of Lieutenant Edward Bellew of the 7th Battalion and Lieutenant Frank

Smith of the 15th, he was off. He slipped through a stable, over a four-metre perimeter fence, and initially headed south in the pouring rain, bound for Switzerland. Later, as he turned towards his real destination, Stettin, he detected two men with tracking dogs in pursuit. Thanks to the rain, the dogs lost his scent and he gave them the slip. At Guben, he boarded a train and decided to portray himself as Peter Jansson, a Swedish-American carpenter grief-stricken that his great German pal, Hans Schmidt, had just died for his Fatherland. No one questioned his grief or troubled him for papers. Near the Danish border, he slipped off the train. Thanks to a drunken, sleepy sentry, Anderson sneaked past a customs post into his old homeland. On Friday, October 22, he was back in London.[1]

Anderson found a cool welcome awaiting him. He was among the first Canadians to escape from Germany, the highest-ranking, and, at forty-seven, by far the oldest. Canadian officials refused to make him a hero. In the paranoid mood of the time, Canadian authorities suspected that the Danish-Canadian officer with the strong accent might well be a German agent. "The green monster of jealousy soon got busy. I was tried, condemned and executed by the yellow element behind my back. I could get no redress or square deal."[2] The hapless Anderson was relegated to staff and training duties at the Canadian base in Shorncliffe. Meanwhile, back in Edmonton, his partners were busy robbing him of the prosperous brick-making business he had taken twenty years to build.[3]

Mervyn Simmons was another Canadian escaper. Long before his capture, with quite unusual foresight, he had secreted a tiny compass in his uniform. At Giessen, he picked out a fellow British Columbian, Frank Bromley who was captured with the 3rd Battalion. They spent time learning about Europe with a British interpreter who had studied at Heidelberg. They also avoided the camp's more notorious double agents and stayed out of trouble. Simmons jumped at the chance of agricultural work and was sent to a farm near Rossbach. As he later confessed, he could have spent quite a pleasant war with a kindly old farmer. Nevertheless, by dawn on October 3, he and Bromley were on the run to the Swiss border. Six days later, a child spotted the cold, hungry Canadians, notified some farm women, and the two men were promptly intercepted by a platoon of German trainees. After interrogation by a German general they were marched back to Giessen to face the consequences.[4]

John Vaughan and Jack Hollett were luckier—or smarter. Captured at Mont Sorrel with the Canadian Mounted Rifles, they were sent to work in a chemical factory in Duisburg. Vaughan stole a map and buried it. He used some of his winnings in a card game to bribe a civilian for a compass, and spent the rest on cloth caps and other clothing that made them look like some of their Belgian fellow-workers. On November 26, 1916, they were ready. While comrades made all the noise they dared over a card game, the pair burrowed under a partition into the Belgian workers' quarters next door. The Belgians kept quiet and let them out. In the street, they almost bumped into a German officer, bowed low, and pushed on. Next, the two men took a boat down river, passed a sentry with a nervous *guten Morgen*, and, like Simmons and Bromley, were spotted by a child. With an eight-hundred-metre lead, they managed to get away into a forest. After two days, they were hungry, exhausted, and close to the Dutch border. After a failed first attempt, they pulled back from the German sentry line to pray that the next night would be darker. At 2 or 3 a.m. on the 30th, it was indeed dark, misty, and very cold. The two men crawled back to the sentry line, heard a soldier cough, and went prone. Then they pushed on as fast as they dared crawl. When they were sure they were in Holland, they hid again until daybreak. When they spotted a Dutch section gang working on the railway, they came out of hiding. Like other escapers, they got food, a bath, medical attention, and a friendly welcome. Within a week, they were in England.[5]

NO ONE CAN NOW TELL HOW MANY TIMES CANADIAN PRISONers in Germany tried to escape. Simmons made two more tries before he succeeded; Collingwood Schrieber got away on his fourth try, but Frederick Rew of the 2nd Battalion failed on all eight attempts. Of postwar reparations claimants, about one in ten reported an escape attempt. Half of those disclosed a second or third attempt.[6] In all, ninety-nine Canadian soldiers and a single officer—Anderson—got away, most of them in the final year of the war.[7] In addition to Anderson, two of them—Victor Britt and Peter Nelson—were of Danish origin.[8] A lone Newfoundlander, Private E. Moyle Stick, managed to get from a camp in Prussia to the Danish border.[9]

Compared to the challenge facing Second World War escapers, getting away from the kaiser's Germany might seem easy. Three neutral neighbours, Denmark, Switzerland, and the Netherlands, shared frontiers with Germany and all were as hospitable to escapers as a nervous neutral power could be. Giessen, Göttingen, and other camps where most Canadians were confined were in the xth Army Corps area around Hannover, only a few hundred kilometres from the Dutch border. Reports survive for seventy of the one hundred Canadian escapers. They were interviewed for evidence of maltreatment, but some prisoners' stories were rewritten by Lord Beaverbrook's staff as colourful tales of Canadian pluck in the face of Hunnish brutality. Forty per cent of escapers were over thirty, older than the CEF average; fourteen came from the 4th Canadian Mounted Rifles and seven were from the 28th Battalion, but the highest proportion, four of thirty captured, came from the tunnellers taken at Mont Sorrel. In all, only twenty-six Ypres prisoners escaped. The first to get away, Sergeant G. F. Mitchell of the 7th Battalion, was a veteran of the British army and the permanent force. Captured at Ypres, he reached Holland on August 7, 1915. Close to half those interviewed (forty-three percent) got away on their first try. Frank MacDonald, a railway fireman, wandered into Holland during a fog and wandered back out again. He had to try once more. Terrible conditions were as much a spur as a barrier: ten Canadians escaped from the notorious Auguste Victoria mine. Work on a bridge over the Rhine at Enger was more congenial, but slack guards and a good plan aided nine Canadian escapers, most of whome got out after a mass break in March 1918.[10]

Canadian authorities may have been embarrassed that only one of 262 officers escaped while almost one in thirty other ranks got away, almost all to Holland. For some officers, it was not for want of trying.[11] Only days after Anderson's escape, the cocky Scudamore tried to get out in a wagon-load of kitchen implements, but an inadvertent motion warned a guard.[12] His accomplice in the escape, Lieutenant John Thorn of the 7th Battalion, became one of the most persistent attempted escapers. Condemned to the punishment camp Fort Zorndorff for his role in Scudamore's attempt, Thorn promptly joined a syndicate of tunnellers who were eventually betrayed, he claimed, by a double agent. At Augustabad, he climaxed a more successful attempt by dressing in widow's weeds. His companion, a French officer, was unfortunately stopped for his papers and, after contemplating the threat of a search by two German ladies, Thorn gave up. At Holzminden, where he rejoined his friend Bellew, Thorn made his third attempt, armed with a passport ably forged by a major in Britain's Indian army. Having gone over three hundred kilometres with only forty to go to the Dutch border, he confessed that he got careless. German sentries stopped him and, next day, he was escorted to Osnabrück "through a hostile and contemptuous population."[13]

Except when they left on *parole*—honour-bound to return and likely to be as condemned by their own side as by the Germans if they failed to do so—officer-prisoners had first to contend with prison walls and guards with orders to shoot to kill. Ingenuity might get a few escapers through the gate: Thorn got out of Augustabad in a wheelbarrow of manure. Later, he tried to escape from Strohen a little more comfortably in a laundry basket, only to be detected. Of course the inevitable answer for escapers was a tunnel. Strohen, a *Straflager* (punishment camp) for officers, was allegedly worm-holed with them.[14] At Clausthal, Wells reported that a first attempt at tunnelling ran into water and a second effort languished after six months for lack of workers. Eventually, their tunnel extended twenty-two metres, some of it through solid rock, but on November 3, 1917, a day before the planned break, it was discovered. "We know how it was given away," wrote an angry Wells, "and there will be trouble for a certain Sinn Feiner (an orderly) after the war."[15]

The most renowned wartime escape exploit was the tunnel at Holzminden, where the other hated Niemeyer brother was commandant. Planned by a Canadian officer, Lieutenant J. G. Colquhoun of the PPCLI, the tunnel began under a staircase and ultimately ran about fifty-five metres, though not in a straight line. Thanks to the limitations of compass work underground, and to the rocks that had once formed a stream bed, the tunnel humped and twisted painfully. The builders shored up the excavation with a judicious selection of bed boards and forced air into the tunnel with bellows made from an old leather flying jacket. To test progress, they occasionally thrust upward with a rag on a length of wire; a watcher at an upstairs window of the main prison building spotted the flag. Crawling to the face of the tunnel to work with table knives and a cold chisel was exhausting and often unpleasant: "There were many rats living in the tunnel, and meeting one of them and seeing the glitter of beady eyes in the semi-darkness was a feeling of revulsion only surpassed when one of the vile and foul creatures scurried over you."[16] Planned for completion in the summer of 1918, the Holzminden tunnel took nine months to build. Even then, it was cut short because it was going too slowly and Niemeyer's *Appelle* hampered the small workforce. On the night of July 23–24, twenty-nine men pushed their bundles down the narrow, humpbacked shaft and out into a bean field. Ten of them made it to the Dutch frontier. Colquhoun was not among them.[17] Long afterwards, Holzminden prisoners revelled in the memory of "Milwaukee Bill's" frantic rage at the mass escape. At the time, Niemeyer's fury was more terrifying than funny, particularly after someone chose the moment of his discomfiture to drop a big log from an upstairs window. "He sent one of the sentries inside—to go and shoot someone," recalled an anonymous prisoner who had the misfortune of being on the stairs. The soldier fired a rifle behind him, though, fortunately for him, the bullet went out a window.[18]

A bigger obstacle to escape than the walls or the guards was the mood of the community. At the more comfortable camps—Friedberg or Bischofswerda—escapes seldom happened. Fellow prisoners could only look forward to cancelled parcels, rooms wrecked by searches, the soaring risk of a week or two in cells, and the certainty of more hours of *Appell*—all so that their livelier colleagues could roam the countryside with just a small hope of reaching neutral territory. Escapers were by no means always popular with their fellow prisoners.

By collecting officers with a resister-mentality in punishment camps like Strohen and Holzminden, the Germans created some of their own problems. Jackson describes a virtual escape factory at an officers' camp at Neuenkirchen, with prisoners busily producing the kit and equipment they would need if they "got loose." To mask the sound of hammering, they built a Wimshurst generating machine to produce the steady cracking sound of static electricity. Their German captors never questioned the need for a standard piece of laboratory apparatus.[19] Walthew gleefully recalled a Holzminden search in which rooms, beds, even the prisoners themselves were stripped bare. "It was a source of great satisfaction to us when two fellows got out two nights later, complete with 'civvy' suits, maps, compasses, etc. which the Huns had been unable to find in their search. I think they must have heard Niemeyer roaring in Berlin when he got wind of it!"[20]

OTHER-RANK PRISONERS WITH ESCAPE ON THEIR MIND WOULD have envied officers a great deal, not least their leisure, better food, and the opportunity to acquire or make useful possessions. Lacking the privacy and the permanency that allowed at least a few officers' camps to set up escape organizations, soldiers were on their own. Major tunnelling efforts were almost out of the question; hungry, exhausted men were not likely to undertake more digging even if they had sufficient time and a secure starting place.[21] However, as Simmons and Vaughan could appreciate, their chief advantage *was* their work. Brutal, exhausting, and dangerous as their labour might be, it took them outside the barbed-wire fences and guard posts of the camps. While armed guards accompanied most of the prisoner *Kommandos* (detachments), over time their vigilance eroded. Civilian workers sometimes joined in assaulting and brutalizing the prisoners of war but, as Vaughan discovered, some of them could be unconsciously and even deliberately helpful. Schoolchildren could sometimes be persuaded to part with maps from their schoolbooks in return for biscuits and chocolate from Red Cross parcels. Rifleman Evanson found an Austrian fellow-worker who, for money and a little sympathy, provided him with passable civilian clothes and some practical advice. Like officers, he also found that the German habit of putting troublemakers together was a blessing. Escapers helped each other with information and hints. At Evanson's camp, a lot of men were caught at a bridge which, naturally, they had tried to cross at night. A failed escaper brought back to his fellow prisoners the words of a careless policeman: Why guard the bridge in daylight? Who would dare cross? Evanson would . . . and did.[22]

Work made another contribution to escaping: it often provided the brutal incentive. Campbell Bell, captured at St. Eloi in 1916, was a big, healthy-looking man whose painful internal injuries were not taken seriously by his captors and who found himself at the notorious Geisweid Iron Works. After several beatings and harsh treatment for not working as hard as his overseers demanded, he attempted two escapes before he was interned in Switzerland as a physical wreck.[23] Colin Earle, the eighteen-year-old student who had been "persuaded" to work at Geisweid by its notorious steam room, bided his time and finally escaped late in the fall of 1915. He was caught after fourteen days; his feet were frozen and he was trying to get food from a farmer's cottage.[24] John Harper of the 1st CMR, badly wounded and captured at Mont Sorrel, spent six months in hospital at Koblenz before being put to work in the bitterly cold weather of January

1917. Conditions drove him to attempt to escape. After three weeks at an iron mine he tried again and, in four days, managed to get close to the Dutch frontier before he was caught. Only during a relatively comfortable interlude working at the kaiser's vineyards on the Moselle did the thought of escaping leave him. Close to the end of the war, crippled with rheumatism and weakened by his dose of the 1918 influenza epidemic, he was half-dead when some advancing American troops picked him up.[25]

Persistence could pay off. A British officer succeeded on his twelfth try. Private Jack Evans of the 4th CMR needed four attempts to get to Holland. On his third, he and a partner were barely a hundred metres from the border when guards intercepted them.[26] Corporal Edwards of the PPCLI made three tries. On the first, his chosen companion lost his nerve and forced him to go back. For the second, at Vehnenmoor in January 1916, he teamed up with Mervyn Simmons and Frank Bromley. Edwards managed to cut through the barbed wire, and the three men made their dash at night. They abandoned Bromley when his legs gave out, and the other two got as far as the River Ems. There they were trapped in an efficient German network of sentries and patrols. Hungry, exhausted, and in rags, the two men were finally caught trying to slip across a bridge. Months later, after cells, semi-starvation, and punishment camps, Edwards and Simmons tried again, armed with some fragments of a map and a tiny compass Simmons's brother had sent him in a package of cream cheese. They waited until August because the days would be shorter, travelled at night, and, apart from the occasional obliging cow, went hungry. Three times they undressed to swim canals or rivers and, by pure luck, they managed to avoid a German patrol at the Dutch frontier. Endurance and a lot of patience helped the two men slip across the border to Holland.[27]

FROM A GERMAN PERSPECTIVE, ESCAPING WAS BOTH PREdictable and a serious military offence. Their *War Book* acknowledged that "attempts at escape on the part of individuals who have not pledged their word of honour might be regarded as the expression of a natural impulse for liberty. . . ."[28] However, escape could not be undertaken with impunity. Once again, the Germans could rely on backing from the Hague Convention: "Escaped prisoners who are retaken before being able to rejoin their own army, or before leaving the territory occupied by the army which captured them, are liable to disciplinary punishment."[29] While the convention implied something well short of the death penalty, the German military repertoire for disciplinary infractions was rich enough. The *War Book* also warned that escapers could be shot by guards and, like insubordination, plotting to escape could be punished by death.[30]

After his first escape attempt, Simmons spent two weeks in *Dunkelarrest*, darkened cells at Giessen. He was released daily for an hour's exercise, and survived on bread and water and, every fourth day, a bowl of soup, and the very occasional treat supplied by a sympathetic prisoner. After his uniform had been "circled" with a red painted ring, he next faced four weeks in the *Strafbaracke*, where prisoners sat stiffly perched on rows of low stools, chests out, heads back, arms rigidly at their sides, for two-hour spells from early morning to evening. Silence and posture were enforced by two guards who condemned offenders to additional days. At intervals, prisoners could walk but not sit. Inmates were deprived of mail, parcels, and the right to send letters.

Edwards and Simmons paid a heavier price for their second escape. According to Edwards, elderly *Landstürmer* marched the two Canadians back to Vehnenmoor past villagers who cursed and spat on them. They waited in cells for eleven days, being fed only thin soup and black bread, until a court martial was convened. Simmons recalled that a friendly guard, a follower of the German socialist Karl Liebknecht, discreetly shared a pot of soup and a loaf of white bread with the two half-frozen prisoners and assured them that the workers of the world would win the war.[31] The court martial sentenced the two Canadians to thirty days of *strenger Arrest* (severe punishment) at the fortress of Oldenburg. To their surprise, the Canadians found that they shared the prison with German NCOs and soldiers under punishment. Their tiny steel-walled cells were dark, unheated, and too high to measure. For three days, prisoners were locked in with a jug of water and a chunk of bread and were given only ten minutes a day to clean their cells and go to the lavatory. On the fourth day, they were allowed light and a bowl of soup. Simmons's first misery was the mid-winter cold, particularly after guards removed his overcoat. Next came the solitude, designed, he concluded, to make him insane or at least docile. Last and worst was the hunger. Helped a little by his skilful amanuensis, the novelist Nellie McClung, Simmons recalled the first of his pangs of starvation: "I was beginning to feel the weariness which is not exactly a pain but is worse than any pain. I did not want to walk—it tired me—and my limbs ached as if I had *la grippe.*" On one of the soup days, the guard apparently forgot him:

> It may have been the expectation of food, together with the hot coffee, which stimulated my stomach, for that day I experienced what starving men dread most of all—the hunger-pain. It is like a famished rat that gnaws and tears. I writhed on the floor and cried aloud in my agony while the cold sweat dripped from my face and hands. I do not remember what I said . . . I do not want to remember.[32]

That night, Simmons recalled, he expected to die, but he survived his sentence. As marked men, Edwards and Simmons suffered a second phase of punishment by being sent to another Cellelager work camp, Parnewinkel. They arrived, by Edwards' description, emaciated, filthy, and bearded to find four to five hundred Russians, eighty French, and eleven British who shared their parcels with the two newcomers. It was, he remembered, the worst of his camps, with surly, vengeful guards and an abusive commandant whose small son climbed the wire fence to shout insults. The British were employed cleaning latrines while the half-starved Russians went out to work on local farms.[33]

By 1917, British and German negotiators had agreed that two weeks' solitary confinement would be the punishment for a straightforward escape attempt. Prisoners guilty of theft or other civil offences during their escape would, of course, be subject to additional penalties. That proviso left room for variations; prisoners complained that they served additional days and weeks for wearing a civilian hat or coat or for damaging property, namely a barbed-wire fence. Simmons and Edwards suffered the normal German penalty for escape: a sentence of from fourteen to thirty days of solitary confinement in a military prison. Being locked in a pitch-black unheated cell on bread and water, with soup and a brief period of exercise every fourth day, was an ordeal that, in Scudamore's recollection, left "the most exuberant spirits remarkably tame."[34]

For officers, *strenger Arrest* was usually followed by months in a fortress. Scudamore, for example, found himself at Halle, a filthy, rat-infested former iron foundry where he and his fellow officers lived on a dirt floor and were served their meals in rusty iron pots. After his escape attempt at Bischofswerda, Lieutenant Thorn shared a cell at Zorndorff in Prussia with forty-two Russian officers. Their efforts to make him welcome did not overcome the smell and stuffiness of the room, and, after breaking the window with his boot, Thorn was sent to join French officers in a cell that included the captured French air ace and future escaper, Roland Garros.[35] Thorn took part in building a tunnel that eventually led him to Augustabad, where his impersonation of a widow earned him a stay in the notorious Fort 9 at Ingolstadt in Bavaria. Conditions there were bad enough that he successfully petitioned Ambassador Gerard to pay a visit. Strohen, near Magdeburg, another officers' punishment camp where Thorn spent time, was so bad it was condemned by neutral observers. Officers were crowded into wooden huts that were unheated in winter and unventilated in summer. The camp itself was built on sand, claimed an inmate, "and the sanitary arrangements were awful—a large hole in the centre of the camp acted as a cesspool into which all the drainage of the camp flowed." According to Captain John Streight, another Canadian escaper, the commandant boasted that he would treat his officer-prisoners like Prussian recruits:

> He did so. I have known him to keep us on Roll Call for 2½ hours, not allowing any of us to sit down or smoke under a boiling hot sun. Some fainted, others who had been badly wounded and ventured to sit down, were rushed off to the cells. All kinds of sentences were carried out without a trial of any sort and punishments awarded.[36]

Apart from formal punishment, many escapers also experienced savage beatings from guards who had frequently faced their own punishment for negligence. Captain Streight of the 3rd Battalion, a Toronto lumber dealer in civilian life, jumped through a window of the train carrying him and other officers from Bischofswerda to Crefeld in the Rhineland. He got to the Dutch border and, he claimed, was caught in the barbed wire when guards recaptured him. They were not amused. At the police station, he was well worked over by troops and border police, and spent his first weeks at Crefeld in the punishment cells. He tried again, this time trying to slip over the border when the gate was lifted for a motor lorry. In the ensuing struggle, he got a rifle butt full in the face. The result was a broken nose, a fractured jaw, and a split forehead. As an additional punishment, he spent the rest of his captivity at Strohen.[37]

Brutality to officer-escapers seems to have been exceptional; for other ranks it was more routine. Edward Hyde had a badly deformed ear to remind him of the beating he suffered after his first escape; on his third attempt, guards smashed his nose and his jaw, and he did not try again.[38] At the Beienrode salt mine, according to Haley Jones, escapers were systematically thrashed by guards after their recapture and, to avoid missing work, they served their fourteen days of *Dunkelarrest* on Sundays in a locally built "black hole." For his first escape, Lance-Corporal Edward Conoghen was beaten with a rubber hose that doctors later agreed had contributed to his epileptic seizures. Fortunately for him, his second escape attempt, from Burgsteinfurt, was more successful.[39] After Charles Taylor failed to get away from Geisweid, guards beat him with a knotted rope before officers sentenced him to twenty-one days in solitary confinement.[40] Another Geisweid escaper, Joseph Gareau of the 2nd Battalion, was compelled by guards to crawl five kilometres on his hands and knees.[41] Thomas Dewdney, a twenty-one-year-old landscape gardener in civilian life, escaped twice in desperation after repeated beatings for failing to complete his loadings. Both times he was recaptured and beaten again, once with a stick, the second time with rifle butts. As a final blow, a guard kicked him in the groin. He needed two weeks in hospital before he could walk again. Charles Davis was brought back to the cement factory where he worked, beaten by guards, served his solitary confinement, and was beaten a second time for failing to disclose where he had obtained his map. For good measure, the guards threw cement in his eyes, affecting his vision for the rest of his life.[42] Two years later, Private Adair still bore the mental and physical scars of head injuries he suffered after a 1917 escape attempt.[43] At Stuttgart, a tough camp where the commandant believed that he could make his own rules for punishing escapers, Philip L'Abbé and Homer Patterson survived three months in solitary confinement for their attempt to get away, with a further seven-month sentence hanging over their heads when they were released. Both men complained that the fear of the further ordeal had affected their hearts and nerves.[44]

Those suspected of helping escapers came in for their own share of beatings and official punishment. Sergeant J. V. Carroll, a middle-aged NCO of the 7th Battalion, might have had a comfortable life in charge of one of the huts at Giessen. Instead, he faced punishment cells and a number of beatings for failing to inform on the ringleaders of a major escape.[45] George Frost, a middle-aged former tugboat skipper captured with the 10th Battalion at Ypres, was sent to Friedberg as an officers' orderly. For helping a British officer become one of that camp's few escapers, he spent twenty-one days at Butzbach prison, a notoriously harsh institution, and emerged a marked man. Having forfeited the protection of his advanced age, he was sent to Geisweid to suffer the full force of beatings and overwork. After a beating left him with a fractured shoulder, guards still forced him to carry on.[46] Another officers' orderly, Corporal George Fraser McAlister of the 15th Battalion, began badly with his captors when he claimed to be Scottish, not Canadian. He helped officers at Crefeld build a tunnel, and endured fourteen days on bread and water at Cellelager when the project was discovered. For some reason, his past was overlooked and he again found himself an orderly at the officers' prison at Holzminden. Once again, McAlister became a humble assistant in a more successful tunnelling project. He was, of course, left behind by the escapers to face Captain Niemeyer's wrath. He suffered a permanently damaged wrist from trying to protect his head during the inevitable beating—and earned an ultimate Distinguished Conduct Medal recommended by grateful escapers.[47] As on the battlefield, those who took the risk and paid the price of helping other ranks to escape were less likely to be decorated than those whose courage had an officer as a witness.

Whatever their formal punishment, persistent escapers sooner or later found themselves on the worst work sites. Sergeant William Alldritt, the YMCA secretary from Winnipeg, was sent to Isernhagen after his second attempt. Without food parcels and half-starved, prisoners failed to complete their tasks in an eleven-hour day. Overseers insisted that Alldritt and the others work even longer. When they refused and asked to see an officer, the NCO in charge simply ordered his men to attack with clubbed rifles. The assault left cuts, gashes, two broken arms, and two shattered rifles, one of them broken on Alldritt's back. His punishment was a transfer to a salt mine at Schende in April 1917. His own account is eloquent enough:

> I worked at this salt mine till December 1917—about 18 British prisoners here—the work was very hard. Practically everyone suffered a great deal from boils. I have been forced to work when I was covered with masses of them—up to a 100 or more at once on legs, thighs, under the arms. I have worked when I couldn't lower either of my arms—and when I got working, matter would be running from boils in both armpits. This with saltpetre in the sores was of course very painful. Our barracks were very crowded here and the air got very impure. For the first three months we got no parcels—after that they came fairly regularly. Your task was always so large you had to work like a demon to get it done. In October I escaped from here by making a duplicate key to a door—was at large 110 days—was captured at Münster, was taken back to salt mines—beaten into insensibility wth rifles by the soldiers. Given extra work at the mines—put in prison on Sundays. In December I was sent bach to Hameln, completed my imprisonment (one week I think) and stayed in Hameln till I was exchanged.[48]

NOT ALL PRISONERS WANTED THE RISKS OR THE CONSEQUENCES of escaping or even resisting their captors. History is dominated by the exceptional groups and individuals who defy the norms. At its best, wartime captivity was a drab, monotonous, frustrating existence, lived too close to other human beings. Even when parcels arrived regularly, prisoners would soon have wearied of the four official assortments of canned food if they had not constantly realized that other prisoners, and even their captors, were worse off. Why risk relative comfort by trying to escape or even by challenging German authority? Escapers were not necessarily approved.[49] Their bold exploits could bring their fellow prisoners hours of standing in the rain and snow while roll-calls were taken, checked, and taken again. An angry commandant could assign hours of *stillgestanden*, or cut off parcels, mail, and letter-writing privileges, or whatever collective punishments his fury and imagination suggested.

In his 1931–32 hearings, to counter the tales of beatings and cruelty from ex-prisoners, the reparations commissioner, Errol McDougall, made a point of collecting statements from ex-prisoners who believed that troublemakers got what they deserved. Lance-Corporal Charles Cooke of the 7th Battalion, already fifty years old when he was captured at Ypres, concluded that those who had been brutally treated "brought punishment and ill usage upon themselves by truculent behaviour to their guards."[50] Men who behaved properly were not knocked about, admitted Sergeant Robert Stewart of the 13th Battalion, "but when they looked for trouble, they got it."[51] Even a youthful survivor of Beienrode, Alex McLeod, admitted to McDougall that "prisoners were not badly treated when they conformed to the rules and did the work assigned to them."[52]

Such prisoners had accepted that, for them at least, the war was over. So far as possible they avoided trouble though, in spite of themselves, they sometimes suffered brutality. The same Alex McLeod who did his best to stay out of trouble at Beienrode lost two teeth to a rifle butt when German guards went berserk after an escape. Like other Beienrode prisoners, McLeod could not escape salt sores and a lifelong battle with bronchitis and indigestion after three years of chronic hunger.

Places like Beienrode and Geisweid were exceptional in their misery. There *were* prisoners who fared comfortably, if monotonously, on a steady diet of Red Cross canned food and German soup, kept reasonably warm in Red Cross clothing and blankets, and enjoyed congenial work and tolerant guards. At least until 1917, when Germany's desperate labour shortage forced a harder look at how prisoners were employed, some men found comfortable places to work.[53] Particularly when they learned what fellow-prisoners had experienced at Bohmte, Beienrode, or behind the lines, such men were not likely to talk of brutality and maltreatment.[54] Prisoners who obeyed orders, did their work, and tolerated the *Schweinerei* (eyewash) encountered in all armies could usually look forward to their mail and parcels and they were less likely to end up at Beienrode, Vehnenmoor, or Captain Niemeyer's nasty fiefdom at Holzminden. They could not escape all the cold, hunger, and misery of a prisoner's life, though they could blame prolonged *Appelle* in the rain and other collective punishments on troublemaking compatriots as much as on the Germans.

The traditional assumption that soldiers in captivity were honour-bound to continue their battle and try to escape at every opportunity might be stood on its head. If the majority went along with their captors, however grudgingly, why were there exceptions? Why did some individuals choose to defy their guards? One of them did so in all innocence. Harry Mitton, a Toronto salesman and church organist, had been corporal of the 1st CMR's signallers when captured at Mont Sorrel. Eminently fair-minded, he even claimed that Canadian patients had been better treated than German soldiers during his time in hospital. At Friedrichsfeld, the German authorities put him in charge of a school for the younger prisoners. A mild-mannered man with some command of German, Mitton also began serving as a prisoners' advocate at courts martial, causing, as he himself admitted, some resentment among German officers whose cases he refuted. It seems never to have occurred to Mitton that their wrath could have consequences until, in the autumn of 1917, he was suddenly transferred to the grim punishment camp at Hestenmoor to cut peat and perform weary hours of *stillgestanden.*[55]

At Giessen, the first resistance among the Canadian prisoners came from trivial acts of defiance—refusal to salute German NCOs or saluting with the wrong hand. The greater defiance of refusing to work at Geisweid led to courts martial and two-year sentences at Butzbach and Cologne for at least five Canadians. It also helped inspire the only other-rank resistance organization. The so-called Iron Twenty banded together to show the Germans that they could take their punishment without giving in. One of them, the presumed ringleader of the Geisweid mutiny, was Charles Riley, a pre-war acrobat from Montreal. He suffered four thorough beatings, a broken wrist, and fourteen months in solitary confinement. Having finished his two-year term, he got three more months for refusing to work in a heavy rainstorm.[56] Riley's friend Lawrence Kane survived five days in the notorious Geisweid steam room and two badly broken ribs without giving in on his vow not to work.[57] Another of the Iron Twenty was James Martin, a twenty-six-year-old timber cruiser from British Columbia. At Valcartier in 1914, he had almost been rejected because of a chronic heart condition. Captured at Ypres with the 7th Battalion, he carried stab wounds received on the march to Roulers. For his part in the Geisweid mutiny, Martin's head was slashed by an officer's sword, two of his ribs were shattered by rifle butts, and he was thrown into a coal bin and kept there in solitary confinement. Percy Sedore, a Toronto shingler, was another of the group. A fellow prisoner later claimed that he could never have imagined anyone surviving the kind of beatings inflicted on Sedore and Martin.[58] A fifth member, Vince Nicholson from Nova Scotia's 25th Battalion, made six escape attempts and endured severe beatings after each try.[59] Arthur Corker, also a member and a former mill manager, succeeded on his sixth escape, though it was then June 1918.[60] Other prisoners might see little but masochism in such suffering, but members of the Iron Twenty took what pride they could in preserving their defiance in the face of pain.

Most prisoners who resisted faced a lonelier experience, without even the moral backing of like spirits. Sapper Joseph McLean, a thirty-three-year-old miner, "was in trouble all the time" and really decided to escape out of desperation. Rather than send him away and lose his labour, his guards made McLean walk barefoot and in his underwear from one end of the camp to the other for two hours until he was half-frozen. Predictably, he got sick, but guards routed him out in three days and put him back to work breaking rocks.[61] Another prisoner, at a peatbog camp, was stripped naked and forced to carry lumps of peat on his head until his guards tired of the fun.

Was resistance or escape motivated by patriotism? The authors, real or ghost, of conventional wartime escape literature suggested that men like Anderson, Simmons, or Edwards returned to battle imbued with a fresh hatred of kaiserism and Prussian militarism. Having experienced its sadistic cruelty and, as escapers, triumphed over its control, they could arm themselves and others for the struggle. In fact, Canadian escaped prisoners were not returned to the front but were used as instructors in England or were frequently repatriated to Canada and released. On the whole, as Moynihan suggests, escapers and other resisters among the prisoners were instinctive rebels. Stephen O'Brien, whose battles with the Germans began on the march back from Mont Sorrel and continued when he struck out at a German nurse who spat on him, already had a crowded conduct sheet in his Canadian army file.[62] Anderson, the sole officer-escaper, had bitter memories of helping to bring a full battalion from Edmonton to Valcartier in 1914 only to have his men taken and himself left displaced and friendless.[63] Nicholson, Sedore, and other members of the Iron Twenty had all had their own brushes with Canadian military discipline.

In the Second World War, soldiers were often reminded of their duty, if taken prisoner, to continue the war in whatever way they could and certainly to take any opportunity to escape. The RAF provided aircrew with ingeniously designed maps, compasses, and other equipment to help them in the task. That was not how the Hague Convention intended prisoners to behave. Apart from immunity from punishment if they successfully escaped, the convention subjected prisoners to the full military authority of their captors. Defying that authority, even in the shape of an elderly *Landstürmer*, ranked as mutiny and escape was equivalent to desertion.

Traditional military discipline had not been strong in the Canadian contingent. On Salisbury Plain, the absence-without-leave rate, like the incidence of venereal disease, had soared out of control and senior officers struggled almost in vain to impose such traditional rituals as saluting. Prisoners raised in Canadian and British homes often shared some old-fashioned assumptions. Children's literature in the Edwardian era, from the *Boy's Own Annual* to the endless series of books by G. A. Henty, featured capture, defiance, and escape as a standard test of the youthful hero's "pluck" and resourcefulness. Those who had lived through the South African War period would remember how Winston Churchill had achieved fame and a political career by escaping from his Boer captors. Such cultural baggage helped shape resister attitudes. At the least, British and Canadian prisoners felt entitled to ridicule goose-stepping soldiers and the apoplectic rages of German officers. Once free of battlefield terror, they regained the conviction that the Germans would never carry out their more blood-curdling threats against British prisoners.

Reality was harsher. The Germans had not created the best-disciplined army in Europe by accident. As young conscripts years before, the *Landstürmer* had experienced beatings with fists and bayonet scabbards, and some of them could remember cells and starvation too, even for minor offences. The German generals who harangued officers at Strohen or Canadians at Dülmen, promising to teach them Prussian discipline, meant what they said and knew how to do it. Until 1917, when the practice was abolished in the German army, recalcitrant prisoners were frequently tied to posts for two-hour periods, sometimes with their arms raised and their toes barely touching the ground, causing agony as circulation drained from the extremities.[64] Prisoners performed hours of *stillgestanden*, often collectively though sometimes individually, facing a wall or a mirror. "Our men were not used to being shouted at," Scudamore recalled, "and when they were, they usually responded with spirit, and that together with an ignorance of the language, was largely responsible for the punishments that followed—punishments that were designed to break a man's spirit and which were fairly successful in their results. . . ."[65]

THE MOST FAMOUS INCIDENT OF CANADIAN RESISTANCE occurred at Bokelah in the spring of 1916. For a moment at least, it seemed that a Canadian might become the first of Germany's

"British" prisoners shot for mutiny. It also illustrated the inevitably clouded perception of justice at the hands of an enemy.

From the perspective of Harry Howland, a central figure in the events and their chief Canadian chronicler, Bokelah was not a bad camp. Russian and British prisoners had separate quarters and the work was not heavy—digging drainage ditches and spreading fertilizer. "Farmer Bill," the elderly Prussian warrant officer who ran the camp, wanted a quiet life; some of the prisoners did not. By German standards, discipline was slack, the pace was slow, and escapes were all too frequent. Prisoners sometimes amused themselves by releasing the cars of a light railway on a steep grade so they derailed with a glorious crash at a sharp turn. Such was the feeling of comfort and self-confidence that a group of British and Canadian prisoners felt entitled to protest, one wet June morning, when they were ordered out early to move rails. Faced with defiance, "Farmer Bill" turned angry and threatening. The prisoners refused to take him seriously.

At the noon *Appell*, some of the men refused to move. The dumb-major or prisoners' leader, caught in the middle, warned them that the Germans were angry and determined. Some men moved to fetch tools; others, emboldened by calls and jeers from bystanders, stayed put. A platoon of armed guards appeared and, as the prisoners reluctantly began to move, they attacked. The result was a brutal scrimmage. Guards beat, jabbed, and drove the prisoners. One of them pinned a British prisoner to the ground with his bayonet. By the time Howland returned to the enclosure, the man was dead.[66]

At the end of June, a German court martial sentenced Howland, six other Canadians, and several British soldiers to ten-year prison terms. At the army corps headquarters, General von Hanisch insisted that the ringleader be found and executed. The obvious man was Private Fred Armstrong of the 13th Battalion. He was big enough to be called "Tiny," was a McGill University student from the Danish West Indies, and he had come out of the group, fists clenched, trying to speak to the furious "Farmer Bill." Armstrong faced the death penalty. However, a German appeal court reduced his sentence to thirteen years in solitary confinement, raised the other Canadians to twelve years, and gave the British prisoners shorter terms.[67] Discipline at Bokelah Camp 3, German authorities assured an American observer, had been undermined after the Canadians' arrival. There was no point in an appeal, advised the U.S. embassy, "as the offence was clearly established."[68]

Howland and his comrades spent eleven months at the German military prison in Cologne, joining eighty British prisoners, some of them there since early in the war. They worked stripping barbed wire from the local defences and survived on whatever remnants of their food parcels a German officer at the prison decided they could have.[69] One of the their number, Billy Brooke, got nine days in the punishment cells for concluding his description of their conditions, "Mother, you know I am not George Washington." The censor, a former salesman in the United States, got the double meaning. It was no joke for Brooke: alone and freezing in an unheated cell, he died of pneumonia.[70] "Tiny" Armstrong barely survived the effects of solitary confinement, semi-starvation, and the fear of an impending death sentence. He died in England soon after his release.[71]

They were not the only Canadians to find their lives shortened by the hardships and "harshing" of German prison camp existence. Nor were they the only Canadians to pay a price for resistance.

6

Going Home

WHETHER OR NOT PRISONERS OF WAR WERE HUMANELY treated, no one believed that long periods of captivity were good for their health and morale. The Hague Convention, drafted by people convinced that modern wars would be terrible but short, offered no solution. In characteristic wartime style, each side blamed the other for failing to find one. "Just so long as Germany's oft-repeated appeal remains unheard—that prisoners of war either be exchanged or entrusted to the hospitality of neutral states," claimed the anonymous authors of *Kriegsgefangene in Deutschland*, "just so long will the heavy burdens of imprisonment have to be borne."[1]

In earlier wars, after slaughter or slavery had become unacceptable, exchanges, to say nothing of fever and starvation, relieved captors of masses of war prisoners. In the early years of the First World War, despite their propaganda, the Germans felt little incentive to release their captives. Handing back the regular soldiers captured in the retreat from Mons or at the first Battle of Ypres would have given Britain veteran professionals to train her raw recruits. As for the French, keeping a third of a million of their soldiers in captivity was a perceptible drain on France's shrinking manpower. By 1916, three-quarters of Germany's prisoners—all who were fit and eligible to work—were busily employed in the Second Reich's war industries.[2]

The Germans were willing to exchange civilian internees, but only on an "all-for-all" basis. The British, with five times as many civilians in custody and relatively few German soldiers, preferred to keep whatever cards they had.[3]

No side, of course, found any benefit in caring for enemy sick and wounded. Already the shrewder philosophers of war-making had grasped a brutal fact: disabling an enemy made him a continuing burden on those who had to care for him while a dead enemy needed no more than some eventual digging by a burial squad. Wounded prisoners required hospital beds, drugs, and medical manpower at a time when even the cotton for bandages was in such desperately short supply that Germany was reduced to using paper. The Germans even ignored their Geneva Convention obligation to repatriate captured medical personnel, even though in practice they were little used. Hundreds of captured doctors, thousands of orderlies, and even some female members of Red Cross societies were kept in captivity waiting for the kinds of epidemics that actually occurred at Wittenberg and Gardelagen. Strenuous efforts by the International Committee of the Red Cross continued until October 1916, before all the French (and reciprocally the German) medical personnel captured in 1914–15 were finally released.[4]

The Hague Convention encouraged belligerents to make their own arrangements to exchange wounded on the battlefield or to transfer them to a neutral country. The Swiss were the necessary catalysts. By February 15, 1915, with a little pressure from Pope Benedict xv, France and Germany had reached an agreement to repatriate proportional numbers of their most seriously sick and wounded prisoners. Beginning from March 2 to 11, with the Swiss Red Cross providing the trains and medical personnel, the first prisoners began shuttling between Lyons and Konstanz. By November 1916, at a rate of about 500 a month, 2,343 Germans and 8,668 French had been repatriated. Once the initial Franco-German agreement was working, Britain and Belgium sought parallel arrangements. An agreement on October 27, 1915 established similar severely restrictive conditions for prisoner exchanges. Only those sufficiently sick or disabled to be of no further service would qualify for release—and officers and NCOs also had to be useless for training or headquarters duties. Necessary disabilities for officers included loss of both eyes, advanced tuberculosis, "damage to the brain with serious results," permanent debility, and "incurable mental disease."[5] Under the terms of the agreement, some of the most seriously wounded Canadians from Ypres had reached England as early as August 1915. By the end of the war, close to 300 Canadians had been repatriated directly from German camps, usually by way of Holland.[6] Among them was Private Cleeton, whose double pneumonia in 1916 had left him unfit for work. His turn came on August 16, 1918:

> They lined us up quickly; I never had a chance to say good bye to the others. All I had time to do was collect my personal things, my watch, for instance, that I had kept throughout and a lot of notes that I had made as I went sewn into my jacket. They loaded us on the train and we went on through the Dutch border, crossing at Aachen on August 17th, my birthday.[7]

The nervous diplomacy that opened a path for at least some prisoner repatriation made it easier to resolve a few other issues through neutral intermediaries. In December 1915, the two enemies promised to keep official record of illnesses suffered by prisoners "to obtain unprejudiced reports for establishing subsequent claims for support." The bureaucratic thirst for information was common ground for two deadly enemies. On January 8, 1916, the agreement was reached to exempt NCOs from labour except as overseers. More negotiations led, in the summer of 1917, to the agreed limits on punishment for escapers to fourteen days or up to two months "if combined with punishable actions in respect to property." German authorities promised that younger prisoners would "be kept away from all unfavourable influences to which they might be subject by being brought into contact with adult prisoners."[8]

The Swiss were willing to do more. Even before the war, Louis de Tscharner, a Berne journalist, had proposed that, in the likely event of a European war, Switzerland should offer to care for equal numbers of wounded soldiers from each side—not least as a further guarantee that Swiss neutrality would be respected. With the worst cases being repatriated, what about the less seriously sick and wounded? Gustave Ador, president of the Geneva-based International Red Cross, took the initiative. The Swiss government found a further and more practical incentive: scores of tourist hotels, emptied by the war, could be filled again with the belligerents paying their hotel and medical bills. A humanitarian message from the pope helped budge the suspicious Germans. As further reassurance, both sides agreed that any prisoner who escaped from Switzerland would be returned by his own side. In late January 1916, Germany and France each dispatched a hundred prisoners suffering from acute tuberculosis. The Germans went to Davos; the French to Leysin. That helped break the ice. Next, negotiators agreed on eighteen acute medical conditions that would qualify prisoners for Swiss internment. The list ranged from diabetes to dismemberment, pernicious anemia, acute bronchitis and asthma, paralysis, and the two staples of wartime psychiatry, hysteria and "neurasthenia." A Swiss medical commission would visit prison camps in France and Germany to judge eligibility for internment, but the captor's representative had the final voice in the decision.[9] As before, when the French and Germans had reached an agreement, the British tagged along. In March 1916, British and German negotiators agreed that prisoners "insufficiently incapacitated to justify repatriation" would be transferred to Switzerland. A commission of two Swiss doctors and a chairman from the captor power would be the judge. All costs of internees would be borne by their home country and any who escaped would be handed back to the Swiss.[10] Having gone that far, the British and Germans did a small and belated good deed for civilian internees. In April 1916, the two belligerents agreed to release women, children, men over fifty-five years of age and under seventeen, and all those in between who were obviously unfit for military service. Seven thousand Germans and six hundred British civilians went home by way of Holland.

On May 25, 1916, the first Canadians reached Switzerland. For prisoners themselves, the process of selection could be anguishing. Acceptance by the commission seemed to promise virtual release from captivity; rejection meant more months and even years of crowded huts, barbed wire, and monotonous manual labour. Lieutenant J. H. Douglas, who spent a month at Konstanz waiting for a decision, remembered that his mood was not helped by renewed dependence on German rations. Parcels, of course, had not kept up.[11] Though the Germans had good reason to rid themselves of useless mouths, both they and the Swiss adopted a rigid view of the agreed conditions. As with most tribunals, luck and manner played a part in the outcome. The artist Allan Beddoes claimed that one of his guards rewarded him for a portrait by advising the young Canadian to play stupid when he came before the medical commission. Beddoes obliged and went to Switzerland. Failing eyesight gave Captain Scudamore a chance at internment but, when his party of forty reached the German border, he and others were sent back because the British had sent only twenty-five Germans. A British major broke down and cried. The experience of appearing before a succession of Swiss–German commissions persuaded Scudamore to try more assertive tactics when officials reappeared in mid-December 1916:

> I marched up to the table, banged it with my fist, and asked who was the head of the commission. A small white-haired man turned out to be the head. I addressed him as "Herr Professor": and shouted that I was going blind and that it was a "schweinerei" to keep a blind man in prison, and carried on so violently that he tried to soothe me and told me I would be leaving shortly.[12]

By Christmas, Scudamore and several dozen disabled Canadians were in Switzerland. When Lieutenant Colonel Claude Bryan of the

Canadian Red Cross visited Switzerland a year later, he found Scudamore helping to manage his fellow Canadians, with no apparent difficulty with his eyesight.[13]

FOR SOME PRISONERS, THE PROSPECT OF GETTING TO Switzerland seemed so close to freedom that it replaced escape. After five attempts to get away, even the redoubtable Thorn concluded that he had suffered enough and that he would wait quietly for exchange or repatriation. However, internment, as many of the former prisoners of war were reluctant to realize, was still a form of captivity. The friendly welcome for "fannigans" at Berne, where the local British community faithfully turned out, seemed a little chillier when internees found their way, via funicular railways or narrow mountain roads, to isolated resorts at Mürren and Chateau d'Oex. The sight of the Eiger and the Jungfrau palled when prisoners explored the limited attractions of what Douglas called "a one-horse hotel town." So did the compensations of adequate food, sheets, and warm blankets and even short visits by small parties of mothers and wives. "On the whole," claimed a British report in 1917, "the prisoners in Switzerland do a great deal of grumbling. They grumble at the work, six hours a day, they grumble at not being paid, they grumble at having to pay duty on things received from England, they grumble at the number of mothers allowed to visit Switzerland being restricted."[14] Jealous rumours spread that the Swiss had given the best hotels to the French. The British paid the Swiss six francs a day per officer and four francs for other-rank internees. By pre-war standards the rate was generous, but prisoners ignored wartime inflation and assumed that the Swiss *commandant de place*, normally a doctor, was in cahoots with profiteering local innkeepers.

One problem was administrative authority. The camps were, in effect, Swiss military hospitals, commanded by uniformed doctors from Switzerland's famous part-time army. Unlike prisoner-of-war camps, British officers shared the same locations with other-rank internees, though they were in separate quarters and, like Colonel Ussher of the 4th CMR, many summoned their wives to join them.[15] Could they exercise the authority of their rank? Would other ranks obey? Much depended on the Senior British Officer (SBO). At Mürren, Lieutenant Colonel F. H. McNeish of the Gordon Highlanders exerted effective authority; at other camps the SBOs—who would not have been in Switzerland except for very poor health—did much less.

The Swiss saw no reason why prisoners fit to work should not be kept busy. Douglas was allowed to use part of his time to attend the University of Geneva. Some internees worked at Lady Duff's bakery in Berne, dispatching three thousand loaves a day to prisoners in Germany; others studied tailoring and other trades. A school in motor mechanics, with extra instruction in vulcanizing rubber tires, was sponsored by the Red Cross, financed by the British magazine *Autocar* and run by a Canadian, Lieutenant A. C. McClurg from Sault Ste. Marie.[16] The most fit were put to work at Swiss wages. British prisoners grumbled that French internees took jobs in factories at wartime wages while they were relegated to road-mending and unskilled labour. At Mürren, Lieutenant Colonel McNeish was condemned for sending men to shovel snow under the command of British officers and NCOs. This was not what the "fannigans" had expected when they were transferred to Switzerland. "Some soldiers fear that they will be sending home for rifles to make them drill."[17]

Until September 1916, Canadian troops had been classified as part of the British army, categorized under the Army Act as "imperial." While Canada paid for its own troops and looked after their administration in England, lines of authority were almost deliberately confused by Sir Sam Hughes, the Canadian minister of Militia, so that he could personally settle any and every issue affecting "his boys." The results were chaotic, embarrassing, and expensive. With the appointment of Canada's High Commissioner to Great Britain, Sir George Perley, as minister of the Overseas Military Forces of Canada, based in London, Sir Robert Borden began to achieve effective administrative control of Canadian troops in Britain and France.

In November, Perley brought Major General Richard Turner back from France and began to overcome the chaos.[18]

One side-effect of creating the Overseas Ministry was an overdue interest in the welfare of CEF prisoners of war and internees, hitherto entirely left to the British. In the summer of 1917, Perley sent Brigadier General Lord Brooke, one of Hughes's protégés, and Major G. R. Geary, a former mayor of Toronto, to investigate the grumbling from Switzerland. They found 137 Canadians, most of them bored and all of them eager to come home. At Chateau d'Oex, the food, discipline, and hotel-keeper were all bad. The Swiss might like macaroni but their guests were tired of it. After consultation with Swiss authorities and the Senior British Officers, Brooke suggested that British and Canadian soldiers had rather more spending money than was wise. Another problem was the Swiss military code: "Offences which are of minor importance in our view are regarded as serious and the punishments are much more severe than under our code." The solution had already been arrived at: "A considerable amount of power has been placed in the hands of our own officers."

A few months later, in December, Lieutenant Colonel Bryan, deputy overseas commissioner of the Canadian Red Cross, visited the Swiss camps. At Berne, he met the British ambassador, called on the Swiss authorities, and visited the Canadian-run school for motor mechanics. At Chateau d'Oex, complaints from Brooke and Geary had led the Swiss army to take over administration and the British Red Cross now ran the canteen. At Mürren, he found most of the Canadians cheerful, busy, and grumbling chiefly about the meagre continental breakfast of coffee and bread. They wanted a supply of their own badges and members of the 15th Battalion (Toronto's 48th Highlanders) petitioned for kilts. They wanted more money. After consulting with Swiss and British officers and seeing for himself that most of the spending was on liquor, Bryan agreed that two pounds ten shillings a month was "on the liberal side." He got back to Berne in time to share in welcoming a party of British prisoners, including thirty-one Canadians. Most, he noted, were in "pretty fair physical condition." He gave the credit, appropriately enough, to regular Red Cross food parcels.[19]

Though they could visit their men in Switzerland and modestly improve their conditions, there were limits to what Canadian authorities could do. In the 1917 general election, efforts to poll every possible military vote extended to Switzerland and an officer was dispatched to oversee the balloting. A belated check with the Foreign Office revealed that the Swiss were by no means ready to cooperate. Since foreigners were excluded from their politics, it followed that Switzerland did not meddle in other people's elections. Borden, satisfied with his victory, asked the Governor General to have Switzerland advised of Canada's "surprise." The United States, after all, had allowed twenty-five polling places for Canadian soldiers to vote.[20]

When the United States joined the Allied cause in 1917, the Dutch replaced the Americans as the "protecting power" for British interests while the Germans turned to Switzerland. The Netherlands had many desperate wartime worries. Full-scale mobilization seemed necessary in light of Belgium's fate, but the cost of keeping half a million men under arms fell on a ruined economy. Dutch rivers, canals, and seaports had provided one of the major routes for German exports, but the British naval blockade effectively froze Dutch trade. Despite a highly developed agriculture, the Netherlands were far from self-sufficient in food and the British allowed only enough shipments to meet what they considered as minimal needs. That left the Dutch very little to barter with Germany for their other needs and the German policy of unrestricted submarine warfare, adopted in January 1917, meant that even the ships the British allowed were likely to be sunk. By the end of the war, the Dutch were as hungry as their once-powerful neighbour.

Diplomatic calculation as well as humanitarian concern made it wise to make some positive contribution to the welfare of prisoners of war. In June 1917, after a few months of adjustment, ill-feeling, and the well-publicized reprisals for alleged work behind the lines, British and German negotiators met in The Hague to resume negotiations. The Dutch government helped with an offer to accept up to 16,000 internees, provided both sides met the cost and provided the food. Medical criteria were extended to include the psychological malady of "barbed-wire disease," at least for those who had already served eighteen months in captivity. Since officers, senior NCOs, and civilian internees added nothing to the labour force, both sides agreed that they, too, would be eligible for internment provided they had already endured eighteen months in the camps. Of the 16,000 vacancies in the Netherlands, 7,500 would be reserved for sick and wounded, 6,500 for officers and NCOs, and 2,000 for civilians. A collateral agreement permitted repatriation from Switzerland of internees who were taking a long time to recover. Their places could then be taken by other prisoners. By the end of the war, 55 officers and 338 Canadian other ranks had been interned in Holland and, for medical reasons, some of them had moved the further step to freedom in England.[21]

Internment in the Netherlands was a special benefit for Canadian officers and NCOs captured at Ypres in April 1915. Among them were men whose health had been undermined in the camps and *Arbeitskommandos*, including the Winnipeg YMCA leader Sergeant Alldritt, Corporal F. W. Newberry, who had spent almost two years at Salstedt, a Saxon salt mine, and Private Alfred Blake, who later boasted that he had kept out of trouble.[22] In May 1918, the Germans finally released Dr. Béland—ostensibly in exchange for a relative of a former German foreign minister interned in England.[23] He could go back to Canada; military prisoners had to stay. Corporal Jack Finnemore, who had survived serious wounds and endless hours of drill at Grossenweidenmoor, confessed that being put on the train to Holland was "a damned good feeling," while The Hague was a lovely place to spend the summer.[24] The senior Canadian in Holland, Major Byng-Hall of the 7th Battalion, urged Sir Richard Turner, chief of staff of the Overseas Military Forces of Canada, to allow officers' wives to join them in Holland. Otherwise, he claimed, the hotel rooms would be filled by vacationing Germans.[25]

The prospect of internment in Switzerland or the Netherlands encouraged prisoners' friends and relatives to bring influence to bear on their politicians. As early as 1916 a wealthy Montreal stockbroker warned Borden that unless his son, a Black Watch captain, was exchanged for a prominent German in Canada, he would reveal what he knew of the government's corrupt wartime dealings.[26] Frank Keefer, the MP for Port Arthur, explained that a constituent's son would have been an officer if he had not reverted to the ranks and that sort of made him an NCO and he should be in Holland. Anyway, it was unfair. As the son had written, "It's a damned shame that the N.C.O.'s are all being exchanged and we're still here."[27] Howard Ferguson, an Ontario cabinet minister and future premier, wrote on behalf of Lance-Corporal John Hewitt, a prisoner since Ypres, whose widowed mother was in precarious health. Lieutenant C. B. Pitblado's father, a Montreal stockbroker, sought support from the prime minister and Sir Edward Kemp, Perley's successor as minister of Overseas Military Forces. Dysentery, he explained, was common in his son's camp. Based on the government's painful experience in trying to liberate Henri Béland, Kemp had a shrewd answer, at least for Ferguson: "Any attempt to urge a particular case is dangerous, as it is apt to prejudice it."[28] Word that the British would again meet with the Germans in June 1918 persuaded Mrs. Rivers Bulkeley of the Red Cross Prisoners' Bureau in London to insist that Borden demand the same treatment for Canadians that the French and Germans had already agreed upon. "Many of them have been prisoners for over three years and most of them have suffered more than human endurance can bear."[29]

When the British and German representatives met again in The Hague between June 8 and July 4, much had changed over the year. The powerful German offensives of March, April, and May had added hundreds of thousands of British and French prisoners to the

German totals, but the Allies had survived the series of setbacks and American troops had continued to flow across the Atlantic. The convoy system, belatedly adopted, had countered the German U-boat threat. At the same time, Germany—and her prisoners—faced acute hunger and both sides knew it. As the British had insisted throughout, prisoners would now be exchanged head for head, rank for rank, provided that they had been held for eighteen months and that they must not serve again within thirty kilometres of the front. Both sides also knew a lot more about the ordeal prisoners had experienced in Germany and, in some cases, in France and Britain.

Much of the 1918 negotiations centred on camp conditions, with the Germans in some cases agreeing to conditions they were in no position to keep. Prisoners "must be treated humanely." They could not work more than ten hours a day, six days a week, with a one-hour, mid-day break. They must have a minimum twenty-five-hundred-calorie diet for workers and twenty-eight-hundred calories for those doing heavy work. Prisoners under punishment must be held in a "light, dry, ventilated room" and officers under punishment were not to be deprived of their mattress, two blankets, and food. Other ranks could eat bread and water and lose their bedding for three days out of four, but only if they were not working and the temperature stayed above 7° C. Unfortunately, disputes about British treatment of captured U-boat crews and German concerns about their captives in China and Japan meant that the July 14 agreement was not ratified.[30]

By the end of the war, the Dutch had accepted 40,000 internees. Among them were 53 Canadian officers and 314 other ranks. As the British had discovered in Switzerland, not everyone appreciated internment. At Scheveningen, where most Canadians had been sent as part of "Group 6—Colonials," there was little to do. Major Fred Palmer of the 1st CMR took charge of training British prisoners in agriculture and poultry-rearing and Captain F. Vernon-Jones organized other internees to pack emergency parcels for camps in Germany. Canadian officers rented a seafront building and organized an "Officer's Club" as a cheaper alternative to Dutch cafés. The British

YMCA started a canteen. Sick and injured officers had the benefit of a special Red Cross hospital at Clingendaal, the country estate of the kindly Baroness de Brienden; other ranks had the more austere benefit of two hospitals run by the Dutch army, one of them for "nervous" cases. A few Canadians organized a baseball team and took on the American legation in The Hague. On July 1, 1918, most Canadians in Holland got together to celebrate Dominion Day with sports and a little entertainment at the expense of their officers. Several thousand spectators looked on.[31]

Food, boredom, and the cost of living were the curses of Dutch internment, as they had been in Switzerland. By agreement, internees were fed the same rations as Dutch civilians, and though they could use their pay to supplement their meals, bread was not for sale and prices for the little that was available struck soldiers as very high. Lieutenant Wells, released from the Niemeyer tyranny at Clausthal, found the country flat but pretty and his banking experience was soon put to use dealing with the pay of eight hundred interned British officers and four thousand other ranks. However, like others he soon complained that the cost of living was too high. "The expense of The Hague is the greatest drawback. Prices are extortionate and it is almost impossible for a subaltern to live."[32] Corporal Raphael Ménard of the 22nd Battalion, released to Holland in April 1918, profited from his leisure to find his future wife.[33] Others read voraciously, learned a trade, or discreetly found a way to earn a few gulden. They were the minority. Corporal Newberry's diary records a dreary routine of aimless walks, cleaning his room, and conversations, interspersed with occasional "parades" for sightseeing tours and spells of work at the YMCA hut.

For Canada's new Union government, discontented internees represented a potential issue. A cabinet colleague, Arthur Meighen, warned Kemp that a Winnipeg MP had heard from his internee son that Canadians in the Netherlands believed that Canada had simply ignored them. Moreover, the general assigned to oversee the British internees allegedly regarded Canadians as little better than the "venereals" he had once commanded at a base camp in England.[34] In June 1918, a report from W. R. Plewman to the *Toronto Daily Star* declared, "Canadians in Holland Starving for Food." Canadians, claimed Plewman, had been well received by the Dutch but their own government had left them bootless and in rags. A sergeant major from Toronto complained that all he had received from Canadian authorities since arriving in Holland six weeks earlier was a pair of socks, a boot brush, and a tin of blacking. Meanwhile the soles had worn off his boots. "The grub here is awful," complained Corporal F. P. O'Donoghue. "It is not only none too good but by no means enough, though we have had meat twice since we have been here. What little money we get we have to buy biscuits or whatever we can get for it and have to pay them through the nose for everything." "What we receive all day would only make a decent breakfast," reported Corporal G. B. Edie. "We are expected to live on sea breezes and love," Corporal C. R. Lyall reported to his mother. Still, he admitted, it was a great improvement on bread and water in a German cell.[35]

It was a measure of the remarkable evolution of Canadian autonomy during the war that, by 1918, Canadians in Holland expected their own government to act on their behalf and the OMFC in London responded. Major Hume Blake, a staff officer with solid political connections, was despatched to The Hague to investigate and report. He found the Canadians in far better shape, physically, mentally, and morally, than he had expected. He also encountered plenty of complaints he considered legitimate. Officers grumbled that their pay was once again being docked, this time for the monthly allowance of 120 gulden granted to the Dutch to cover the cost of their food. Other ranks denounced high prices, a lack of recreation, and, above all, boredom. With a pound sterling worth about a third of its face value in Dutch currency, the cost of living was indeed high.

Food, the core grievance, was a complex problem. Since the Dutch population had to submit to strict food rationing, it would create severe tensions if their British guests were seen to be conspicuously better fed.[36] Even after making allowances, however, Blake agreed that "the soldiers' food has been not only altogether insufficient but often so dirty and badly prepared as to be altogether uneatable." A change of contractor had not produced significant improvement.[37] As remedies, Blake recommended higher allowances for officers and other ranks, a supply of badges, boots, and uniforms to help Canadians distinguish themselves from their British allies, and a special YMCA hut for Canadians, preferably with "a few Canadian ladies" to help. Canadians must also resist Dutch proposals to send some of them to a new internment area at Leeuwarden.[38] Lieutenant Colonel Gerald Birks, Canadian head of the overseas YMCA, was reluctant to spend £3,000 for a few hundred Canadians in the Netherlands but he did not have to be converted to their strong desire for a national identity:

> Life in the colonies has developed our men along sufficiently different lines from life in the Old Country, that they call for special treatment, not only in connection with educational work, but on the physical side, in their games and even in the matter of food supplies. . . .[39]

BY THE TIME THE OVERSEAS MINISTRY COULD RESPOND effectively to conditions in Holland, the war was over. Beginning on August 8 with the highly successful joint Australian-Canadian advance at Amiens, the Canadian corps had been one of the spearheads of the Allied advance. Switched from the Amiens front before it bogged down, the corps had broken through some of the toughest sections of the Hindenburg Line, crossed the Canal du Nord, and taken Cambrai. In its last battle of the war, the corps had smashed through the Germans' last defensive line by capturing Valenciennes. Canadians had arrived at Mons on November 11 when news reached them that the guns would be silent after 11 a.m.[40]

At his last camp, Soltau, W. J. Chambers had used borrowed

corporal's stripes to get himself a job in the camp post office. That meant a daily trip to town, under escort, to collect the day's mail. It also meant a daily glimpse at a store window where Germany's military fortunes were displayed. He was not wholly surprised when, on November 8, his little party was met by guards from the camp announcing the outbreak of revolution and the kaiser's abrupt departure. The red flag hoisted by the guards, he noted, had been stitched together from red handkerchiefs supplied in Red Cross parcels.[41]

Article 10 of the armistice, signed by the German delegates at Marshal Ferdinand Foch's headquarters in the Forest of Compiègne, required "immediate repatriation without reciprocity" of all Allied and United States prisoners of war. In the chaos of post-armistice Germany it was not easy to repatriate prisoners but, for all but the hapless Russians, the task was well underway by the end of December.[42] Private William Bouvier and Private Robert Gray of the 16th Battalion, captured at Cambrai on October 1, had loaded barges and looked after horses behind the German lines until November 12 when they were simply told to leave. Three days later, they reached the British lines. Thousands of the ragged, starving men who had been kept behind the lines did the same—leaving a bitter impression on the advancing Allied troops who encountered them. In Germany, authority broke down in some camps. Gunner Wilf Hand, a Mont Sorrel prisoner, was working in a paper factory when the war ended. He walked forty kilometres to his *Stammlager* at Friedrichsfeld and simply boarded a train for Holland.[43] Another Friedrichsfeld prisoner, Corporal Arthur Speight, recalled that authority and rations both ceased. He befriended a German corporal who had been decent to him and shared Red Cross parcels with him. In return, the corporal took them to the nearby town of Wesel, where a tin of cocoa or a couple of bars of Sunlight soap "would supply six men with beer for as long as they cared to stay."[44]

Captivity did not end as smoothly for everyone. At least one prisoner, Private James Wall, got his last beating in Germany for deciding that the armistice released him from further work.[45] Another Canadian, Andrew Cowie of the 31st Battalion, claimed that Germans shot three prisoners in his camp during a post-armistice strike.[46] Other prisoners, awaiting courts martial or long prison sentences, could suddenly go free. Some prisoners nursed the hope of postwar vengeance on oppressive Germans, and the Niemeyer brothers vanished from their respective camps even before the war ended. Vengeance sometimes went the other way. John Carndew, a St. Eloi prisoner, had had a relatively easy job in a hat factory at Oberhausen. Shortly before the armistice, his fellow workers went on strike. In one of the resulting mêlées, the interpreter, a German civilian, hit him on the face and broke his nose.[47] Peter Thornton, never very strong, claimed that he was locked in a shed by the angry farmer who employed him, fed on bread and water, and not released until late in December 1918.[48]

As Germany's front-line troops retreated, civil order broke down, particularly in coastal regions and in the north German states where most of the remaining Canadian prisoners were confined. In some camps, delegates of Soldiers and Workers' Councils appeared, hoisted improvised red flags, and stripped officers of their rank badges. Claude Beesley, the former divinity student, was at Langensalza on November 11. Nothing changed. Two weeks later, camp authorities ordered French prisoners to dismantle their theatre. As the men carried sets and costumes out of the building, a milling crowd persuaded nervous guards that a riot was brewing. German troops, hurriedly assembled, opened fire. Later, Beesley claimed that he had counted nine bodies. A little weakly, the Germans blamed the French for trying to set up a revolutionary Soviet among the prisoners.[49] Alvin Ferguson, in an officer's camp near Stralsund, met the real thing. Within a few days of the armistice he found that his fate was controlled by a Soldiers and Workers' Council which terrorized German officers and prisoners alike. On the night of December 5–6, two of his fellow prisoners were shot for straying out of bounds. "Everybody agrees it was absolute murder. . . . Another act of

Hunism."[50] Three days later, Ferguson was on his way by train and ferry to Denmark, and on December 17, he landed at Leith.

At Soltau, nothing changed for weeks beyond a softening in the attitude of the guards. Finally, prisoners made up their minds that they would simply break out of the camp and march if nothing better happened. Whether in response or by coincidence, a train arrived on December 22, ready to remove some of the prisoners. All of them insisted on piling aboard and, though flags had been strictly forbidden throughout their captivity, Chambers recalled that every man seemed to have one. Two days later their train reached a silent and seemingly empty Hamburg. At the docks, a British destroyer and a small steamer waited for them.

> The German guards were lining us up, wagging their fingers at us, and numbering us off when a British petty officer bawled at him to quit, he would take charge. What a thrill it gave us when that burly guard subsided when the sailor yapped at him. For nearly four years, they had ordered and controlled our every action and this was the first time one of our own side was the top dog. Freedom, what a sweet taste it had.[51]

As early as August, the British had made plans to repatriate their prisoners. Special camps would be opened at Calais and at Ripon in Yorkshire, each with enough accommodation to quarantine any ex-prisoners who might bring typhus and other infections into an island already suffering from the 1918 influenza epidemic. Troop-ships and liners chartered from neutral countries made their cautious way into Dutch, German, and Belgian ports. Trains collected a thousand or more prisoners a day from Friedrichsfeld, Limburg, Mannheim, and other prisoner concentration camps and took them to the docks at Danzig, Hamburg, Rotterdam, and Antwerp. Canadians remained, as they had through the war, with their British, Australian, and South African counterparts. As the

Overseas Ministry's staff officer now responsible for prisoners of war, Blake organized small staffs to handle pay and records for Canadians arriving at Ripon and Dover and to interrogate them on their experiences.[52]

OMFC records indicated that, as of October 31, there were 78 officers and 2,248 Canadian other-rank prisoners in Germany, 106 internees in Switzerland, and 42 officers and 286 other ranks in the Netherlands. Eventually, statistics showed that 28 officers and 255 other ranks had died in German hands and, of course, Major Anderson and 99 other ranks had managed to escape. By February, 149 Canadian officers and 2,767 other ranks had been part of a flow of tens of thousands of British ex-prisoners who passed through the repatriation camps at Ripon and Calais.[53] Camp staffs processed men through medical examinations, distributing new uniforms and kit, settling back pay and allowances, and issuing passes to other ranks for a standard twenty-eight days' leave. The Prisoners of War Committee supplied forms for an official interview with ex-prisoners, seeking evidence of maltreatment and, later, signs of revolutionary subversion. Once they were free of the camp, the delights of London lay ahead. The Red Cross Prisoner of War Bureau even turned its quarters into a hostel for the men they had fed and worried about since 1915. Then the ex-prisoners joined the stream of a quarter-million Canadians heading for home and civilian life.

If returned prisoners had only realized how important their medical board and their interview might be for the rest of their lives, they might have controlled their impatience, endured more of the primitive diagnostic tests available in 1918, and replied more systematically to the questions. Perhaps fewer men would have returned with medical forms declaring cheerfully "all systems normal" and repatriation forms that asserted simply "treatment good." For most men at that stage of their lives, a patient attention to the requirements of bureaucracy would have tested human nature too hard. Even most of the staff at Dover and Ripon were already thinking more of the future than of the dismal wartime past.

7

Afterwards

AT RIPON, CAPTAIN E. J. THOMAS LAY IN WAIT FOR IMPATIENT homesick Canadian ex-prisoners. Blake's representative had a serious military function. Captivity was a taint on a soldier's honour, expunged only by evidence that it was due to the sad fortune of war. More practically, military pay regulations insisted that soldiers were only entitled to be paid as prisoners of war if they had not contributed to their own captivity by cowardice or neglect.[1] Admittedly, such questions were low on Captain Thomas's agenda. Questions about what happened at Ypres or Mont Sorrel were ancient and potentially embarrassing history.[2] The Allies were convinced that the Germans had treated their prisoners with criminal brutality. Now, having helped establish an international law for the protection of prisoners of war, the victors would sit in judgement on the vanquished offenders. Former prisoners were expected to furnish the evidence for the modern world's first war-crimes trials. As Thomas reported to the director of the Canadian War Records Office, "I am working on the principle that what your department and the Overseas Ministry want is the truth, the whole truth and nothing but the truth—and that any errors that are allowed to creep in may only weaken the case of our martyred prisoners against the Hun by leading some to doubt the real facts. God knows there is enough that can be proved to the hilt for the most incredulous."[3]

It was not as easy as he had expected. "There are so many parades for the men that I am having difficulty in finding an opportunity to examine them and have to rush their statements through and I find too it is quite impossible to enter up an individual's statement by following the printed list of questions."[4] British authorities had wisely limited repatriation processing to a twenty-four-hour period and, with pay parades, clothing parades, medical boards, and the prisoners' own eagerness to escape the last phase of constraint after years of imprisonment, the interview was a low priority. Thomas confessed that he had seen barely one in five of the returning Canadians. Even then, getting the real story took hours of exhaustive questioning: "Often some of the most vivid details will come out as an aside after 20 minutes or half an hour of examination." He took pains, he explained, to avoid revealing that he already knew of the notorious Fort McDonald at Lille or the dreaded salt mine at Beienrode: "I lead each man to believe I have never heard the story before and get it fresh from him and in his own words."[5]

IN THE END, LIKE SO MUCH IN WAR, BOTH THE EFFORT AND the suffering were largely in vain. Soldiers eager to get home may have told Thomas less than they knew—or their later stories grew with time and the long-term consequences of beatings, overwork, and malnutrition. Thomas's accumulated documentation was buried in the British evidence. In December 1918 British voters backed politicians who promised to hang the kaiser and to squeeze Germany "until the pips squeaked." However, neither was the deposed kaiser hanged nor, as many Germans would have hoped, did the Allies hold him solely and personally responsible for all that had ensued. At Versailles, German delegates found, to their helpless indignation, that they were required to accept collective national responsibility for the war, and that Germans had to pay the full costs of the war in reparations. If put into practice, that meant paying for crimes against civilians, damage to private property, and, among other specific evils, "the maltreatment of prisoners of war."[6]

A further consequence of the treaty's distribution of blame to the German people and not merely to their former emperor was that individual Germans would be compelled to answer charges of violations of the Hague and Geneva conventions, though they would do so before German courts. Of forty-five cases, the British chose to proceed with six, three of them associated with maltreatment in prison camps and three with submarine warfare, including the sinking of the Canadian hospital ship, *Llandovery Castle*.[7]

The war-crimes trials were held in 1920 before the German Supreme Court at Leipzig under the aegis of President Friedrich Ebert's shaky and unpopular Socialist government.

Claud Mullins, one of the British counsel, later explained that German justice had its quirks. Was Robert Neumann, a camp guard, a sadist or a disciplinarian? The court accepted twelve of the seventeen assault charges against him—and sentenced Neumann to six months in prison. Sergeant Karl Heyen, a burly cooper, had beaten and tortured prisoners at a mine in Westphalia, but he was responsible for discipline and getting his reluctant charges to work. If he had assaulted prisoners claiming to be sick, he was only obeying a doctor's orders to ensure that they were not malingering. His penalty was ten months in prison.

Captain Emil Müller, a Karlsruhe lawyer and reserve officer, had taken over the former British prisoner cage at Flavy-le-Martel during the March offensives of 1918. His military superiors had filled it with a thousand British prisoners and left them to die of hunger and dysentery. It was left to the British to explain why the two unfloored huts and the barbed-wire enclosure had been located in a swamp. If the survivors were hungry, verminous, and demoralized, was that their condition while they were part of the British Fifth Army and was that why they had surrendered so quickly?

Müller had left the camp on sick leave on May 5, 1918, just before the death rate became notable. His successor should have been charged with that responsibility. The court recognized Müller's effort to improve conditions, criticized the general staff's insistence on using prisoners for dirty work behind the lines, and sentenced the former officer to just six months' imprisonment. As weighty a matter with German judges as the violence was evidence that Müller, Neumann, and Heyen had used such words as *Schweinehund* (swine) and *Dreckschwein* (dirty pig). Vulgar abuse, Mullins explained, might be irrelevant in English law, but in German courts it was a matter of concern because it affected the victim's honour.[8]

LIKE OTHER CANADIAN VETERANS, FORMER PRISONERS OF WAR came home to a country that had prepared a set of tough-minded institutions and programs designed to move them into the freedom and hard consequences of civil life as swiftly as possible. Politicians and officials were conscious of the billions of dollars a year American governments lavished on the aged but well-organized veterans of their Civil War. Canada could afford no such extravagance. The Military Hospitals Commission (MHC), established in 1915, did more than provide convalescent beds and medical treatment; it launched an ambitious, innovative program of vocational training and placement so that disabled soldiers could be restored to the civilian work force better trained and perhaps even better paid than before the war.

A new Board of Pension Commissioners (BPC), created in 1916, implemented the ideas of one of its first members, Major J. L. Todd, a McGill professor of parasitology. With the American "pension evil" as a warning and French and British experience as models, Todd offered a simple basis of pension rating. A soldier, he insisted, brought nothing but a healthy mind and body to the public service. "For practical purposes, the market for healthy bodies is said to be the general market for untrained labour."[9] Assuming doctors could assess such bodies, Canadian pensions were based on the percentage of fitness lost during active service. Todd's principle sharply distinguished between what a veteran *actually* earned and a veteran's earn-ing power. Without an incentive to work, many veterans would lapse into dependence and, ultimately, Canada would have its own "pension evil."[10]

Pensions and retraining were for the disabled. The promise of "full re-establishment," made by the Borden government in the 1917 election and delivered through a new Department of Soldiers' Civil Re-establishment, was not based on generosity, as soldiers might have imagined, but on a rapid transition from military to civil life. The cure for too many years of military discipline and dependence was a brisk immersion in the responsibilities of civilian life. The opposition leader, Sir Wilfrid Laurier, set the tone for the government: "I would rather trust the manhood of the man, if he comes back sound in limb and body, than depend upon the existence . . . of a paternal government."[11] There was one apparent but illusory exception. Historically, Canada had met any special debt to its returning soldiers by distributing more of its seemingly limitless public lands. In fact, the last distribution, after the South African War, had more than exhausted the supply of arable land. Many returned men had difficulty grasping that the Soldier Settlement Acts of 1917 and 1919 were large-scale loan schemes to allow men (women were explicitly excluded) to borrow enough money to become successful homesteaders. Soldiers, enthusiastically buying land, livestock, and equipment on five per cent loans from the Soldier Settlement Board, would soon discover that they had bought at the top of a grossly inflated market. It wasn't until another world war erupted that farm prices even approached the levels of 1919.[12]

The policy-makers who planned for Canada's returned soldiers were accurate in one prediction: their fellow citizens would soon grow tired of them. Veterans who depended on goodwill and sympathy to get them resettled would have a very short respite. A sharp depression in 1921 wiped out thousands of jobs that depended on patriotic memories. Veterans who imagined that their reminiscences, real or fictitious, would command a national literary market were badly deceived.

Ex-prisoners had no special status. Most returned men found comfort in their own organizations: the Great War Veterans' Association, the bonus-seeking Grand Army of United Veterans, or the conservative, officer-dominated Army and Navy Veterans. Though many of the early veterans' leaders were Ypres survivors, repatriated to Canada in 1916, ex-prisoners seem to have had no major role in these organizations. J. P. Cathcart, a psychiatrist with the DSCR and its successor, the Department of Pensions and National Health, commented that former prisoners played very little part in veterans' organizations and old comrades' associations.[13] While Cathcart might theorize about possible neuroses, it was not hard to find practical reasons. Men captured in 1915 and 1916 had little in common with soldiers who had shared the triumphs of the Canadian corps. Contemporaries in the 3rd or 15th Battalions who avoided capture at Ypres or Mont Sorrel had as little as a fifty per cent chance of outliving the war. Their deaths were a standing reproach to those who had lived, however painfully, in the camps.

Like their fellow veterans, ex-prisoners had to rebuild their own lives. Brigadier General Victor Williams, having returned to the command of the military district covering Toronto and central Ontario, quietly found a new career as the second commissioner of the Ontario Provincial Police.[14] In 1921, when William Lyon Mackenzie King formed his first Liberal government, the former postmaster general from Beauce, Henri Béland, seemed the best choice as minister for Soldiers' Civil Re-establishment.[15] Lieutenant Edward Bellew discovered, on his release, that he had earned a Victoria Cross for his courage at Ypres. However, he also found that captivity had left him unable to pursue his engineering career. Through the 1920s, he ranched and guided in the Rockies. Allan Beddoes found a niche for himself in the precarious world of Canadian art and a more secure position as a founder of the Canadian College of Heraldry. Lieutenant Conn Smythe, captured when his aircraft crashed, boasted that his prison camp experience was a valuable preparation for his brilliant career in the business of sports. At

Schweidnitz during the last year of the war, he confessed, he had played bridge for eight to ten hours a day.[16]

It is hard to generalize about the 616,636 men and women who enlisted in the Canadian Expeditionary Force.[17] They ranged in age from the early teens to the late sixties, from wealthy professionals to unemployable drifters, from professional wrestlers and a former world heavyweight boxing champion to men whose health was so precarious they belonged in a hospital, not a tent. Survivors of years of infantry service at the front were equal claimants with men who had spent a few days in an armoury before release for poor health or misconduct. Ex-prisoners were almost as varied.

Returned soldiers who had worked as civil servants or for large companies like Eaton's or the Canadian Pacific Railway usually found their pre-war jobs waiting for them. One escaper, Edward Edwards, went back to Consumers Gas and got a raise from his pre-war fifty cents an hour to sixty cents. Albert Campbell, who had survived the cold and hunger of Norderney Island, went back to driving a bus for the Toronto Transportation Commission at $30 a week. Preferential treatment of veterans made the post office a major employer of returned men. So were police and fire departments. Others, even those with apparently secure jobs, caught the epidemic of restlessness that touched most returned men. Arthur Corker, the persistent and ultimately successful escaper, had managed a flour mill at Nanaimo before the war. Afterwards he tried farming, railroad construction, and carpentry. Robert Brown, a former checker in a carpet factory, took a chance on music as a new career. Eventually, he found work as a hospital attendant. Wartime experience in German factories, and perhaps the lasting impact of hunger and overwork, persuaded a lot of industrial and construction workers to try something else. Many tried their own businesses, only to fall victim to the postwar depression. Even established businesses foundered. Captain John Streight had earned $5,000 to 12,000 from his lumber business before the war. In 1921 he was lucky to escape with modest savings.[18] Thomas Scudamore reopened his real estate business in Vancouver only to close it down in 1921 and again in 1927, when he was forced to choose between a complete rest or a nervous breakdown.

Students who had left school to enlist often found it hard to return to classrooms four or five years later, and the government had few programs to encourage them. Robert Russell, a former clerk with the Grand Trunk Railway, used his wartime savings to complete law school and Robert Bradley abandoned schoolteaching to become a dentist. They were the exceptions.[19] Lieutenant Alvin Ferguson, who had survived serious wounds and the Soldiers and Workers' Councils' deputies at Stralsund, enrolled at the London School of Medicine, but came home to Toronto with tuberculosis and died in 1920. This was also the fate of many others, who blamed their infection on gas at Ypres or the crowded, stuffy barracks in German *Gefangenlagern.* A common complaint was the mental and nervous breakdown that contemporary psychiatry labelled "neurasthenia." A number of ex-prisoners were among the inmates of the DSCR's mental hospitals at London and Ste. Anne-de-Bellevue. Dr. Walter Haight, captured at Mont Sorrel and held until February 1918, found it even more difficult than other army doctors to establish a civilian practice. Bischofswerda, Crefeld, and Holzminden had left him with severe acne and acute indigestion, and without most of his teeth. Months of living in fear had left such a paralysis of will-power that he could no longer support his wife and two small children.[20]

AMONG THE GREAT ILLUSIONS OF THE WAR AND ITS IMMEDIATE aftermath was the expectation that the vanquished would pay its costs. In the wake of the Franco-Prussian War of 1870, the new German Empire had imposed a seemingly crippling indemnity of five billion francs on a shattered, strife-riven France. That bill was paid within a few years, persuading both the guileful and the gullible that there was no limit to the amount Germany itself could raise. German reparations could rebuild France, pay off Britain's debts to the United States, and cover the huge military pension costs that Canadian and other taxpayers would otherwise have to assume.

That was not, in fact, what the Treaty of Versailles ultimately promised or delivered, and even its demands on Germany were soon eroded by the manifest inability of the former enemy to pay. To bring an end to the continuing Allied blockade and the resulting mass starvation, German delegates had reluctantly accepted responsibility for the war, but Germany's financial obligations, though vast, were specific. Under sections 231 and 232 of the treaty, as President Woodrow Wilson had insisted, Germany's payments were to be based on the cost of damage to civilians. A reparations commission estimated the bill in April 1921 at the then-stupendous figure of $33 billion.

Since Canada's external affairs were still essentially managed by Great Britain, Canadians had little to do with the complex and bitter reparations negotiations that dragged on through the 1920s between Germany and her increasingly divided victors. Ottawa's reponsibility was limited to securing its part of the British share and distributing it according to its interpretation of the treaty. The task had begun immediately after the war when the government ordered the undersecretary of state to compile a list of claimants. With much else on its collective mind, Arthur Meighen's government waited until October 31, 1921 to do more. Since many of the claims related to merchant shipping lost through enemy action, a politically sympathetic Maritimer was a logical choice. Sir Douglas Hazen, a former cabinet colleague and now the Chief Justice of New Brunswick, was appointed a royal commissioner to investigate and report on claims arising from the treaty of peace with Germany. A few weeks later, when Meighen's government was soundly defeated, Hazen discreetly resigned. It took the new Liberal government until March to name a successor: New Brunswick's former Liberal premier, MP for Saint John, and later lieutenant governor, William Pugsley. He inherited a healthy and growing collection of claims, ranging from torpedoed schooners to luggage lost on the *Lusitania*. German air raids on England had damaged Canadian dependents or their property. While military prisoners had to demonstrate actual maltreatment, civilian internees, from Henri Béland to crewmen of the horse-boat SS *Mount Temple*, were eligible for German reparations merely by virtue of having been confined. Somewhat past the prime of life, the new commissioner held leisurely hearings at Saint John and several smaller Maritime seaports, continued to Montreal and Ottawa, and was in Toronto when he suddenly fell seriously ill and died on March 31, 1925. A successor—James Friel, a Moncton lawyer—was appointed a few months later. He inherited 280 decisions, 167 of them signed.[21]

Friel soon discovered that his predecessor had followed a kindly policy of giving claimants what they wanted with a minimum of argument. Instead, Friel attempted to establish some legal standards by borrowing from the British, the Americans, and the common law of damages. As a first step, he disposed of a long list of claimants from the Halifax Explosion: no one had ever demonstrated that the Germans had been responsible for the devastating blast. Pugsley had awarded his old cabinet colleague, Béland, $30,000 for his suffering and heart damage without demanding medical evidence. Lacking any such evidence, the British would probably have allowed him $1,500. Still, Friel was not unreasonable: two letters from prominent Montreal and Toronto heart specialists got Béland his money and an extra $5,000.[22] British precedents limited awards to less prominent civilian internees. David Scherman, a Jewish-Canadian shopkeeper imprisoned at Lille in 1916, got a solatium of $500; Hugh Young, the Copp Clark representative stranded in Nuremberg, was granted $2,200. William Flint, who had chosen the summer of 1914 to visit Leipzig where his mother and sisters were studying music, was awarded $2,000 plus $250 for the lumbago he had acquired at Ruhleben. Ernest Macmillan was granted $1,100 with the reminder, shared with other younger internees, that if he had not been interned, he might well have ended his life in the trenches.[23]

In his report, Friel dealt with only a handful of military prisoners and reached decisions on only six cases. Philip Barnden of the Fort

Garry Horse, captured during a famous cavalry charge at the Battle of Cambrai, had shared the hardships and beatings of prisoners held behind the line, and ended the war with pleurisy and tuberculosis. Friel granted him $3,000. Friel also gave $2,500 to Fred Whittaker, one of the Geisweid resisters who had spent two years in prison at Butzbach and Cologne. Alex Douglas, another Ypres prisoner who had worked for almost two years at the Geisweid blast furnace, got $6,000 for "outrageously severe treatment." George Adams, sent to a salt mine for failing to salute a German officer, must have been disappointed to receive only $2,000. The average award for the six cases was $3,400.[24] Friel's full recommendations added up to $4,246,868.75 plus five per cent interest from the official end of the war.

James Friel's first report was his last. He got into a legal dispute over his attempt to reduce some of Pugsley's more generous awards and he settled no more cases.[25] Meanwhile, however partial and inadequate German reparation payments might seem to her former enemies, they slowly mounted up. By 1927, the Canadian government was confident that it would receive $7,798,947. In 1929, when Parliament was asked to approve a partial payment of the Friel awards, Canada had $21,259,649 in its reparations account. Pressed by Harry Stevens and the Conservative member for Lunenburg, W. G. Ernst, to make immediate payment in full, Prime Minister W. L. Mackenzie King and his government gracefully agreed.[26]

SUCH PRUDENCE COULD NOT SAVE THE LIBERALS FROM A deepening Depression and their own complacency about larger matters. The Conservatives, under R. B. Bennett, won the 1930 election and soon discovered, like all new governments, that they had inherited much messy and unfinished business. While war reparations continued to bedevil international indebtedness and the solvency of some major powers, spending the money was at least a minor unsolved problem in Ottawa. Friel had left 150 claims pending and newly elected MPs promised many more. The combination of available money and increasingly desperate times added to demand, but Bennett tackled it with characteristic energy. Friel's resignation was accepted even before it was offered and on September 6, within a month of taking office, a Montreal lawyer, Errol M. McDougall, was appointed in his place.

Born in Trois-Rivières in 1881, the son and grandson of judges, educated in Scotland and Montreal, McDougall had practised law since 1906 in the respectable Conservative firm of McGibbon, Casgrain and Mitchell.[27] A no-nonsense, tough-minded lawyer with his own judicial ambitions, McDougall was determined to get the job done. He promptly notified potential claimants through the press, hurried through the existing dossiers, and discovered, on his deadline of January 15, 1931, that he had acquired 529 new cases, 340 of them from former prisoners of war. He set those aside until he had resolved the civilian claims. Soon he was off across Canada, from Yarmouth to Vancouver and even down to Boston, where schooner captains found it easier to meet him. At St. Catharines he met lawyers for Armenian Canadians, eager for a share of Turkish reparations for parents and property lost in the notorious 1915 massacres. McDougall was brisk, courteous, and, in contrast with the easy-going Pugsley, firmly judicial. Of course he did not expect the Armenians to have deeds to the missing property, but neither would he accept their unsubstantiated claims. What if the property had vanished into Russia with other relatives?[28] Interned seamen, already compensated by the British Board of Trade, had no right to ask Canada for a second payment. Nor was he sympathetic to relatives claiming damages for the loss of loved ones on the torpedoed *Lusitania*. Ida Paint, whose Vancouver dress shop had been destroyed by a rioting mob of soldiers hunting for German businesses, could take her claims elsewhere.[29] So could Mrs. Daniel Hamilton, a kindly woman who had taken an insane veteran into her home only to have him burn it down. The Treaty of Versailles had made no provision for her.[30]

By the summer of 1931, McDougall had disposed of outstanding civilian claims in three separate reports and turned to the prisoners of war. By now, it was apparent that he did not intend to emulate Pugsley's easy-going ways and Friel's generosity.[31] In Article 231, Germany had assumed responsibility "for causing all the loss and damage to which the Allied and Associated Governments and their nationals have been subjected as a consequence of the war . . . ," but what German reparations had to cover was set out only in Article 232 and, so far as military prisoners were concerned, that was limited to "damage caused by any kind of maltreatment of prisoners of war." That may have sounded all-inclusive in 1919, but it had a more specific meaning to McDougall in 1931. Armed with British precedents, McDougall insisted that damage meant demonstrable pecuniary harm. Relatives had no claim. Since imprisonment of prisoners of war was legal, maltreatment could not extend to the injuries to life and health that were among its consequences. It did not, for example, include malnutrition at a time when all of Germany was short of food: "A hardship arising from necessity and which was borne alike by the captured and the captors does not constitute 'maltreatment'." Nor did maltreatment include any reasonable punishment for malingering, escaping, or defying German authority. "To shoot and kill or maim a prisoner in the act of escaping, is not illegal and to punish him, even severely, upon recapture cannot be termed 'maltreatment'; unless the punishment, by its violence and inhumanity, transgresses the rules applied to the treatment of prisoners by civilized nations." Even a strict construction of the Hague rules would be unreasonable, given the enormous burden of prisoners Germany had acquired early in the war.

In the fall of 1931, McDougall set off across Canada and south to Chicago and Seattle on another round of hearings. By listening to all the prisoners before responding to their claims, McDougall argued, he would get a better grasp of their overall experience and find corroborative linkages.[32] Meanwhile, commission staff unearthed the repatriation statements Captain Thomas had collected in 1918–19 and discovered how some of the tales of German atrocities had grown in the intervening years. McDougall had soon concluded that "a large number of the applicants erroneously regarded this Commission as a means to obtain an initial or increased pension." As a result, Dr. J. P. Cathcart, chief neuro-psychiatrist of the Department of Pensions and National Health, accompanied McDougall on his tour of western Canada and his department tracked down medical records as a check on each applicant. Ex-prisoners who imagined that they had only to fill out a form and collect a doctor's certificate would discover that they were in a hearing where learned counsel, medical witnesses, and documentation were expected. For Errol McDougall, dispensing with the full rigour of due process and the rules of evidence was only relative. Claimants would finally discover the cost of a rushed medical and a hurried statement at Ripon or Calais twelve years before.

The ensuing years had been brutally hard on most veterans. The claim form required applicants to report their pre-war and postwar occupations and earnings. Given the span of years, the altered value of money, and the expectations of youth and middle age, it was easy to see that most were hardly better off than they had been in 1914 and many were far worse.[33] By 1930, officials had coined the term "burned-out cases" for men who had enlisted in their forties or older and whose stamina had vanished in their years of service. Scores of ex-prisoners fitted the description, most of them old soldiers who had hurried to re-enlist in 1914 and who had found themselves at Ypres. There were youngsters, too, who had imagined in their early twenties that the injuries, bronchitis, and chronic indigestion from the camps would vanish in a few months of rest, good food, and familiar surroundings. Now in their forties, they knew that bad health, like the fits of morning coughing common among ex-prisoners, would be theirs for life. The mental traumas of camp life—the fear of beatings and cold, dark cells, the hours on stools in the *Straflager* or at *stillgestanden* facing the sun—had permanently manifested themselves in chronic insomnia and nervousness. In a supposedly light-hearted article written in 1926, Scudamore suggested that

German punishment had often broken prisoners' spirits but the effect had been delayed until long after their captivity.[34] Cathcart, who met two hundred of the claimants and studied the files of three hundred more, observed how often the appearance of good health was deceptive. Compared with other veterans, ex-prisoners suffered from gastro-intestinal problems, bronchitis, recurring rashes, a reduced resistance to infection, even sterility. They were touchy, pent-up, and emotional. "The symptom which appeared most frequently was that of fatigue towards the end of the day. In a great many this fatigue was probably present at all times and explains the frequent complaints of irritability and lack of initiative and 'pep'. Annoyance with trifles, tendency to avoid company, or rather very jovial or noisy company, were often mentioned."[35]

McDougall was not profoundly sympathetic to his prisoner-claimants. Harry Howland recalled encountering a portly lawyer in a drab Vancouver hotel room, obviously impatient to get to the next case. He was furious that McDougall accepted the American claim that the Bokelah court martial had been fair and the finding of serious disobedience amply proved. The dislike was mutual. "Claimant's demeanour before this Commission was truculent and defiant and not such as to arouse sympathy but rather created the impression that he was not only capable of inciting hostility but did arouse the active enmity of his captors."[36] Howland was lucky to get $500. "Truculence" was a common experience and the commissioner was careful to draw out any evidence that prisoners who minded their manners with their captors faced little likelihood of punishment. Officers usually received a politer reception than other ranks, even when they had to be disappointed. McDougall's second most generous award, $2,000, went to Major Clyde R. Scott, the army's director of Records, who had plainly used his bureaucratic skills and the best of medical advisors to assemble a satisfactory case. Captured at Ypres as a young lieutenant, he convinced McDougall that his ankylosed knee was the result of German medical neglect.[37] Few other claims of medical neglect, cruelty, or mismanagement, including a man whose injured eyes had been removed without anaesthetic, got anything at all. William Lickers, the Mohawk prisoner at Beienrode, *was* successful in arousing the commissioner's sympathy. His physical presence made an impact few others could match and he received the commission's highest award, $3,000.[38] His presence at Beienrode helped. Armed with Justice Robert Younger's report, McDougall granted virtually every claimant who had laboured in German salt mines at least $500 in reparations. Thanks to Younger's reports, there was a similar presumption of suffering for men who had laboured behind the German lines. William Evans of the Royal Canadian Dragoons, captured during the March retreat in 1918, had been forced to work behind the lines "in conditions which are almost indescribable" and was beaten insensible with a pick handle. He was awarded $600.[39] Those of Giessen's Iron Twenty who survived to demonstrate continuing disabilities received between $800 and $1000 though, like Howland, they were reminded that they had been, at least partially, the authors of their own misfortune.[40]

Nevertheless, awards were exceptional and Friel's generosity was no precedent. Alfred Todd, whose treatment at Geisweid, Butzbach, and Cologne was virtually identical with Fred Whittaker's, had expected $2,500. Lacking better evidence of damage than his discharge medical board report that "all systems [were] normal," he got nothing. "I can only deal with the case as it has been submitted to me," wrote McDougall, "and I find that claimant has failed to discharge the burden of showing a medical disability resulting from maltreatment whilst a prisoner of war."[41] Many ex-prisoners received similar assessments.

McDougall would have insisted that sympathy was not at issue, though neither would he waste it on men who, according to his carefully mustered evidence, claimed wounds from German bayonets that were suspiciously close to scars recorded on their enlistment documents in 1915 or on ex-prisoners whose friends corroborated their sufferings in identically worded affidavits. When the former escaper Edward Edwards sought compensation for the rheumatism and frayed nerves he had inherited from Vehnenmoor and Parnewinkel, McDougall noted that he now claimed to be the victim of maltreatment that, in his book, he had attributed to Russians or fellow prisoners. "Claimant," he explained, "created a very favourable impression before the Commission and I have dealt at length with his two statements to show the unfortunate and perhaps pardonable exaggerations which creep into stories of this kind after a lapse of years." As a man approaching his sixties, Edwards might expect a little rheumatism and "nerves."[42] He was harsher with a Toronto policeman who, in 1919, had blamed a mining accident at Recklinghausen on a fallen log and who, by 1931, insisted that his injury was due to a German guard who had torn the skin from his shin with a blow from a rifle butt.[43] In one of the few cases that burst through the obscurity of the commission's proceedings, a former flyer claimed that Baron Manfred von Richthofen had joined others in torturing him for information, with the result that his injured arm had turned gangrenous. Before the reputation of the famous Red Baron was utterly lost, the German consul general hurriedly brought convincing evidence that no member of the Richthofen family had been anywhere in the vicinity.[44]

One price of reserving judgement until he heard all the cases was that McDougall received hundreds of additional claims during 1931 and 1932. Having rushed 340 cases to completion by the end of 1931, McDougall was confronted by almost five hundred more that had turned up after the deadline. Predictably, the government insisted that he deal with them. The continuing Depression was almost certainly a factor: unemployment and relief were far more common among the later claimants than they had been among those who filed in 1930. In a rare collective effort, seventy-six unemployed Toronto ex-prisoners, "in dire financial straights [*sic*]," petitioned the prime minister for quick action. Penniless, unemployed, and "burned out," William Sharpe pleaded for payment so he could put a down payment on a poultry farm and feed his family.[45] By 1932, it was also apparent that Germany would be paying no more reparations and any payments in excess of the money Canada had already received would be paid by the taxpayer. McDougall noted, with evident approval, one ex-prisoner who had withdrawn his claim rather than be a burden on the Canadian treasury.[46]

In the end, Sharpe and most other ex-prisoner claimants were disappointed. Of 862 claims for maltreatment, McDougall made awards in only 201 cases, most of them for $500 with, as usual, five per cent interest from January 10, 1920.[47] Major C. G. Power, the Liberal critic on veterans affairs, briefly contrasted the treatment of baggage on the *Lusitania* with the meagre awards to former prisoners. *The Legionary*, official organ of the country's largest veterans' organization, remained consistent in its policy on the reparations issue by making no comment at all. Determined to switch its sights away from unhappy minorities to the vast problem of unemployment afflicting most of its members, the Canadian Legion was not to be distracted by men who, on the whole, played little role in its ranks. McDougall, meanwhile, earned the reward of judiciousness: a judicial appointment.

With no one to lead or organize them, ex-prisoners of war fared as well as they could through the hard Depression years. When war with Germany came again in 1939, some of them could enjoy the ironies of history as middle-aged members of the Veterans Guard of Canada, guarding German prisoners of war at Antler, Gravenhurst, and Bowmanville. Captain John Streight, the one-time escaper, served as a commander of prisoner-of-war camps in Canada. Inmates found the experience of captivity in Canada sufficiently bearable, however, that numbers of them returned after the war—a migration no known Canadian "fannigan" made after 1918.

By then, the Hague Convention had become the Geneva Convention of 1928. Thanks to bitter experience, under the convention prisoners could no longer be compelled to labour. The conditions of imprisonment that the British and German delegates had debated at

The Hague in 1918 became part of the new convention. Sadly, at least two major countries, Japan and the Soviet Union, were not among the ratifiers.

Anyone considering the experience of Canadian prisoners in Germany in the First World War will be tempted to give them a more cosmic role as the advance guard of the slave labour armies of the Third Reich. Were Giessen, Soltau, and Gardelegen the forebears of Dachau and Bergen-Belsen? Were Simmons and Edwards premature members of the army of "Peatbog Soldiers" whose song would be one of the anthems of Hitler's victims?

There are seldom categorical answers to such questions.[48] The war years gave German employers experience in using large armies of prisoners in unskilled and sometimes dangerous labour. German workers showed that it was possible to keep their distance from the ragged, poorly fed *Ausländer* (foreigners) and, on occasion, to assist in teaching them proper discipline and respect. The treatment of prisoners behind the line, however understandable and driven by hunger and imminent defeat, was a deplorable chapter in German military history. It is also sometimes argued that work camps were the brainchild of penal reformers, eager to liberate convicts from the prison dungeons where some Canadians also spent part of their German captivity. What is durably true is that the degradation of half-starved, brutalized prisoners came too easily. The German military system during the war years tolerated physical violence and humiliation as disciplinary techniques, and yet many armies, including Canada's, have been admirers of what German military discipline accomplished.

Applying the future to the past is the sin of anachronism, but all futures grow out of the past. The hideous crimes of Naziism would have been impossible without the kind of people who ran and guarded wartime prison camps, but any country and any culture can produce their sadistic counterparts, and people in most societies can find good reasons to look the other way. In his own judicial way, perhaps that was Errol McDougall's message.

As we look back across seventy-five years of mass murder, torture, and industrialized savagery, contemporary claims about "martyred prisoners" brutalized and starved by barbaric Huns tend to fade into the degraded status of war propaganda. Yet in allowing prisoners of war to be compelled to work without enforceable constraints, the Hague Convention was flawed. The improved protection of prisoners in the Geneva Convention became the prisoners' sole memorial. Canadian prisoners in Hitler's war were among the beneficiaries. Otherwise, the prisoners of 1915–18 were forgotten; their experiences had no place in an official record that preferred to ignore why so many raw, poorly led soldiers had surrendered at Ypres and Mont Sorrel. The prisoners' own bitter memories were eclipsed by the desire to forget and a postwar belief that any talk of German brutality was a resurrection of wartime lies. Besides, some Canadian consciences might also have been troubled.

Appendix A

Canadian Prisoners of War

In the summer of 1917, as the Overseas Ministry gradually expanded its administrative responsibility for Canadians, the Canadian War Records Office in London began keeping track of Canadian prisoners of war. Until then, statistical records were maintained by the War Office and no systematic totals were maintained for the "imperial" contingents.

Beginning in the summer of 1918, separate records were kept for Canadian officers in captivity and the CWRO statistics referred only to other ranks. Whatever the administrative reason for the change, the new system helped conceal the fact that most of the officers and senior non-commissioned officers captured in 1915 and 1916 had been interned in Switzerland and the Netherlands and a disproportionate number of those who remained in actual prison camps were rank and file. Such a revelation might have demanded an explanation.

TABLE A1 **Location of Canadian Prisoners of War**

	31 October 1917 officers – other ranks	31 January 1918 officers – other ranks	31 October 1918 other ranks only
In Germany	113–2510	107–2484	2248
In Turkey	1	—	—
In Bulgaria	1	—	—
Interned			
In Switzerland	6–60	17–138	102
In Holland	—	—	312
Escaped	1–37	1–48	81
Repatriated to England	5–120	8–155	307
Died as Prisoner	22–197	24–218	246
Total	149–2924	157–3043	3296

TABLE A2 **Canadian Prisoner of War Statistics, August 1917 to November 1918.** (Other ranks only)

	New POWS	Died	Escaped	Interned		Repatriated		
				Holland	Switzerland	Germany	Holland	Switzerland
1917								
August	17	9	3	—	—	—	—	—
September	63	4	—	—	—	—	—	59
October	109	14	12	—	—	—	—	—
November	4	6	5	—	4	—	—	—
December	61	9	2	—	70	6	—	—
1918								
January	68	2	2	—	—	—	1	1
February	3	4	1	—	—	8	—	—
March	11	3	8	143	30	1	—	—
April	13	—	5	32	—	10	—	1
May	32	1	4	112	3	9	—	—
June	24	—	1	22	—	3	—	30
July	3	3	4	11	—	2	—	—
August	10	3	1	4	—	8	3	—
September	56	4	6	—	25	1	18	—
October	82	5	4	11	—	1	26	—
November	179	9	12	3	4	161	238	—
Total	735	76	70	338	136	210	286	91

Table A3 Canadian Prisoners of War by Unit and Formation

	Prisoners in August 1917	August - December 1917	January - July 1918	August- November 1918**
1st Canadian Division				
1st Battalion	1	1	7	2
2nd Battalion	2–110	9	1	19
3rd Battalion	5–239	4	—	79
4th Battalion	1–7	1	1	4
5th Battalion	19	4	12	5
7th Battalion	7–218	1	1	46
8th Battalion	4–181	5	2	10
10th Battalion	2–26	—	1	2
13th Battalion	5–188	—	17	30
14th Battalion	75	3	21	13
15th Battalion	11–199	7	—	84
16th Battalion	152	1	32	8
2nd Canadian Division				
18th Battalion	4	9	1	2
19th Battalion	2–18	7	1	6
20th Battalion	4	17	—	1
21st Battalion	—	4	2	1
22nd Battalion	5	1	6	3
24th Battalion	10	1	—	1
25th Battalion	16	1	—	1
26th Battalion	8	3	12	—
27th Battalion	2	—	—	2
28th Battalion	2–87	—	1	7
29th Battalion	1–57	6	1	16
31th Battalion	25	11	1	4
3rd Canadian Division				
Princess Patricia's	1–44	1	11	15
Royal Cdn. Regt.	1–67	—	6	6
1st Cdn. Mtd. Rifles	8–134	1	9	13
2nd Cdn. Mtd. Rifles	4	2	—	2
4th Cdn. Mtd. Rifles	9–310	4	—	75

	Prisoners in August 1917	August - December 1917	January - July 1918	August- November 1918**
5th Cdn. Mtd. Rifles	3–16	2	16	1
42nd Battalion	2	5	—	1
43rd Battalion	27	1	9	4
49th Battalion	1–16	1	—	2
52nd Battalion	8	3	2	—
58th Battalion	9	1	5	1
60th Battalion	—	2	—	—
116th Battalion	—	—	34	2
4th Canadian Division				
38th Battalion	1	—	17	3
44th Battalion	1–8	1–105	—	6
46th Battalion	1–3	9	—	2
47th Battalion	4	2	2	1
50th Battalion	18	2	4	3
54th Battalion	5	4	3	—
72nd Battalion	1–10	1–2	5	1
75th Battalion	1–41	17	3	13
78th Battalion	7	1	32	2
85th Battalion	1	—	—	—
87th Battalion	6	1–15	2	4
102nd Battalion	5	2	5	1
Canadian Cavalry Brigade				
Royal Cdn. Dragoons	—	27	—	6
Lord Strathcona's Horse	1	4	9	3
Fort Garry Horse	2	47	3	—
Yukon Machine Gun Brigade	—	3	—	—
Other Units				
Canadian Light Horse	3	—	—	—
Royal Canadian Horse Artillery	—	1	—	—
Canadian Field Artillery	29	—	—	5
2nd Tunnelling Company	4–59	—	—	12

	Prisoners in August 1917	August - December 1917	January - July 1918	August- November 1918**
Canadian Army Medical Corps	2	—	—	1
Canadian Pioneers	7	—	—	—
Cdn. Machine-Gun Corps	1	1	3	—
Canadian Railway Troops	—	—	9	—
Royal Flying Corps/ Royal Air Force	17	12	—	15

Note: officer – other ranks

* The figures do not include prisoners who escaped, died, or had been interned or repatriated.

** These figures do not include officers taken prisoner.

Appendix B

Analysis of Reparations Claimants

Who were Canada's prisoners in the First World War? The National Personnel Record Centre is reluctant to provide information because of both the Privacy Act and the extensive work involved. One largely unused public source is the data provided by the McDougall commission. In reporting only those cases which proceeded to adjudication (setting aside cases which were incomplete, withdrawn, or over which the commissioner did not accept jurisdiction), McDougall usually revealed details of each claimant's age at enlistment, pre-war and current employment, pension classification, and marital and family status. Lapses occur at the outset of his reporting, when he tended to give less information about office claimants. Many applicants were ex-British soldiers.

Of the 862 prisoner-of-war claimants, 645 usable cases were selected from claimants captured while serving with units of the Canadian Expeditionary Force, and their applications had included information about age, service, family circumstances, and employment. Of these, 286 were wounded at the point of capture, 107 claimed to have made one or more attempts to escape, and 26 of them had succeeded. Thirty-six prisoners among the claimant group had been compelled to work in salt mines and seven had been part of the reprisal party sent to Libau in 1916–17. Although ages at enlistment ranged from 13 to 58, the average was 24.6 years, consistent with other recorded CEF data.[1] About 44 per cent of claimants had received disability pensions.

To analyse pre-war and postwar occupations, 318 of the 340 cases dealt with in McDougall's first report on maltreatment of prisoners of war were examined. Those set aside included British claimants who had emigrated to Canada after the war and those whose claims were withdrawn. These claimants had submitted their applications before January 15, 1931. While subsequent claimants have been considered in a more general profile of Canadian prisoners of war, their employment information tends to show how the Depression affected the economic position veterans had achieved in the 1920s, as reflected in the earlier group.

For comparison with the larger group of claimants, 124 of the original claimants had been wounded at the time of capture, 57 reported escape attempts (14 were successful), 36 had worked in salt mines, and 5 had been in the Libau reprisal.

The prisoners of war were not a fair cross-section of the CEF, as revealed in surveys of enlistment records conducted by Colonel A. F. Duguid's staff between the wars. After all, three of the units contributing the largest numbers of prisoners, the 3rd and 15th Battalions and the 4th Canadian Mounted Rifles, were recruited largely from the Toronto area; the 13th Battalion came from Montreal, the 8th from Winnipeg, and the 7th, predominantly, from Vancouver.

1. In some cases, McDougall recorded admitted discrepancies with the attestation form, but the age stated on the claim form has been used.

Table B1 **Canadian Prisoner of War Claimants for Maltreatment**

Place and Date of Capture	
Ypres, April 1915	293
St. Eloi, April 1916	9
Mont Sorrel/Hooge, June 1916	141
Somme, September–November 1916	32
Vimy Ridge, April 1917	19
Fresnoy, May 1917	10
Lens, August–September 1917	19
Passchendaele, October–November 1917	11
Cambrai, November 1917	7
1918 Retreats	9
Amiens, August 1918	5
Miscellaneous (raids, etc.)	11
Air crashes 1916	2
1917	4
1918	11

Table B2 **Canadian Prisoner of War Claimants for Maltreatment by Rank at Capture**

Officers	27
Senior NCOs	30
Corporals	40
Other ranks	484
Total	581

Table B3 Canadian Prisoner of War Claimants for Maltreatment by Age of Enlistment

Under 20 (minimum 13)	105
20-29	352
30-39	103
Over 40 (maximum 60)	17
Not provided	4
Total	581

Table B4 Canadian Prisoner of War Claimants for Maltreatment by Marital and Family Status

Married pre-war	82
Married postwar	374
Unmarried as of 1931	117
Not provided	8
Total	581*
Family size (children)	
none	68
one	113
two	136
three	80
four or more	60
Total	457

* includes widowers, one divorced.

TABLE B5 **Canadian Prisoner of War Claimants Receiving Disability Pensions**

Pension Classification	100%	60–95%	20–55%	5–15%	Total
Number	28	27	115	121	291
Percentage of total	9.6	9.3	39.5	41.6	100

(For comparison with all disability pensions, see Morton and Wright, *Winning the Second Battle*, p. 237. Pensions were granted in five per cent gradients.)

TABLE B6 **Pre-war and Postwar Employment of Pre-Deadline Prisoner of War Claimants for Maltreatment**

Category	Pre-war	Postwar
Professional	8	13
Commerce	6	8
Sales	13	23
Clerical	54	54
Service	32	58
Transportation	25	21
Industrial	74	46
Mining/Forestry	21	9
Farming	15	14
Construction	34	13
Students	11	–
Apprenticeship	13	–
Unemployed	1	23
Semi-employed	–	25
Unknown	2	2
Total	309	309

REFERENCES: Errol M. McDougall, *Reparations, 1930–1931: Report on Maltreatment of Prisoners of War* (Ottawa: King's Printer, 1932); *Further Report* (Ottawa: King's Printer, 1933), and *Final Report* (Ottawa: King's Printer, 1933).

Notes

Introduction

1. On numbers of Canadian prisoners, see *Report of the Overseas Military Forces of Canada* (London: n.p., 1919), p. 58, table II, p. 468. See also National Archives of Canada, Record Group 9 III, v. 1123, P-48-4. More accurate figures were compiled by the Historical Section, Canadian General Staff, between the wars and were made available to me by Professor R. C. Brown. On prisoners in German hands, see C. R. M. F. Cruttwell, *A History of the Great War, 1914–1918* (Oxford: Clarendon Press, 1936), pp. 630–31; N. N. Golovine, *The Russian Army in World War I* (New York: Archon, 1964), pp. 74, 81–92. A bibliography of prisoners' reminiscences can be found in W. D. B. Kerr, "Historical Literature on Canada's Participation in the Great War," *Canadian Historical Review*, 14 (December 1933): 414–15, 429, 432–33; 15 (June 1934): 183–84; 16 (June 1935): 365. An anthology of prisoners' memories can be found in William D. Mathieson, *My Grandfather's War: Canadians Remember the First World War, 1914–1918* (Toronto: Macmillan, 1981), chap. 11.

2. Revealingly, the work of the reparations commission was virtually ignored in the issues of *The Legionary*, official organ of the Canadian Legion, during the months of McDougall's hearings although matters affecting veterans' welfare and legislation were staples in several regular columns. (Author's review of issues from 1930 to 1933.)

3. The word does not appear in Nicholson's index: G. W. L. Nicholson, *Canadian Expeditionary Force, 1914–1919: The Official History of the*

Canadian Army in the First World War (Ottawa: Queen's Printer, 1962). Duguid had prepared notes which might well have appeared in the never-published second volume of his proposed series.

4. Mary M. Moore, *The Maple Leaf's Red Cross: The War Story of the Canadian Red Cross Overseas* (Lon-don: Skeffington & Son Ltd., 1919), p. 107.

5. Errol M. McDougall, *Report of the Commission on Reparations, 1930–1931: Report on Maltreatment of Prisoners of War* (Ottawa: King's Printer, 1932), p. 77. Herbert Franks' own troubles after forty-two months of twelve-hour days in German stone quarries included general debility, gastritis, acute nervousness, and a nose so badly smashed by a German guard that it affected his speech.

6. Michael Moynihan, *Black Bread and Barbed Wire: Prisoners in the First World War* (London: Leo Cooper, 1978), p. x.

7. Modern German scholarship, understandably, has found other subjects for historical research. One useful exception, though of an Austrian camp that held Italians and then Russians, is Rudolf Koch's *Das Kriegsgefangenerlager Sigmundsherberge, 1915–1919* (Dissertationen des Universität Wien, 1981) no. 181. The German Federal Archives at Stuttgart and the Bundeswehr's Historical Archives at Freiberg confirmed that almost all publications on the subject dated from the war or its immediate aftermath. However, reflecting the common German practice, they did not commonly distinguish between British prisoners and the imperial contingents.

8. Daniel J. McCarthy, *The Prisoner of War in Germany: The Care and Treatment of the Prisoner of War with a History of the Development of the Practice of Neutral Inspectorate* (New York: Moffat, Yard, 1918).

1 Prisoners and Covenants

1. *Daily Express*, 4 Jan. 1919.

2. Frank Maheux to Angeline Maheux, 19 May 1915, Maheux Papers, NAC, Manuscript Group 30 E 297.

3. Harold R. Peat, *Private Peat* (Indianapolis: Bobbs-Merrill, 1917), p. 154.

4. Thomas William Gosford Recollections, p. 145, NAC, MG 30 E 475. (Gosford was ninety-five when he recorded his reminiscences.)

5. Maria Tippett, *Art in the Service of War: Canada, Art and the Great War* (Toronto: University of Toronto Press, 1984), p. 65.

6. Freiherr Langwerth v. Simmern, Wireless Press, serial 8194, 10 Feb. 1919, Kemp Papers, vol. 133, NAC.

7. Ibid., vol. 167, Statement "In the Matter of Canada's 'Golgotha',"

1 April 1919, by Bandsman Leonard Vivian, 3rd Bn., Middlesex Regiment, and Cpl. William H. Metcalfe V.C., 16th Battalion.

8. As Sir Robert Borden explained to Kemp after meeting Currie in Paris: "He could never obtain the slightest evidence to lead him to believe that such an incident had occurred and he did not believe that it ever did occur." Borden to Kemp, 17 Feb. 1919, p. 55804, NAC, MG 26 G I, OC 414. A typical story, reported by an American civilian who had shared a lengthy train journey with a Canadian soldier, insisted that the victim, discovered by Sgt. G. Lyons and forty-two others, was a Sgt. Brant of the 16th Battalion. Only the soldier, Lyons, and one other had allegedly survived the war. Currie personally interviewed Lyons, a former business associate in Vancouver, and discovered the story was groundless.

9. H. W. Brown, acting Deputy Minister of National Defence, to the Director, National Gallery of Canada, 13 May 1930, NAC, RG 24, vol. 817, HQ 54-21-8-48. On the sculture and history, see Tippett, *Art in the Service of War*, pp. 81–87.

10. Ibid., p. 111 citing Werner Schaefer, *Englische Lügen in Weltkrieg* (Berlin, 1941), pp. 34–39.

11. Bruce Trigger, *Children of the Aatensic: A History of the Huron People to 1660* (Montreal: McGill-Queen's University Press, 1976).

12. His captor, Edward III, had to settle for a tenth of the amount before John went free. See D. M. Broome, "The Ransom of John I, King of France, 1360–1370," *Camden Miscellany*, xiv (1926).

13. Hugo Grotius, *The Rights of War and Peace, Including the Law of Nature and of Nations*, trans. A. C. Campbell (London: W. Walter Dunne, 1901), p. 346.

14. Ibid., p. 358.

15. Richard Speed, *Prisoners, Diplomats and the Great War: A Study in the Diplomacy of Captivity* (New York: Greenwood, [1990]), p. 5 and *passim.*

16. Charles I. Bevans, ed., *Treaties and Other International Agreements of the United States of America, 1776–1949* (Washington: United States Government Printing Office, 1971), vol. I, pp. 7–11.

17. Ivan S. Bloch, *The Future of War in its Technical, Economic and Political Relations* (Boston: Gima, 1902).

18. James Brown Scott, *Documents Relations to the Program of the First Hague Peace Conference . . .* (Oxford: Humphrey Milord, 1921), p. 1.

19. The Hague Convention, Chapter II, Article 4 in James Brown Scott, ed., *The Hague Conventions and Declarations of 1899 and 1907 Accompanied by Tables of Signatures, Ratifications and Adhesions of the Various Powers and Texts of Reservations*, 3rd ed. (New York: Oxford University Press, 1918), p. 104.

20. Ibid., Article 7.
21. Ibid., Article 8.
22. Ibid.
23. Ibid., Article 6.
24. The 1907 amendment to Article 6 seems a difference without much distinction; however, it may be worth citing because of the later significance of the issue: "The tasks shall not be excessive and shall have no connection with the operations of the war." Scott, *Hague Conventions*, p. 109.
25. Ibid., Article 17.
26. Ibid.
27. Ibid., Article 15.
28. Ibid., p. 112–13. (The 1899 convention had required only a "bureau for information relative to prisoners of war.")
29. André Durand, *From Sarajevo to Hiroshima: History of the International Red Cross* (Geneva: Henri Dunant Institute, 1978), pp. 21–36.
30. Coleman Phillipson, *International Law and the Great War* (London: T. Fisher Unwin, 1916), p. 252.
31. On the mood in Canada at the outset of the war, see Barbara Wilson, *Ontario and the First World War, 1914–1918: A Collection of Documents* (Toronto: University of Toronto Press, 1977), pp. xvii–xix, 3; Desmond Morton and J. L. Granatstein, *Marching to Armageddon: Canadians and the Great War, 1914–1919* (Toronto: Lester & Orpen Dennys, 1989), pp. 8–9; Mason Wade, *The French Canadians, 1769–1967* (Toronto: Macmillan, 1968), pp. 642–45. See also Ramsay Cook, *The Politics of John W. Dafoe and the Free Press* (Toronto: University of Toronto Press, 1963), pp. 66–67.
32. PC 2721, 28 Oct. 1914; W. D. Otter, *Internment Operations: Report, 1914–1919* (Ottawa: King's Printer, 1921), pp. 3–4; Desmond Morton, *The Canadian General: Sir William Otter* (Toronto: Hakkert, 1974), pp. 324–32.
33. McCarthy, *Prisoner of War*, p. 271.
34. Ibid., pp. 12–21.
35. On early grievances, see Phillipson, *International Law*, p. 254 and notes.
36. On conditions at Wittenberg, see Robert Jackson, *The Prisoners, 1914–18* (London and New York: Croom Helm, 1989), pp. 1–3; J. W. Garner, *International Law and the World War* (London: Longmans Green, 1920), vol. II, pp. 18–20; J. W. Gerard, *My Four Years in Germany* (New York, 1917), p. 172–74; McCarthy, *Prisoner of War*, pp. 105 ff; *London Times Weekly*, 14 April 1916, NAC, RG 24, vol. 6993, ch. XIII, p. 12.
37. Speed, *Prisoners, Diplomats and the Great War*, pp. 66–67; *Report on the Typhus Epidemic at Gardelagen by the Government Committee on the Treatment by the Enemy of British Prisoners of War during the Spring and Summer of 1915* (London: His

Majesty's Stationery Office, 1916), Cd. 8351, pp. 1–7. A Canadian in the British army, Private Robert McKie, was one of the typhus victims. See Errol M. McDougall, "Royal Commission for the Investigation of Illegal Warfare Claims and for the Return of Sequestered Property in Necessitous Cases," *Further Report* (Ottawa: King's Printer, 1933), p. 113.

38. Gerard, *Four Years*, p. 160. See also Speed, *Prisoners, Diplomats and the Great War*, pp. 21–24, and on the inspection system in Germany, pp. 26–30 and Gerard, *Four Years*, p. 161 ff.

39. Speed, *Prisoners, Diplomats and the Great War*, p. 25.

40. Gerard, *Four Years*, p. 164.

41. On inspection, see Gerard, *Four Years*, p. 169; Charles Hennebois, *In German Hands: The Diary of a Severely Wounded Prisoner* (London: Heinemann, 1916), p. 232.

II CAPTURED

1. He was the kind of person internment was designed for since he joined the Royal Naval Air Service for a successful wartime career until he crashed and died in 1917. S. F. Wise, *Canadian Airmen and the First World War: The Official History of the Royal Canadian Air Force*, vol. I (Toronto: University of Toronto Press, 1980), pp. 171, 176; Ken Bell and Desmond Morton, *Royal Canadian Military Institute, 100 Years, 1890–1990* (Toronto: RCMI, 1990), p. 43.

2. *Toronto Globe*, 14 Aug. 1918.

3. Ibid., 15 Feb. 1919. See also J. D. Ketchum, *Ruhleben: A Prison Camp Society* (Toronto: University of Toronto Press, 1965). Ketchum, twenty-one when arrested, confessed that he initially considered Britain's involvement in the war "a terrible mistake" and continued his studies. However, a desire to undergo "a war experience" persuaded him to leave his passport at home. He was arrested, jailed, and transferred to Ruhleben on Sept. 9, 1914, to remain there until Nov. 24, 1918.

4. Cases taken from James Friel's *Report of the Royal Commission . . . to investigate and report upon all claims which may be submitted to the Commission for the purpose of determining whether they are within the First Annex to Section 1 of Part VIII of the Treaty of Versailles . . . 14 December 1927* (Ottawa: King's Printer, 1928), vol. II, pp. 511–41 *passim*.

5. Israel Cohen, *The Ruhleben Prison Camp: A Record of Nineteen Months' Internment* (London: Methuen, 1917), pp. 40–50. "Pro-Germans" were also segregated when relations with other prisoners grew unpleasant. Cohen believed that treatment of the group was, if anything, less favourable because guards resented men who might be patriotic but who used their citizenship to escape German military service (pp. 102–09).

6. Robert Jackson, *The Prisoners, 1914–18* (London: Routledge, 1989), p. 55. Jackson deplores the emphasis on hardships at Ruhleben.

7. Cohen, *Ruhleben Prison Camp*, p. 42 ff. See also Garner, *International Law*, vol. II, pp. 16–17.

8. Desmond Morton, "Sir William Otter and Internment Operations in Canada During the First World War," *Canadian Historical Review*, 15 (March 1974): pp. 32–58.

9. C. H. Mellor report, pp. 29219-20, Borden Papers, NAC, OC 261.

10. The fellow prisoner was Eric A. Keith, whose memoir, *My Escape from Germany*, recalled Béland as "a man of great personal charm" (p. 125). The Stadtvogtei was a criminal prison largely taken over by the army as a detention barracks.

11. Wilfrid Laurier to Borden, 29 August 1917, Borden Papers, NAC, p. 29147 *et passim*. Henri Béland, *My Three Years in a German Prison* (Toronto: Briggs, 1919), is a book without rancour.

12. On air crew prisoners, see Wise, *Canadian Airmen in the First World War*, pp. 647–48.

13. On the suspected deserter, see NAC, RG 24, vol. 6992; also John Cooke in McDougall, *Further Report*, p. 56.

14. On the battle, see Nicholson, *C.E.F.*, pp. 295–96; E. S. Russenholt, ed., *Six Thousand Canadian Men: Being the History of the 44th Battalion, Canadian Infantry, 1914–1919* (Winnipeg: De Montfort Press, 1932), pp. 109–12.

15. Nicholson, *C.E.F.*, pp. 336–37; 369–72. On Canadian losses in the last sixteen months of the war, see Appendix A, Table 2.

16. The first time was on July 1, 1916 when the unit had been nearly annihilated on the first day of the Battle of the Somme. On Newfoundland prisoners, see G. W. L. Nicholson, *The Fighting Newfoundlanders: A History of the Royal Newfoundland Regiment* (London: Thos. Nelson, 1964), p. 391; William Quinton, *Twenty Months in Germany* (St. John's: n.p., n.d.).

17. Canada's minister of Militia, Colonel Sam Hughes, had scrapped the pre-war mobilization plan and summoned the entire Canadian militia to send contingents to the new camp at Valcartier, near Quebec City. Close to 33,000 men had come and the minister had reorganized contingents ranging from a few dozen to a thousand men into seventeen ad hoc infantry battalions. Some militia units, notably Montreal's 5th Royal Highlanders, Toronto's 48th Highlanders, and Winnipeg's 90th Rifles were strong enough to impose their own identity on their new unit.

18. On the fate of the 15th Battalion, see Daniel Dancocks, *Welcome to Flanders Fields: The First Canadian Battle of the Great War: Ypres, 1915* (Toronto: McClelland & Stewart, 1988), pp. 162–64. (The commanding officer of the 15th, Lieutenant Colonel John A. Currie, a fifty-eight-year-old militia veteran and MP for Simcoe North, spent some of the day trying to collect his scattered unit but the 15th had ceased to exist before he left the battle, undoubtedly a victim of what the war had already defined as "shell shock." He was found in Boulogne a few days later. To avoid scandal, he was promoted and returned to Canada. NAC, MG 30 E 8, notes by Col. A. F. Duguid; see also Dancocks, ibid., p. 177.)

19. John C. Thorn, *Three Years a Prisoner in Germany: The Story of Major J. C. Thorn, A First Canadian Contingent Officer who was Captured by the Germans at Ypres on April 24th, 1915, Relating His Many Attempts to Escape (Once Described as a Widow)* . . . (Vancouver: Cowan & Brockhouse, 1919), pp. 3 ff. Dancocks, *Flanders Fields*, pp. 176–79.

20. On the battle, see Nicholson, *C.E.F.*, pp. 66–83; Duguid, *History of the Canadian Forces*, pp. 285–367; Dancocks, *Flanders Fields*, pp. 159–226.

21. The 3rd "Torontos" had been formed from some of the militia's oldest units: the Governor General's Horse Guards, the 2nd Queen's Own Rifles, and the 10th Royal Grenadiers.

22. In Dancocks' *Flanders Fields*, published in 1988, he is still presumed dead (p. 216). We will meet him later.

23. Postwar casualty returns for the Second Battle of Ypres were compiled by Colonel A. F. Duguid's staff. See NAC, RG 24, vol. 1874, file 211. The official history discreetly avoids references to casualty totals as does a recent popular history of the battle. See Nicholson, *C.E.F.*, p. 92; Dancocks, *Flanders Fields*, pp. 226–28.

24. Nicholson, *C.E.F.*, p. 149.

25. For an account of a wounded officer of the 4th CMR, see J. Harvey Douglas, *Captured: Sixteen Months as a Prisoner of War* (Toronto: McClelland, Goodchild & Stewart, 1918), p. 28–41. Douglas was captured with his friend Lieutenant N. L. Wells, of whom see below. See also Captain Alan Crosman Papers, NAC, MG 30 E 36, for a description of the 4th CMR's neighbour, the 1st CMR. Unfortunately, Crosman's narrative, prepared to justify his surrender, ends with the start of his captivity.

26. Ussher's account of the circumstances of his capture is in NAC, MG 30 E 376.

27. Prisoner totals for the battle at Mont Sorrel have been ascertained from prisoner lists at the end of 1916 in Argyll House file P-249-33, NAC,

RG 9 III, vol. 2921. These exclude those who had died or escaped by then. On Wilken, see "A Short Record of Twenty-One Months Captivity in German Prison Camps," NAC, MG 30 E 33; Ypres League to Director of History, 23 Feb. 1926, and reply, 10 March 1926, RG 24, vol. 1494, HQ 683-1-12 (vol. 6). Another Mont Sorrel prisoner was Lieutenant Harvey Douglas. See *Captured.*

28. In their training, Canadians were not encouraged to accept German surrenders. "We are not anxious to add the extra burden to the country of keeping prisoners," one man wrote to his sister (Curtis Papers, 18 June 1915, NAC, MG 30 E 505). Lieut. C. V. Williams, newly arrived at Le Havre, reported to his clergyman-father, "You will very seldom now hear of the Canadians taking prisoners, they take them to some quiet spot and then it is a case of the dead may march." (Williams' letters in author's possession.) See above for the durable trench myth of the "crucified Canadian." In the official history, there is a suggestion that Canadian soldiers took fewer prisoners than they might have at their final battle of the war, Valenciennes. (Nicholson, *C.E.F.* pp. 474–75.)

29. See "March With Me," an unpublished manuscript in NAC, MG 30 E 204, p. 95.

30. George Pearson, *The Escape of a Princess Pat: Being the full account of the capture and fifteen months' imprisonment of Corporal Edwards of the Princess Patricia's Canadian Light Infantry and his final Escape from Germany into Holland* (New York: George Doran, 1918), pp. 46–49.

31. McDougall, *Maltreatment,* pp. 138, 276.

32. Major G. Wilken, "A Short Record," NAC, MG 30 E 33, pp. 4–5.

33. Since Meakin emerged from the war (and perhaps entered it) mentally unbalanced, his story may be doubted, as it was by the reparations commissioner. See McDougall, *Maltreatment,* p. 293.

34. McDougall, *Final Report,* p. 159.

35. Interrogation report, Pte. F. J. Hamilton, 26th Battalion, Canadian War Records Office (CWRO) file, NAC, RG 9 III, vol. 4737, folder 152, file 1.

36. Dancocks, *Flanders Fields,* p. 178. T. M. Scudamore, *Lighter Episodes in the Life of a Prisoner of War* (Aldershot: Gale & Polden, 1933), p. 9.

37. Private G. Scott, "Three Years and Eight Months in a German Prison," NAC, MG 30 E 280, p. 3. (Cited in Matheson, *Grandfather's War,* p. 228.)

38. Major T. M. Scudamore, "Lighter Episodes in the Life of a Prisoner of War," *Canadian Defence Quarterly,* vol. VII, no. 3 (April 1930), pp. 395–96.

39. Pte. M. C. Simmons as told to Nellie L. McClung, *Three Times and*

Out as told by Private Simmons (Toronto: Thos. Allen, 1918), pp. 9–10.

40. "March With Me," NAC, MG 30 E 204, p. 94.

41. McDougall, *Maltreatment*, pp. 86, 132. (McDougall noted that Walker had never mentioned his experience at repatriation in 1918.)

42. Peter Anderson, *I, That's Me: Escape from German Prison Camp and Other Adventures* (Ottawa: Bradburn Printers, n.d.), pp. 81–83.

43. Arthur Gibbons, *A Guest of the Kaiser: The Plain Story of a Lucky Soldier* (Toronto: J. M. Dent, 1919), pp. 117 ff. (Like other wartime accounts of prisoners, Gibbons' bitter memories may have been affected by his later role as a recruiting sergeant and an official in the Canadian Legion. The reparations commissioner clearly had strong reservations about his credibility. See McDougall, *Maltreatment*, pp. 90–91.

44. Cited in Gordon Reid, ed., *Poor Bloody Murder: Personal Memoirs of the First World War* (Oakville: Mosaic Press, 1980), p. 83; also in Mathieson, *Grandfather's War*, p. 226.

45. Pearson, *Princess Pat*, p. 58.

46. Captain Lyman Gooderham to parents, 6 June 1916, NAC, RG 9 III, vol. 1120, CWRO file P-48-4.

47. A British officer, who later had the experience of being a prisoner of war, recalled "it was great fun watching the Canadoos with the prisoners. They went through their pockets and relieved them of everything souvenirable." (Imperial War Museum, memoirs of Lt. Col. N. E. Tyndale-Siscoe, RFA.) For others see ibid., A. M. Munro Papers, letter to his father, 14 June 1917; NAC, Frank Baxter Papers, 6 July 1918.

48. Pearson, *Princess Pat*, p. 58. On evacuation from the Mont Sorrel area, see Corporal Fred McMullen and Private Jack Evans, *Out of the Jaws of Hunland* (Toronto: Briggs, 1918), pp. 31–33.

49. McDougall, *Maltreatment*, p. 291. Perhaps he was the man O'Brien claimed to have seen shot in his own captivity account. See O'Brien Papers, NAC, MG 30 E 426.

50. Reminiscences in D. S. O'Brien Papers, NAC, MG 30 E 426. (O'Brien claimed three escape attempts and succeeded in 1918.)

51. Private Thomas Hogarth claimed reparations for two teeth knocked out by an Uhlan lance on the march to Roulers. See McDougall, *Maltreatment*, p. 276.

52. Anderson, *I, That's Me*, p. 83.

53. Ibid., pp. 84–85; William Quinton, "Twenty Months," NAC, MG 30 E 162, pp. 1–2.

54. O'Brien ms. p. 3, NAC, MG 30 E 426.

55. Wilken, "Short Record," p. 7.

56. Jackson, *Prisoners*, p. 11. A year later, Captain H. Champion and his observer fared similarly at Courtrai: "The smell of humanity in the cell was nauseating. The basin had not been emptied for days. It was not long before I discovered that I was not the only occupant of the cell. Their numbers were legion and of three distinct species." Ibid., p. 12.

57. McDougall, *Maltreatment*, p. 39. The matter remained private until he sought reparation for an experience which had obviously affected his physical and mental health. Another Canadian officer, Captain Harold Davis, claimed that he was sent to Strohenmoor, an officers' punishment camp, and subjected to three weeks' solitary confinement because his aircraft carried leaflets—something the Central Powers seemed to regard with special disapproval. Since Davis had been wounded in the buttock by an explosive bullet, this was painful as well as unpleasant. (Ibid., p. 314.)

58. Hauptstadtarchiv Stuttgart, MI/11/BN 800. Copy of remarks made in the course of conversation with the Canadian Brigadier General Victor Williams by Capt. Tettenborn, Grenadier Regiment Queen Olga, 26 June 1916, trans. Stephen Brown. Williams' evidence for Canadian attitudes was based, he claimed, on the preference for referring to the German enemy as "Fritz" rather than "Huns" or "Boche." An attendant German intelligence officer gravely confirmed that these were the words they found in Canadian letters. Having no artillery of its own in June 1916, the 3rd Division was supported by the artillery of a former Indian Army division. The Allied offensive began on July 1 at the Somme, then the juncture between the British and French armies and well to the south of Ypres.

59. In *The Great War, 1914–1918* (London: Routledge & Kegan Paul, 1973), Marc Ferro refers to the intense emotion of German reaction to Britain's unexpected entry into the war. It was an emotion Canadians were soon to encounter from German soldiers and civilians.

60. Scudamore, "Lighter Moments," p. 397.

61. Scott, "Three Years and Eight Months," p. 4 (cited in Mathieson, *Grandfather's War*, p. 231).

62. Pearson, *Princess Pat*, pp. 65–66.

63. McClung, *Three Times and Out*, p. 17–18.

64. Scudamore, "Lighter Episodes," p. 397.

65. Anderson, *I, That's Me*, p. 85.

66. Harry Howland, "Come March With Me," NAC, MG 30, E 204, p. 99.

67. Anderson, *I, That's Me*, p. 84; Pearson, *Princess Pat*, pp. 71–77; McClung, *Three Times and Out*, pp. 20–23; Account of Lieutenant J. E. McClurg, 2nd Battalion, CWRO file, NAC, RG 9 III, vol. 4738, folder 153, file 1.

68. O'Brien ms. p. 3, NAC, MG 30 E 4260. While such a tale seems far-fetched, Gerard recalled reading in an official paper that people in a small town near the Danish border had been fined and imprisoned for improper conduct towards prisoners of war. He assumed that they had been guilty of brutality but discovered from the U.S. consul at Kiel that they had been guilty of passing prisoners food and drink. (Gerard, *Four Years*, p. 166.)

69. G. W. L. Nicholson, *Fighting Newfoundlanders*, pp. 362–63.

70. See McDougall, *Maltreatment*, pp. 54, 141, 193, 206.

71. Anderson, *I, That's Me*, pp. 85–86; Scudamore, "Lighter Episodes," pp. 397–98; Account of Lieutenant McClurg; Thorn, *Three Years a Prisoner*, p. 3. In a *note verbale* of 11 Jan. 1915, Germany had argued: "Since England does not blush to use coloured troops of all races against Germany in the present war, English officers must not be surprised if they are brought into close contact with their comrades in arms." (See Garner, *International Law*, p. 23.) In practice, black internees at Ruhleben were segregated and a special camp at Zossen was reserved for Moslem, Indian, and black prisoners. A large mosque in the centre of the camp, built "at the Kaiser's command," was a feature of German prison camp propaganda. So were photographs of the "racial types" arrayed against Germany by her enemies. See McCarthy, *Prisoner of War*, on the Moslem camp at Zossen-Wunsdorff, which he found "pleasant and agreeable"; see Jackson, *Prisoners*, pp. 130–34.

72. W. F. and M. Chambers, "The Unwilling Guest": unpublished manuscript in the possession of George Chambers, made available to the author, p. 1. Chambers noted that, like the railway cars that carried Canadians troops across France, these were marked for eight horses or forty men.

73. Anderson, *I, That's Me*, p. 87. Thorn, *Three Years a Prisoner*, pp. 3–4.

74. Pearson, *Princess Pat*, p. 81.

75. Howland, who returned to Cologne to spend months at the prison, claimed that the boy was the son of a German soldier and his English wife and was well known to the British sergeants in the prison. (Howland, "March With Me," pp. 224–25.)

76. John Vaughan, *Halifax Herald*, 12 September 1917, in CWRO file, NAC, RG 9 III, vol. 4737, folder 150, file 1; account of Captain A. Crosman, NAC, MG 30 E 36.

III Barbed-Wire Disease

1. See John H. Morgan, *The War Book of the German General Staff Being "The Usages of War on Land"*

Issued by the Great General Staff of the German Army (New York: McBride, Nast & Co., 1915), p. 91; cited in the British *Report on Treatment of Prisoners of War by the Enemy*, Comd. 8988, p. 11.

2. Report of Dr. Karl Ohnesorg, NAC, RG 24, vol. 6993.

3. Gerard, *Four Years*, p. 165.

4. McCarthy, *Prisoner of War*, pp. 73–74; Dr. Ohnesorg, the assistant attaché for prison inspections at the U.S. Embassy, regarded Giessen as a very good camp when he visited at the end of 1915. See Report, n.d., NAC, RG 24, VOL. 6993. See CWRO, P-48-4; NAC, RG 9 III, vol. 1122. (In all, there were 105 "parent camps" by the end of 1916 and 165 by the end of the war, 75 for officers and 89 for other ranks. See McCarthy, *Prisoner of War*, p. 53; Speed, *Prisoners, Diplomats and the Great War*, p. 75.)

5. Inoculation was a common theme among ex-prisoners who approached the Canadian reparations commissioner. See McDougall, *Maltreatment*, p. 43.

6. Journal of an unidentified prisoner, contributed by James Robb (Ottawa: n.p.), p. 2.

7. Vaughan, *Halifax Herald*, 12 Sept. 1917. See also McCarthy, *Prisoner of War*, pp. 51–53.

8. McCarthy, *Prisoner of War*, p. 47.

9. Unlike most Britons and Canadians, who regarded Kitchener as the acme of experience and wisdom, most insiders believed that the secretary of state for War should have been able to win the war and had failed. His departure for Russia cleared the way for the aggressive and successful minister of Munitions, David Lloyd George.

10. Jackson, *Prisoners*, pp. 42–43. Jackson cites the experience of a young rifleman who arrived at Langensalza to find that members of the Brigade of Guards had long since organized his new hut for their benefit. Once they learned that, despite his six-foot height, he was not of their number, he was left to shift for himself.

11. Wilken, "Short Record" and CWRO, NAC, RG 9 III, vol. 4738, file 36-1-w; McCarthy, *Prisoner of War*, pp. 76–86. In contrast, a British prisoner, Ernest Evanson, recalled Minden as the "happiest days of my captivity." A British chaplain (presumably Wilken) preached on Sundays, there was a library, a school, a choir, a band, and congenial work (for a London accountant) in the camp office. It was certainly preferable to the coalmine he faced in March 1917. See Moynihan, *Black Bread*, p. 62.

12. A Canadian medical officer captured at Ypres, unlike those captured at Mont Sorrel in June 1916, was repatriated within a few months.

13. Howland, "March With Me," p. 106.

14. Ibid., p. 24.
15. McCarthy, *Prisoner of War*, described German camps in ch. v, pp. 55 ff. See also McClung, *Three Times and Out*, pp. 34–39.
16. Ibid., pp. 54–55.
17. Ibid., pp. 45–46. (The slogan, widely seen in the early war years, meant "God punish England.")
18. Edwards, *Princess Pat*, p. 92; Vaughan, *Halifax Chronicle*, NAC, RG 24, vol. 2660.
19. McCarthy, *Prisoner of War*, pp. 122 ff.; Garner, *International Law*, p. 21. Garner claimed that the Germans also ignored epidemic tuberculosis after the Irish prisoners had proved recalcitrant. See also Speed, *Prisoners, Diplomats and the Great War*, p. 65.
20. McDougall, *Maltreatment*, case 17899, p. 75; see also *Final Report, 1932*, p. 179, case of Pte. Albert McCluskey, 15th Battalion. Both prisoners were "marked men" for the rest of their captivity, suffering repeated beatings and punishment. Both also suffered after escape attempts. On the Irish Brigade, see *To Make Men Traitors: Germany's Attempt to Seduce Her Prisoners of War* (London: His Majesty's Stationery Office, 1918) and, on a broader scale, Arnold Krammer, "Soviet Propaganda Among German and Austro-Hungarian Prisoners of War in Russia, 1917–1921," in Samuel R. Williamson and Peter Pastor, eds., *Essays on World War I: Origins and Prisoners of War* (New York: Brooklyn College Press, 1983), pp. 239–40.
21. Howland, "March With Me," pp. 134–36.
22. McCarthy, *Prisoner of War*, p. 273.
23. Report of Dr. Karl Ohnesorg, n.d., NAC, RG 24, vol. 6993. Evans reported that, while the Red Cross was normally efficient in providing properly sized clothing for British soldiers, his came three months late, reducing him to rags. See McMullen and Evans, *Out of Hunland*, p. 73. Report of Lt. Col. Claude G. Bryan to Colonel C.A. Hodgetts, 15 Dec. 1917, NAC, RG 9 III, vol. 2922, P-254-33.
24. Speed, *Prisoners, Diplomats and the Great War*, p. 72.
25. Chambers, "Unwilling Guest," p. 2.
26. Ambassador Gerard's expert, Dr. Alonzo Taylor, was a forceful critic and, according to Gerard, "could use the terms calories, proteins etc. as readily as German experts and at a greater rate of speed." (Gerard, *Four Years*, pp. 184–85.)
27. Anderson, *I, That's Me*, p. 90. Private Ashbourne memoir in Reid, *Poor Bloody Murder*, p. 88.
28. O'Brien ms., NAC, MG 30 E 426.
29. Durand, *From Sarajevo to Hiroshima*, ch. I, *passim.*
30. Jackson, *Prisoners*, pp. 62–63.
31. Chambers, "Unwilling Guest," p. 3.

32. Cited by Nicholson, *Fighting Newfoundlanders*, p. 364.
33. McClung, *Three Times and Out*, p. 173.
34. Chambers, "Unwilling Guest," p. 6.
35. Jackson, *Prisoners*, pp. 63–64. On Lady Evelyn, see ibid., p. 68. On prisoners' attitudes: Howland, "March With Me," p. 127. On British policy: Maj. Gen. Sir W. G. Macpherson, Col. Sir W. H. Horrocks, and Maj. Gen. W. W. O. Beveridge, *History of the Great War Based on Official Documents: The Medical Services: Hygiene* (London: HMSO, 1923), vol. II, p. 148.
36. Macpherson, *Medical Services: Hygiene*, vol. II, pp. 148–49; High Commissioner to the Postmaster General (P.E. Blondin), 15 Jan. 1917, Borden Papers, NAC, RLB 1081.
37. Mrs. G. H. Stott to Borden, 3 Nov. 1916, 119415, Borden Papers, NAC, RLB 1081, C–4400.
38. Ibid., extract of letter from Company Sergeant-Major A. E. Thompson, p. 119463.
39. Perley to Postmaster General, 15 Jan. 1917, pp. 1194787 and ff., Borden Papers, NAC, RLB 1081 C-4400. The discrimination between officers and other ranks, a focus for particular fury, was soon dropped. One man with two sons in camps—both architects, one a captain and the other a private—complained that he could feed one while the other could starve. (Ibid., P. J. Watt to Borden, 6 Feb. 1917, p. 119525.)
40. Ibid., Memorandum 8 April 1918, p. 119589; list on p. 119609. Both sides were concerned about the transmission of contraband and the British were also worried lest the very large flow of parcels of food and clothing might help subvert their own blockade of Germany. At the same time, widespread concern about the state of British prisoners gave Germany a pressure point on the British. See Macpherson, *Medical Services: Hygiene*, p. 149.
41. On the management of the parcel system, see Moore, *Maple Leaf's Red Cross*, pp. 115–17.
42. *Canadian Active Service Pay Book*, para. 5 (in Royal Canadian Military Institute, Toronto).
43. Bulkeley to Captain Law, 16 Nov. 1916, NAC, RG 9 III, vol. 30, f. 8-1-48; see also NAC, RG 24, vol. 6993, chap. XIII, p. 12.
44. The British issued four different parcels, ranging from 9,669 to 13,323 in caloric value. Parcel "C" included a tin of bully beef, a tin of salmon, a tin of condensed milk, ¼ lb. of tea, ½ lb. of sugar, a jar of marmite, 4 oz. of chocolate, an 8 oz tin of beef loaf, a 1 lb. suet pudding, 8 oz. of dripping, 4 oz. of Quaker oats, 2 oz. of soap, a tin of baked beans, and a 1 lb. tin of jam. (*Macpherson, Medical Services: Hygiene*, p. 151.)
45. Moore, *Maple Leaf's Red Cross*,

p. 109. See Pearson, *Princess Pat*, pp. 90–91; Gilbert T. Taylor in Mathieson, *Grandfather's War*, pp. 237–38.

46. *Toronto Daily Star*, 14 June 1918.

47. Tony Strachan, ed., *In the Clutch of Circumstances: Reminiscences of Members of the Canadian National Prisoners of War Association* (Victoria: Cappis Press, 1985), p. 200.

48. "A Year in German Military Hospitals," *Saturday Westminster Gazette*, 6 Jan. 1917.

49. Arthur Gibbons, *A Guest of the Kaiser* (Toronto: J. M. Dent, 1919), pp. 122 ff. (Gibbons sought reparations in 1932. McDougall rejected the claim essentially on the grounds of Gibbons's credibility. See *Maltreatment*, pp. 90–91, case 1923.)

50. Private Alexander Clarke, taken at Ypres, sought reparation because his leg had been removed without his permission. Medical evidence showed that the Germans had operated five times to save a badly damaged ankle, that opening a wound to drain it was common surgical practice, and that his treatment had been conscientious. McDougall, *Maltreatment*, pp. 24–25.

51. Ibid., p. 162.

52. Cited in Canadian Bank of Commerce, *Letters from the Front*, vol. 1 (Toronto: Canadian Bank of Commerce, 1919), p. 271.

53. CWRO interrogation reports, Private A. M. Allan, NAC, RG 9 III, D-1, vol. 4737.

54. Statement by Private C. W. Baker, CWRO file, NAC, RG 9 III, vol. 4737, folder 150, file 2; see statement by Lieutenant J. E. McClurg, ibid., vol. 4738, folder 153, file 1. McMullen and Evans, *Out of Hunland*, pp. 57–65, also refer to the combination of roughness and skill McMullen's surgeon demonstrated.

55. Cpl. F. W. Newberry diary, 8 May 1915, 11 May 1915, NAC, MG 30 E 525.

56. McDougall, *Maltreatment*, p. 72.

57. Ibid., pp. 173–74.

58. Ferguson diary. For further experiences in German hospitals, see Douglas, *Captured*, pp. 62–135. For a less benign account see "A Canadian Sergeant" and "A Year in German Military Hospitals," *Sunday Westminster Gazette*, 6 June 1917, though some would dismiss any account printed in wartime as propaganda. McCarthy, *Prisoner of War*, pp. 105–20, comments on health conditions in the German camps, notably Wittenberg, Minden, and Limburg. On plague camp, see Thorn, *Captivity*, pp. 100–01.

59. Account of Captain F. S. Park, NAC, RG 9 III, vol. 3751.

60. Anderson, *I, That's Me*, pp. 87–90; Scudamore, "Lighter Episodes," pp. 400–01; Lt. J. H. Douglas, *Captured*, pp. 144–56, describes other experiences encountered during his wait at Konstanz for transfer to Switzerland. Major Thorn, captured with Scudamore, had a more adventurous time: Thorn, *Three Years a Prisoner*.

61. McCarthy, *Prisoner of War*, p. 272.
62. Anderson, *I, That's Me*, pp. 89–90.
63. In *Letters from the Front*, vol. 1, p. 275.
64. Niemeyer's brother, Karl, commanded the officers' camp at Holzminden. His nineteen pre-war years in the United States earned him the nickname "Milwaukee Bill," but his command of English was imperfect. Holzminden veterans remembered one harangue: "You think, gentlemen, I know nothing of your little plans, but I tell you I know damn all." Since the prisoners were busy with a lengthy tunnel which would allow some twenty-nine of their number to escape, Niemeyer was, in fact, literally correct. See Moynihan, *Black Bread*, p. 105 and Jackson, *Prisoners*, pp. 94, 96.
65. Garner, *International Law*, pp. 8–12.
66. Duguid notes, NAC, RG 24, vol. 6993; Chief Paymaster to Major P. Byng-Hall, 19 Jan. 1916, NAC, RG 9 III, vol. 102, file 10-16-5; A/Paymaster General to Byng-Hall, 23 March 1916, ibid.
67. Moynihan, *Black Bread*, p. 113.
68. Lieutenant Alvin Ferguson, diary (in possession of the author).
69. McCarthy, *Prisoner of War*, pp. 275–78 for regulations at Burg.
70. Jackson, *Prisoners*, p. 51. See also Lt. N. L. Wells in *Letters from the Front*, vol. 1, pp. 274–75.
71. For descriptions of Ingolstadt Fort 9, Holzminden, and Strohen, see Thorn, *Three Years a Prisoner*, pp. 49–94, Lt. Frederick Walthew in *Letters From the Front*, vol. 1, p. 461.
72. McCarthy, *Prisoner of War*, p. 191–92.
73. Jackson, *Prisoners*, p. 77; Gerard, *Four Years*, pp. 168–71.
74. Vaughan, *Halifax Chronicle;* Simmons, *Three Times and Out*, p. 39.
75. McCarthy, *Prisoner of War*, pp. 60–61. See also ibid., pp. 47–48; Pearson, *Princess Pat*, p. 101; Gilbert Taylor in Mathieson, *Grandfather's War*, pp. 237–38.
76. McCarthy, *Prisoner of War*, p. 48.
77. Pearson, *Princess Pat*, p. 101; Gilbert interviewed by Mathieson, *Grandfather's War*, p. 239.
78. A. J. Cleeton cited in Strachan, *Clutch of Circumstances*, p. 192.
79. McDougall, *Maltreatment*, pp. 139–40.
80. Account of Captain F. S. Park, NAC, RG 9 III, vol. 3751.
81. Cited in *Letters from the Front*, p. 322.
82. A more clinical term was "Captivity Neurosis." See Durand, *From Sarajevo to Hiroshima*, p. 45.

IV Labour and Pain

1. Bernadotte Schmidt and Herbert C. Vedeler, *The World in the Crucible, 1914–1919* (New York: Harper &

Row, 1984), p. 698. (German casualty figures were based on numbers of wounded evacuated behind their military formations whereas the British and Canadians included those who were cared for in field hospitals and could expect to return to duty in a few weeks. This affected the prisoners, whose wounds were judged by German standards of triage.)

2. The problems of labour in Germany's wartime economic mobilization, though with slight reference to the role of 1.5–4 million prisoners, is dealt with by Gerald D. Feldman, *Army, Industry and Labor in Germany, 1914–1918* (Princeton: Princeton University Press, 1966).

3. McCarthy, *Prisoner of War*, pp. 136–38.

4. Morgan, *War Book*, p. 93. (Cited in "Treatment by the Enemy," Comd. 8988, p. 11.)

5. He found that he had been given two enormous feather beds. When he found them suffocating and reverted to his blankets and greatcoat, the two young women of the house gratefully retrieved them. Even a prisoner had taken priority over their comfort. (Chambers,"Unwilling Guest," pp. 11–12.)

6. Speed, *Prisoners, Diplomats and the Great War*, p. 77.

7. McCarthy, *Prisoner of War*, p. 178.

8. Cleeton recalled: "We had learned a few wrinkles during some of the wettest and rainiest days on Salisbury Plain about the conditions meted out to prisoners-of-war, that under war conditions prisoners could not be forced to work in German factories that were supplying munitions to the enemy."(Strachan, *Clutch of Circumstances*, p. 195.)

9. McDougall, *Maltreatment*, p. 290.

10. Ibid., p. 61.

11. Ibid., p. 64. The journal of an anonymous soldier echoes Seaman's experience. Men of his party resisted for three weeks, going down the mine but not working, much to the anger of German miners and guards. See *Journal*, pp. 6–15.

12. Chambers, "Unwilling Guest," p. 3.

13. McDougall, *Final Report, 1932*, pp. 154–55.

14. Strachan, *Clutch of Circumstances*, p. 196–97.

15. Ibid., pp. 195–98.

16. Cited in NAC, RG 24, vol. 6993, chap. XIII-12.

17. Wilken, "Short Record," NAC, MG 30 E 33; also RG 9 III, vol. 4738, file 36-1-w.

18. McDougall, *Maltreatment*, p. 157.

19. Ibid., p. 261.

20. Ibid., p. 67.

21. For example, Corporal Fred Clark, who had been recommended for medical repatriation but had to endure eleven more months of drill on clogs until the marching affected his heart. (McDougall, *Further Re-*

port, p. 50.) See also ibid., p. 101, 103–04.

22. McDougall, *Final Report*, p. 67.

23. Ibid., pp. 164–65. His status was restored. See also L/Sgt Ronald Kennedy to OIC Records, CEF, 4 May 1918, NAC, RG 9 III, vol. 2921, asking that ranks be confirmed for two Canadian prisoners whose captivity he had shared. One of them was Cpl. Bruce.

24. McDougall, *Maltreatment*, p. 28. Another of the Giessen "mutineers" was Frederick Whittaker. See reparations commission, *Report*, 1927 (Ottawa: King's Printer, 1928), case 1383. Edwards repeated a different version of the story in his wartime memoirs. See Pearson, *Princess Pat*, pp. 108–38. Punishments varied. William Adair, a thirty-six-year-old former CPR brakeman, refused to do munitions work at Mühleim. He was transferred to farm work but his food parcels were cut off. See CWRO interrogation reports, William Adair, NAC, RG 9 III, D-1, vol. 4737.

25. Ibid., pp. 96–97.

26. McDougall, *Final Report*, p. 130.

27. Ibid., p. 130.

28. McDougall, *Further Report*, p. 48; *Final Report*, p. 182.

29. McDougall, *Maltreatment*, p. 185; *Further Report*, pp. 47–48.

30. McDougall, *Further Report*, p. 132.

31. McDougall, *Further Report*, pp. 47–48; *Final Report*, p. 182.

32. McDougall, *Maltreatment*, pp. 306–07.

33. Ibid., p. 304.

34. Ibid., pp. 154–55.

35. McClung, *Three Times and Out*, pp. 118–19.

36. Pearson, *Princess Pat*, p. 116.

37. McDougall, *Maltreatment*, pp. 69–70.

38. Pearson, *Princess Pat*, pp. 119, 121; McClung, *Three Times and Out;* Pte. John Finlay, 14th Bn. CWRO, NAC, RG 9 III, vol. 4737, folder 150, file 3, identified him as RSM. Want of the Cheshire Regiment. "He sold none of my stuff as far as I am aware but the other men told me of their losses and this is the way I came to know of it."

39. Statement of Pte. William Adair, CWRO, NAC, RG 9.

40. Statement by Gunner W. Hand, ibid., folder 152, file 1.

41. McDougall, *Maltreatment*, pp. 166–67.

42. Ukrainian prisoners in Canadian internment camps complained of many of the same forms of violence from their militia guards, including beatings with rifle butts, kicks, and being tied or chained to trees for not working hard enough. Officers in charge of camps routinely denied the charges, but they did not convince the elderly director of internment operations. See Bohdan Kordan and Peter Melnycky, *In the Shadow of the Rockies: Diary of the Castle Mountain*

Internment Camp (Edmonton: Canadian Institute of Ukrainian Studies Press, 1991), pp. 44, 49–50, 56, and *passim.*

43. Chambers, "Unwilling Guest," pp. 7–8.

44. Ibid., p. 11.

45. For a limited occupations profile of a sample of prisoners, see Appendix B.

46. Chambers claimed that earlier prisoners warned them not to indicate any useful occupation. His group put themselves down as clerks or *Schreiber.* When that was challenged, they described themselves as jockeys, prize-fighters, or, in his case, a musician. At Lichtenhorst, this earned him a place playing piano in the camp orchestra and spared him some of the labour.

47. McDougall, *Further Report*, pp. 170–71; Feldman, *Army, Industry and Labor*, pp. 68 ff.

48. Statement of Private W. H. Johnston, 47th Battalion, CWRO, NAC, RG 9 III, vol. 4737, folder 152, file 2. At the reparations commission, Johnston claimed that 135 prisoners had started the project and only 89 survived the ordeal. (McDougall, *Further Report* , p. 198– 99.) Another Canadian who shared the Nordeney experience was Private John Fogarty, 75th Battalion. See McDougall, *Final Report*, p. 66.

49. McDougall, *Maltreatment*, p. 275.

50. Ibid., p. 301.

51. McDougall, *Final Report*, p. 102.

52. McDougall, *Maltreatment*, pp. 212–13.

53. McDougall, *Final Report*, p. 119. (Like others who made claims for the obvious physical side-effects of their work, Hutchison learned that he had not suffered "maltreatment" in terms of the Versailles treaty.)

54. Robert Younger, *Report on the Employment in Coal and Salt Mines of British Prisoners of War in Germany*, Comd. 958 (London: HMSO, 1918), p. 2.

55. Ibid., p. 3.

56. McDougall, *Maltreatment*, p. 282. In his repatriation statement, McDougall reminded him, O'Brien had admitted that for the eight weeks at the mine he and other Canadians had slipped away to a vacant gallery to sleep and chat until their shift returned to the surface. and that work at the coke oven followed their discovery.

57. Ibid., p. 247.

58. Younger, *Coal and Salt Mines*, p. 3. The British White Paper on German treatment of prisoners of war is in NAC, RG 24, vol. 6993. Evans was one of the prisoners forced to work at Auguste Victoria. The experience helped motivate his four escape attempts. See McMullen and Evans, *Out of Hunland*, pp. 85–92.

59. Moynihan, *Black Bread*, p. 63.

60. McDougall, *Maltreatment*, p. 108.
61. Younger, *Coal and Salt Mines*, p. 4.
62. McDougall, *Final Report, 1931–32*, p. 59.
63. Nicholson, *Fighting Newfoundlanders*, p. 364. Martin was later the Hon. Lt. Col. of the Royal Newfoundland Regiment.
64. Statement by Sergeant W. H. Alldritt, 8th Battalion, CWRO, folder 150, file 1A. See also R. B. Bennett Papers, NAC, MG 26 J, M 1309.
65. Statement of Lance Corporal Haley Jones, CWRO, folder 152, file 2. See also McDougall, *Final Report*, p. 57.
66. On medical treatment, see Haley Jones' statement; McDougall, *Maltreatment*, pp. 238, 288 and *passim;* Younger, *Coal and Salt Mines*, p. 7.
67. McDougall, *Final Report*, pp. 33–34.
68. Ibid., p. 40.
69. Statement by Lance Corporal Haley Jones, 15th Battalion, CWRO, NAC, RG 9 III, vol. 4757, folder 150, file 1.
70. Ibid., pp. 39–40. Lickers received the largest single reparations payment made to any maltreated Canadian prisoner: $3,000. A powerfully built man of twenty-six when he enlisted, he was a semi–paralysed physical wreck when McDougall saw him in 1931. On other cases, see ibid. pp. 150, 182, and, for others, *passim.*
71. Younger, *Coal and Salt Mines*, p. 4.
72. Ibid.
73. McDougall, *Maltreatment*, case 1879, p. 56.
74. McCarthy, *Prisoner of War*, p. 168. McCarthy sympathized with British NCOs at Schneidemühl who were punished for trying to protect sick prisoners from labour *Kommandos.* See ibid., p. 94.
75. Wilken, "Short Record," p. 10.
76. It was, claimed Speed, "a fairly typical working camp." *Prisoners, Diplomats and the Great War*, p. 78.
77. McDougall, *Maltreatment*, pp. 120, 170, 233–34.
78. Sir Robert Younger, *Report on the Treatment by the Enemy of British Prisoners of War Behind the Firing Lines in France and Belgium*, Comd. 8988 (British Parliamentary Papers, 1918), vol. XXVI, Misc. No. 7, April 1918, pp. 12–14.; Garner, *International Law*, p. 44.
79. CWRO, NAC, RG 9 III, vol. 4738, folder 254, file 36-I-M and McDougall, *Further Report*, pp. 186–87. Harry Johnson, also of the 75th, lasted eleven months until he was sent to hospital, too weak and emaciated to work. He recalled heavy work, beatings, and starvation while working under shellfire, building German trenches and gun emplacements. (Ibid., pp. 197–98.)
80. "Canadian Prisoners of War," Lager Wahn to High Commissioner

for Canada, 30 April 1917, P-244-31, NAC, RG 9, vol. 2921; Nicholson, *Fighting Newfoundlanders*, pp. 362–63. CWRO, NAC, RG 9 III, vol. 38, file 36-I-T.

81. McDougall, *Final Report*, p. 112.

82. Ibid., p. 78.

83. McDougall, *Maltreatment*, pp. 200–01. The few Canadians captured during the German March and April offensives in 1918 shared a particularly harsh experience. In both victory and defeat, prisoners felt the impact of German emotion as well as suffering from the lack of food supplies. See Moynihan, *Black Bread*, pp. 141 ff. and Jackson, *Prisoners*, pp. 24–26.

84. Even after the final casualty statistics were compiled, 137 officers and 4,273 other ranks were listed as "missing and presumed dead." Some of them may have been prisoners working behind the German lines who died and were buried in unmarked graves, but almost all of them were men whose bodies were never identified or even found. Their names were eventually recorded on huge monuments such as the Menin Gate at Ypres or the Thiepval tower overlooking the valley of the Somme. See Nicholson, *C.E.F.*, p. 548.

85. Younger, *Prisoners Behind the Lines*, pp. 18–19. An Australian escaper claimed to have seen a large stock of Red Cross clothing and of food parcels near a German headquarters near Lille. Most had been opened and looted and many were addressed to Canadians. (Ibid., p. 22.)

86. CWRO, Statistics of Prisoners, NAC, RG 9 III, vol. 2921, file P-248-33.

87. See Claud Mullins, *The Leipzig Trials: An Account of the War Criminals' Trials and a Study of German Mentality* (London: H. F. and G. Witherby, 1921), pp. 68–81; McDougall, *Further Report*, p. 100 (Private James Hilliard Lacey).

88. Wilken, "Short Record," p. 16.

89. Statements of William Adair, Claude Allan Beesley, CWRO, NAC, RG 9 III, vol. 4737, file 36-I-A and 36-I-B.

90. See Appendix B.

91. McDougall, *Maltreatment*, p. 224.

92. McCarthy, *The Prisoner of War*, pp. 143–46.

V Resistance and Escape

1. For the escape, see Anderson, *I, That's Me*, pp. 129–36.

2. Ibid., p. 137.

3. See Anderson file, Public Archives Record Centre, C-922. In Canadian wartime statistics, no officer escaper was acknowledged. Keeping Anderson in England was, however, not unique; as a matter of policy, no escaped prisoner returned to the front. Anderson finally received the Distinguished Service Order for his exploit, but not before winning another DSO for gallantry at Murmansk against the Bolsheviks in 1918–19.

4. McClung, *Three Times and Out*, pp. 48–85.

5. *Halifax Herald* clipping in RG 24, vol. 6770.

6. See Appendix B.

7. See Appendix A2.

8. For the numbers, see *Report of the Overseas Military Forces of Canada, 1918* (London: n.p., 1919), p. 468. On Britt and Nelson, see McDougall, *Maltreatment*, pp. 140, 250.

9. Nicholson, *Fighting Newfoundlanders*, p. 362. See Corporal S. C. Wood to Officer Commanding, 9 July 1919, Argyll House file, P-260-33, NAC, RG 9 III, vol. 2922. On escapes, see Thorn, *Three Years a Prisoner*, pp. 10–12, 38–42, 68–77; Pearson, *Princess Pat*, pp. 105–40, 159–94; McClung, *Three Times and Out*, pp. 61–77, 124–35, 192–239; Vaughan in *Halifax Herald*, 12 Sept. 1917.

10. See CWRO, NAC, RG 9 III, folders 155–58 and vol. 4739–40, especially folders 156/14, 156/15, and 158/IA.

11. Technically, another Canadian officer, Flight Lieutenant Arnold Chadwick of the RNAS, already mentioned as evading civilian internment, escaped from Belgium after crashing behind German lines. He dressed as a woman and slipped into Holland. However, he had not been made a prisoner.

12. Scudamore, "Lighter Episodes," p. 402; Thorn, *Three Years a Prisoner*, p. 10.

13. Ibid., pp. 10–79 and *passim.*

14. Jackson, *Prisoners*, p. 98.

15. *Letters from the Front*, p. 179. (Sinn Fein was the Irish nationalist movement that had spawned the Easter Rising of 1916.)

16. Jackson, *Prisoners*, p. 95.

17. The main account of the tunnel and the camp is H. G. Durnford, *The Tunnellers of Holzminden with a Side Issue* (Cambridge: Cambridge University Press, 1920), pp. 89–147.

18. Jackson, *Prisoners*, p. 96.

19. Ibid., p. 97.

20. *Letters from the Front*, p. 322.

21. Chambers claims that he was part of a tunnelling exercise at Giessen which had to be abandoned a week before completion because prisoners in his section of the camp were virtually all transferred to Lichtenhorst. (Chambers, "Unwilling Guest," p. 7.) No other report of serious tunnelling has been found.

22. Moynihan, *Black Bread*, pp. 66–68.

23. McDougall, *Maltreatment*, pp. 264–65.

24. McDougall, *Maltreatment*, p. 96.

25. McDougall, *Maltreatment*, p. 318.

26. McMullen and Evans, *Out of Hunland*, pp. 130–33, 178–95, 205–17.

27. Both Edwards and Simmons added to wartime literature with "escape books" by popular writers. Pearson was a former PPCLI sergeant who wrote for the *Toronto Daily Star* from overseas; Nellie McClung was a popular novelist and suffrage reformer. Both authors lent their own distinctive touch, with Edwards portrayed as a tough, indomitable resister while Simmons is allowed to admit occasional despair and anguish. He also encounters a few decent Germans, such as a socialist, while reserving his wrath for the "militarists." See Pearson, *Princess Pat*, pp. 108–38 and *passim;* McClung, *Three Times and Out*, pp. 108–230.

28. *War Book*, p. 94.

29. Hague Convention, Article VIII.

30. *War Book*, p. 95. The Germans also legitimized reprisals as a means of discouraging escape.

31. McClung, *Three Times and Out*, pp. 151–54.

32. Ibid., pp. 165–66. Obviously, allowances must be made for colourful prose, but, quite apart from Germany's critical wartime food shortage, controlled starvation appears to have been a deliberate aspect of penal policy. Since it applied to German soldiers as well as prisoners, authorities complied with the Hague Convention.

33. Pearson, *Princess Pat*, p. 149; McClung, *Three Times and Out*, p. 166.

34. Scudamore, "Lighter Episodes," p. 402. See Evans's experiences in Evans and McMullen, *Out of Hunland*, pp. 134–36; 199–202.

35. Garros owed his fame in air warfare to devising a primitive system that allowed him to fire a machine gun forward without hitting his propellor blades, turning his Morane-Saulnier into the first fighter aircraft. When he was shot down, the Germans discovered and perfected the device. Garros eventually escaped, returned to flying, and was killed. See Wise, *Canadian Airmen and the First World War*, p. 349–50.

36. Major J. E. L. Streight to G.O.C. Canadians, 21 May 1918, NAC, RG 9 III, vol. 2921; Thorn, *Captivity*, pp. 94–95; Scudamore, "Lighter Episodes," p. 402.

37. Ibid.; see also McDougall, *Maltreatment*, pp. 40–41.

38. McDougall, *Maltreatment*, p. 92.

39. McDougall, *Further Report*, p. 59.

40. McDougall, *Maltreatment*, p. 290.

41. McDougall, *Further Report*, p. 191.

42. McDougall, *Maltreatment*, p. 269.

43. Statement of Private Adair, CWRO, NAC, RG 9 III.

44. McDougall, *Maltreatment*, pp. 189, 197.

45. McDougall, *Further Report,* p. 184.

46. McDougall, *Maltreatment,* pp. 85–86.

47. Ibid., pp. 47–48.

48. NAC, RG 9 III, vol. 4737, folder 150, file IA. Alldritt was regarded by his friends in Winnipeg's elite as a man of character and integrity. The YMCA took him back after the war, but his back injury and failing eyesight left him increasingly disabled and he died at the age of fifty-two. R. B. Bennett Papers, pp. 383511–26, NAC, MG 26 J.

49. Moynihan, *Black Bread,* pp. xii, 57.

50. Ibid., p. 316.

51. Ibid., p. 106.

52. Ibid., p. 231.

53. McDougall, *Maltreatment,* p. 224.

54. Alan Beddoes, who had submitted a claim to the reparations commissioner, withdrew it before it could be heard. See McDougall, *Further Report.*

55. McDougall, *Maltreatment,* p. 260.

56. McDougall, *Final Report,* p. 45.

57. McDougall, *Further Report,* p. 96.

58. McDougall, *Maltreatment,* pp. 128, 312.

59. McDougall, *Further Report,* p. 204.

60. CWRO, NAC, RG 9 III, vol. 4739, folders 155–60; McDougall, *Maltreatment,* p. 251.

61. Ibid., p. 292.

62. O'Brien, "Narrative," NAC, MG 30 E 426.

63. Anderson, *I, That's Me,* pp. 17 ff.

64. The British counterpart, Field Punishment No. 1, involved "crucifixion" by tying a soldier to a wagon wheel for similar periods, two hours in the morning and two in the evening. The punishment was introduced in the 1880s to replace the cat-o'-nine-tails.

65. Scudamore, "Lighter Episodes," p. 394. At Parnewinkel, Mervyn Simmons saw how far his German guards could go. The Russians, cadaverous and exhausted, finally rebelled at working seventeen hours a day. Next day, German troops arrived in strength. Other working parties were dispatched until only the Russian resisters remained. Then, as guards spread, the Russians were ordered to run in a circle:

> In an hour they were begging for mercy, whimpering pitifully as they gasped out the only German work they knew—"Kamerad, O Kamerad"—to the NCO who drove them on. They begged and prayed in their own language; a thrust of the bayonet was all the answer they got. Their heads rolled, their tongues protruded, their lips frothed, their eyes were red and scalded—and one fell prostrate at the feet of the NCO, who, stooping over, rolled back his eyelid to see

if he were really unconscious or was feigning it. His examination proved the latter to be the case, and I saw the Commandant's motion to kick the Russian to his feet. This he did with a right good will, and the weary race went on. (McClung, *Three Times and Out*, p. 182.)

66. Howland, "March With Me," pp. 183–97. The dead man, Jack Logan, was the father of six children.

67. Howland claimed that he saw Armstrong only once after the June trial. A Canadian escaper met him at Cellelager and learned his version of the story. Statement of Pte. Langlais, CWRO, file P-52-4, NAC, RG 9 III, vol. 1124.

68. The court martial is described by Howland, ibid., pp. 200 ff. The attested judgement of the court is in HQ 240-1-40, RG 24, vol. 1205. On the American opinion, see ibid., OIC Records to Secretary, Militia Council, 9 Jan. 1917; McCarthy, *Prisoner of War*, pp. 101–03. McCarthy refers to Armstrong as "formerly a student at one of the Canadian Universities, confined for months in solitary confinement in a prison cell, without light, with little ventilation, and with the prospects of a capital sentence being passed upon him with-out aid or comfort from anyone, who could speak his own language." (McCarthy, *Prisoner of War*, pp. 101–02.)

69. Under the German regulations, prisoners were entitled to soap, cleaning materials, and some food items in the standard parcel. Howland, with the customary anti-Semitism of his time, assumed that "Jew-Boy," the officer, was helping himself to what he wanted or could sell. ("March With Me," pp. 211–14.)

70. Ibid., p. 216.

71. Pte. Francis Armstrong, personal file, War Service Records, National Public Records of Canada.

VI GOING HOME

1. *Kriegsgefangene in Deutschland* (Freiberg, Librairie de l'université Otto Geschwande, 1918). By the time this edition of a multilingual pictorial depiction of German camps and their happy inmates appeared, a solution had, in fact, been found. (Among the features of the booklet are a hand-tinted photograph of the mosque at Zossen, captions in English, French, Italian, and Russian, and several pages of faces of German's ethnically diverse prisoners, including Africans, Sikhs, Cossacks, Scots, and a lone Korean. British counterpart propaganda emphasized overweight, elderly, and, increasingly, underaged and undersized German prisoners. See also the weekly *Illustrated War News*.

2. McCarthy, *Prisoner of War*, pp. 136–38.

3. When friends pleaded with Sir Robert Borden to arrange an exchange that would release Davidson Ketchum, General Gwatkin, the chief of the general staff in Ottawa, found the proposal fit for irony: "A youthful student of music, recommended by his landlady, sounds harmless enough, and the Kaiser no doubt would gladly swop him for a German, lusty and aggressive." (Gwatkin to Loring Christie, 5 Jan. 1915, Gwatkin Papers, NAC, MG 30 E 51.)
4. Durand, *From Sarajevo to Hiroshima*, p. 52.
5. On policy for exchanges, see Carson file, vol. 32, file 8-1-80, NAC, RG 9 III.
6. Durand, *From Sarajevo to Hiroshima*, p. 56; See Appendix A. (Numbers repatriated before August include those released from internment in Switzerland.) Alexander Clarke, 10th Battalion, was repatriated through Holland on August 8, 1916, with an amputated right leg. (McDougall, *Maltreatment*, case 1677, pp. 24–25.) However, at least one other Ypres prisoner, Richard Codresco of the PPCLI, also an amputee, was repatriated on August 24, 1915, before the agreement was signed. See ibid., p. 155.
7. See Strachan, *Clutch of Circumstances*, p. 199.
8. Duguid notes, Chapter XIII-12, NAC, RG 24, vol. 6993.
9. Speed, *Prisoners, Diplomats and the Great War*, pp. 33–35. McCarthy, *Prisoner of War*, pp. 252–62.
10. Extract from Despatch by Secretary of State for Foreign Affair . . . 25 March 1916, NAC, RG 24, vol. 6993. Ibid., Terms of British–German Agreement; Garner, *International Law*, p. 55.
11. Douglas, *Captured*, p. 153.
12. Scudamore, "Lighter Episodes," pp. 405–07.
13. Report of Lt.-Col. Claude Bryan, 15 December 1917, NAC, RG 9 I, vol. 2922, file P-254-33.
14. Jackson, *Prisoners*, p. 79. Douglas, *Captured*, p. 179.
15. Ussher complained about the cost of keeping his wife in Switzerland and argued that the five-pound monthly advance officers received should be supplementary to his pay. The war ended before his request could be addressed. (Ussher to Major Hume Blake, 14 Dec. 1918, NAC, RG 9 III, vol. 1921, file P-243-33.)
16. McClurg's wife was one of those able to join her husband in Switzerland. (Douglas, *Captured*, p. 168.) On McClurg, see CWRO, NAC, RG 9 III, vol. 4738, file 36-1-MC.
17. Ibid., p. 70.
18. The subject is dealt with in the author's *A Peculiar Kind of Politics: Canada's Overseas Ministry in the First World War* (Toronto: University of Toronto Press, 1982) and, more narrowly, in "Junior but Sovereign

Allies: The Transformation of the Canadian Expeditionary Force, 1914–1918," in Norman Hillmer and Philip Wigley, *The First British Commonwealth* (London: Frank Cass, 1980), pp. 56–67.

19. Report of Lt.-Col. Claude G. Bryan to Colonel C. A. Hodgetts, 15 Dec. 1917, NAC, RG 9 III, vol. 2922, file P-254-33.

20. Borden to Duke of Devonshire, 12 Jan. 1918, Borden Papers, RLB 4411, NAC, MG 26 H, p. 130227.

21. "An Agreement between the British and German Government concerning Combatants and Civilian Prisoners of War," 2 July 1917, Comd. 8590, Misc. no. 12, NAC, RG 9 III, vol. 2922, file P-254-35. On numbers, see Appendix B, Table B1, and RG 9 III, vol. 2921, file P-249-33.

22. Not completely. On a farm labour commando, the German corporal in charge amused himself by performing amateur surgery on Blake's ringworm scars, leaving him with a nasty set of infections that hastened his exchange but remained with him long after his release. (McDougall, *Maltreatment*, p. 153.)

23. Walter Long to the Governor General, 13 May 1918, Borden Papers, OC 261, NAC, MG 26 H, p. 29288; Borden to Béland, 14 May 1918, Borden Papers, NAC, MG 26 H, p. 29288.

24. Finnemore interview in Mathieson, *Grandfather's War*, p. 241.

25. Major P. Byng-Hall to Sir R. E. W. Turner, 12 April 1918, NAC, RG 9 III, vol. 2921.

26. Borden called his threat. McCuaig's son was exchanged to Holland in 1918 and became senior Canadian officer when Byng-Hall was repatriated to England. See Clarence J. McCuaig to Borden, 8 Sept. 1916, Borden Papers, OC 261(1), pp. 29062 and *passim.*

27. RG 9 III, vol. 94, file 10-12-59X Keith Munro to Grace Munro, 16 May 1918, enclosed with Frank A. Keefer MP to Kemp, 20 July 1918, Overseas File, NAC, RG 9 III, vol. 94, file 10-12-59X.

28. Kemp to Ferguson, 14 March 1918, Kemp Papers, NAC, RG 9 III, vol. 94, file 10-12-59X. See also J. Pitblado to Kemp, 25 Jan. 1918, ibid.

29. Evelyn Rivers Bulkeley to Borden, 31 May 1918, Borden Papers, OC 267, NAC, MG 26 H.

30. Speed, *Prisoners, Diplomats and the Great War*, pp. 38–41; "Memorandum on Exchanges," Borden Papers, OC 267; Garner, *International Law*, p. 56.

31. *Report of the Overseas Military Forces of Canada*, p. 465.

32. *Letters from the Front*, p. 270.

33. McDougall, *Further Report*, pp. 117–18.

34. Meighen to Kemp, 16 June 1918, Kemp Papers, NAC, RG 9 III, vol. 94. The MP he refers to as

"Anderson" was Major G. W. Andrews, MP for Winnipeg Centre. His son, Lieutenant G. F. Andrews, 8th Battalion, had been captured at Ypres in 1915.

35. W. R. Plewman, *Toronto Daily Star*, 14 June 1918.

36. H. B. Warner to Secretary, High Commissioner for Canada, 19 June 1918, Borden Papers, OC 267, NAC, MG 26 H.

37. Report of Major Hume Blake, "Visit of investigation of condition of Canadian Prisoners of War Interned in Holland," Oct. 1918, NAC, RG 9, vol. 94, *Report of the OMFC*, pp. 465–67.

38. Report of Major Hume Blake, RG 9 III, vol. 94, OS file 10-12-59. (The War Office was shocked that Canadians would not want to accompany their British comrades to Leeuwarden. "We have hitherto always regarded prisoners of war from whatever part of the Empire they came, as British prisoners of war, without any measure of differentiation," H. J. Creedy complained to Kemp on Nov. 2, 1918. Ibid.)

39. Lt. Col. Gerald Birks to Kemp, 29 Oct. 1918, ibid. (Birks had agreed to the hut in a letter on Oct. 19, soon after returning from Holland with Blake, but presumably his YMCA colleagues had given him second thoughts.)

40. Among the casualties in the Canadian corps during the "Hundred Days" were 317 additional prisoners of war. (NAC, RG 9 III, vol. 2921, file P-250-33.)

41. Chambers, "Unwilling Guest," p. 16.

42. According to Speed, 576,000 of 937,000 non-Russian prisoners were repatriated by the end of December. (*Prisoners and Diplomats in the Great War*, p. 176.)

43. Statement by Private William Bouvier, 16th Highlanders, CWRO, NAC, RG 9 III, vol. 4737, folder 150, file 2; statement by Gunner W. Hand, op. cit.

44. Jackson, *Prisoners*, p. 120.

45. McDougall, *Maltreatment*, p. 109.

46. McDougall, *Further Report*, case 2759.

47. McDougall, *Maltreatment*, p. 278.

48. Ibid., p. 291.

49. Statement of Private Claude Beesley, CWRO, NAC, RG 9 III, D-1, file 4737.

50. Ferguson diary, 7 Dec. 1918. (The German revolutionaries were told that German officers imprisoned in Russia had sided with Russian officers during the 1917 revolution. See Jackson, *Prisoners*, p. 118.)

51. Chambers, "Unwilling Guest," p. 16.

52. See CWRO, NAC, RG 9 III, vol. 4737, folder 150, file 1; *Report of the OMFC*, p. 457; Moore, *Maple Leaf's Red Cross*, p. 123.

53. Statistics are found in NAC, RG 9, vol. 1921, file P-248-33, and leave an untidy statistical miscellany of eighteen officers and twenty-five other ranks. Canadian prisoner-of-war statistics added to their inevitable imperfections by treating officers and other ranks completely separately and sometimes on different dates.

VII Afterwards

1. Private John Cooke sued the Department of National Defence for $3,225 for pay (and accumulated interest) withheld because he was suspected of deserting to the enemy during the Passchendaele offensive. See McDougall, *Further Report*, p. 55.

2. Though not in the case of a small number of prisoners suspected of deserting to the enemy. See McDougall, *Further Report*, p. 53.

3. Captain E. J. Thomas to Lt. Col. N. F. Parkinson, 17 Dec. 1918, NAC, RG 9 III, vol. 4737, folder 150, file 1.

4. Ibid., Thomas to Blake, 9 Dec. 1918.

5. Ibid., Thomas to Lt. Col. N. F. Parkinson, 17 Dec. 1919.

6. Treaty of Versailles, Articles 231, 232.

7. The *Llandovery Castle* was torpedoed on June 27, 1918, while returning to England. Survivors were machine-gunned in the water. Of the crew and medical staff of 258, only 24 survived. All 14 Canadian nursing sisters on board were lost. (Nicholson, *C.E.F.*, p. 398n.)

8. Mullins, *The Leipzig Trials*, p. 205 and *passim.*

9. Canada, *Sessional Papers*, 185, 1916, "Recommendations of the Pensions and Claims Board, C.E.F. as to Pensions and Other Matters," p. 45.

10. The MHC and the BPC and their policies are described in Desmond Morton and Glenn Wright, *Winning the Second Battle: Canadian Veterans and the Return to Civilian Life, 1915–1930* (Toronto: University of Toronto Press, 1987), chapters 2 and 3.

11. Canada, House of Commons, *Debates*, 10 April 1918, p. 613.

12. Morton and Wright, *Winning the Second Battle*, pp. 142–53 and *passim.*

13. Report of Dr. J. P. S. Cathcart in McDougall, *Maltreatment*, p. 15. Of 309 reparations claimants whose postwar occupational careers were traced, one, Arthur Gibbons, had served as a national official with the Canadian Legion. In his wartime book, *A Guest of the Kaiser*, Gibbons had aroused sympathy and horror by his claim that a German surgeon had deliberately twisted and set his wounded leg so the foot pointed backward. See McDougall, *Maltreatment*, case 1923, pp. 90–91.

14. Dahn D. Higley, *O.P.P.: The History of the Ontario Provincial Police Force* (Toronto: Queen's Printer, 1984), pp. 128–30.

15. Morton and Wright, *Winning the Second Battle*, p. 163. *The Veteran*, 17 March 1922.

16. Cited by Mathieson, *Grandfather's War*, p. 236; on his prison camp experiences, see Conn Smythe, *If You Can't Beat 'Em in the Alley* (Toronto: McClelland & Stewart, 1981), pp. 62–66.

17. Though not impossible. See Appendix A.

18. McDougall, *Maltreatment*, p. 40.

19. Ibid., pp. 125, 141.

20. Ibid., pp. 139–40.

21. James Friel, *The Report of the Royal Commission . . . to investigate and report upon all claims which may be submitted to the Commission for the purpose of determining whether they are within the First Annex to Section 1 of Party VIII of the Treaty of Versailles, and the fair amount of such claims and for the return of sequestrated property in necessitous cases. 14 December 1927*, vol. 1 (Ottawa: King's Printer, 1928), pp. 5–18.

22. Ibid., case 1421, vol. 2, pp. 552–54.

23. Ibid., vol. 2, pp. 541–42; 532–35; 510–11; 534.

24. Ibid., pp. 501–39 and *passim*.

25. *Canadian Annual Review*, 1928–29, p. 64.

26. Canada, House of Commons, *Debates*, 14 Feb. 1929.

27. *Canadian Who's Who* and other sources.

28. McDougall granted the claimants compensation for relatives lost in the massacres, but, unlike the Paris Committee which endeavoured to set international standards, he did not support a property claim. See Errol McDougall, *Reparations, 1930–31: Special Report Upon Armenian Claims* (Ottawa: King's Printer, 1931).

29. C. H. Cahan to R. B. Bennett, 15 Jan. 1932, Bennett Papers, p. 383319, NAC, MG 26 H.

30. NAC, RG 14, D 2, vol. 222, file 100, case 1700.

31. His judgement was not infallible. In the case of the schooner *Gypsum Queen*, he accepted the evidence of the owner and of Senator Hance Logan that the ship had been torpedoed off Ireland and granted $70,000. A subsequent royal commission proved that the schooner had been wrecked off the coast of Ireland and that the Liberal senator from Nova Scotia had pocketed half the award for his services. Logan's senate career continued. See *Report of the Royal Commission on the Gypsum Queen* (Ottawa, 1933).

32. Errol McDougall, *Reparations, 1930–31: Supplementary Report* (Ottawa: King's Printer, 1931), p. 3.

33. See Appendix B.

34. Scudamore, "Lighter Episodes," p. 394. On McDougall's view of Scudamore, see *Maltreatment*, p. 88.
35. Cathcart Report in McDougall, *Maltreatment*, p. 14.
36. Ibid., case 2185, p. 262; Howland, "March With Me," pp. 337–38, NAC, MG 390 E 204.
37. McDougall, *Maltreatment*, case 1855, pp. 42–43.
38. Ibid., case 1854, pp. 34–35.
39. McDougall, *Further Report*, p. 189.
40. Ibid., case 1997, p. 128.
41. McDougall, *Maltreatment*, case 1752, p. 28.
42. Ibid., case 2049, pp. 168–69.
43. Ibid., case 2150, p. 245.
44. Ibid., case 1846, pp. 34–35. (McDougall had already noted that no reference to the torture or to Richthofen appeared in the flyer's repatriation report.)
45. Petition of Maltreated Prisoners Regarding Reparation Claims, Bennett Papers, M-1309, NAC, MG 26 H, p. 382884; W. H. Sharpe to Miss A. E. Miller, 15 Sept. 1932, ibid., p. 383404.
46. McDougall, *Final Report*, p. 56. Another ex-prisoner who refused to claim reparations was William Alldritt. Friends discovered in January 1933 that he was going to lose his YMCA job because of physical debility and increasing blindness and persuaded him to submit a claim. Whether or not the government would have considered the claim became moot when Alldritt died in March 1933. See W. E. Davidson to C. H. Cahan, 21 Feb. 1933, Bennett Papers, p. 383504 and ff.
47. McDougall, *Final Report*, p. 6. (The date of the ratification of the Treaty of Versailles marked the official end of the war.)
48. Though Richard Speed does his best to offer one that is only a little softer than I might endorse. See *Prisoners and Diplomats in the Great War*, p. 63.

Bibliography

Books and Articles

Anderson, Lt. Col. Peter. *I, That's Me: Escape from German Prison Camp and Other Adventures.* Ottawa: Bradburn Printers, n.d.

Band, I. *Des Kriegsgefangenen Haltung and Schicksal in Deutschland.* Berlin: Verlag für Politik und Wirtschaft, 1921.

Béland, Henri-Severin. *My Three Years in a German Prison.* Toronto: Briggs, 1919.

Bird, W. R. *And We Go On.* Toronto: Hunter Rose, 1930.

Canadian Bank of Commerce. *Letters from the Front, 1914–1919.* Toronto: Canadian Bank of Commerce, 1919.

Cohen, Israel. *The Ruhleben Prison Camp: A Record of Nineteen Months' Internment.* London: Methuen, 1917.

Cohen-Portheim, Paul. *Time Stood Still: My Internment in England.* London: Duckworth, 1931.

Cruttwell, C. R. M. F. *A History of the Great War, 1914–1918.* 2nd ed. Oxford: Clarendon, 1936.

Dancocks, Daniel G. *In Enemy Hands: Canadian Prisoners of War, 1939–45.* Edmonton: Hurtig, 1983.

Dennett, Carl P. *Prisoners of the Great War.* Boston: Houghton, Mifflin, 1919.

Doegen, Wilhelm. *Kriegsgefangene Völker.* Berlin: Verlag für Politik und Wirtschaft, 1921.

Douglas, J. H. *Captured: Sixteen Months as a Prisoner of War.* Toronto: McClelland, Goodchild & Stewart, 1918.

Duguid, A. F. *Official History of the Canadian Forces in the Great War, 1914–1919.* General Series, vol. 1. Ottawa: King's Printer, 1938.

Durand, André. *From Sarajevo to Hiroshima: History of the International Red Cross.* Geneva: Henri Dunant Institute, 1978.

Durnford, H. G. *The Tunnellers of Holzminden with a Side Issue.* Cambridge: Cambridge University Press, 1920.

Dwinger, Edwin Erich. *Mon journal de Sibérie, 1915–1918 dans les camps des prisonniers.* Paris: Payot, 1930.

Feldman, Gerald. *Army, Industry and Labor in Germany, 1914–1918.* Princeton, N.J.: Princeton University Press, 1966.

Forsythe, David P. *Humanitarian Politics: The International Committee of the Red Cross.* Baltimore: Johns Hopkins University Press, 1977.

Garner, James Wilford. *International Law and the World War.* Vol. 2. London: Longmans, Green & Co., 1920.

Gerard, James. *My Four Years in Germany.* New York: George Doran, 1917.

Gibbons, Sgt. Arthur. *A Guest of the Kaiser: The Plain Story of a Lucky Soldier.* Toronto: J. M. Dent, 1919.

Golovine, N. N. *The Russian Army in World War 1.* New York: Archon Books, 1964.

Grotius, Hugo. Translated by A. C. Campbell. *The Rights of War and Peace, Including the Law of Nature and of Nations.* London and New York: W. Walter Dunne, 1901.

Hay, Malcolm Vivian. *Wounded and a Prisoner of War.* New York: George Doran, n.d. [1917].

Hennebois, Charles. *In German Hands: The Diary of a Severely Wounded Prisoner.* London: Heinemann, 1916.

Jackson, Robert. *The Prisoners, 1914–18.* London: Routledge, 1989.

Keith, Eric A. *My Escape from Germany.* London: Nisbet & Co., n.d. [1918].

Kerr, W. D. B. "Historical Literature on Canada's Participation in the Great War," *Canadian Historical Review* 14 (December 1933); 15 (June 1934); 16 (June 1935).

Ketchum, J. Davidson. *Ruhleben: A Prison Camp Society.* Toronto: University of Toronto Press, 1965.

Koch, Rudolf. *Das Kriegsgefangenerlager Sigmundsherberge, 1915–1919.* Dissertationen der Universität Wien, 1981. no. 181.

Krammer, Arnold. "Soviet Propaganda Among German and Austro-Hungarian Prisoners of War in Russia, 1917–1921." In *Essays on World War 1,* edited by Williamson and Pastor (see below).

Kriegsgefangene in Deutschland. Freiberg: Librairie de l'université Otto Geschwende, 1918.

Lee, Joseph. *Captive at Carlsruhe and Other German Prison Camps.* London: John Lane, The Bodley Head, 1920.

Mathieson, William D. *My Grandfather's War: Canadians Remember the First World War, 1914–1918.* Toronto: Macmillan, 1981.

McCarthy, Daniel J. *The Prisoner of War in Germany: The Care and Treatment of the Prisoner of War with a History of the Development of the Practice of Neutral Inspectorate.* New York: Moffatt, Yard & Co., 1918.

McClung, Nellie. *Three Times and Out as told by Private M. C. Simmons.* Toronto: Thomas Allen, 1918.

MacLeod, J. N. *A Pictorial Record and Original Muster Roll of the 29th Battalion,* C.E.F. Vancouver: R. P. Latta, 1919. [Account by Capt. H. J. Biggs.]

McMullen, Fred and Jack Evans. *Out of the Jaws of Hunland: The Stories of Corporal Fred McMullen, Sniper, and Private Jack Evans, Bomber, Canadian Soldiers Three Times Captured and Finally Escaped from German Prison Camps.* Toronto: William Briggs, 1918.

MacPherson, W. G., W. H. Horrocks, and W. W. O. Beveridge. *History of the Great War Based on Official Documents: Medical Services: Hygiene of the Great War.* Vol. 2. London: His Majesty's Stationery Office, 1923.

Moore, Mary M. *The Maple Leaf's Red Cross: The War Story of the Canadian Red Cross Overseas.* London: Skeffington & Son, 1919.

Morgan, John H., ed. *The War Book of the German General Staff, Being "The Usages of War on Land" Issued by the Great General Staff of the German Army.* New York: McBride, Nast & Co., 1915.

Morton, Desmond. *A Peculiar Kind of Politics: Canada's Overseas Ministry in the First World War.* Toronto: University of Toronto Press, 1982.

—— and Glenn Wright. *Winning the Second Battle: Canadian Veterans and the Return to Civilian Life, 1915–1930.* Toronto: University of Toronto Press, 1987.

Moynihan, Michael. *Black Bread and Barbed Wire: Prisoners in the First World War.* London: Leo Cooper, 1978.

Mullins, Claud. *The Leipzig Trials: An Account of the War Criminals' Trials and a Study of German Mentality.* London: H. F. and G. Witherby, 1921.

Nicholson, G. W. L. *Canadian Expeditionary Force, 1914–1919: The Official History of the Canadian Army in the First World War.* Ottawa: Queen's Printer, 1962.

——. *The Fighting Newfoundlanders: A History of the Royal Newfoundland Regiment.* London: Thos. Nelson, 1964.

Pearson, George. *The Escape of a Princess Pat: Being the Full Account of the Capture and Fifteen Months' Imprisonment of Corporal Edwards of the Princess Patricia's Canadian Light Infantry and His Final Escape from Germany into Holland.* New York: George Doran, 1918.

Phillipson, Coleman. *International Law and the Great War.* London: T. Fisher Unwin, 1916.

Reid, Gordon, ed. *Poor Bloody Murder: Personal Memoirs of the First World War.* Oakville: Mosaic Press, 1980.

Russenholt, E. S. *Six Thousand Canadian Men: Being the History of the 44th Battalion, Canadian Infantry, 1914–1919.* Winnipeg: De Montfort Press, 1932.

Scott, James Brown. *The Hague Peace Conferences of 1899 and 1907.* 2 vols. Baltimore: Johns Hopkins University Press, 1909.

——. *The Hague Conventions and Declarations of 1899 and 1907 Accompanied by Tables of Signatures, Ratifications and Adhesions of the Various Powers and Texts of Reservations.* 3rd ed. New York: Oxford University Press, 1918.

——. *Documents Relating to the Program of the First Hague Peace Conference Laid Before the Conference by the Netherlands Government.* Oxford: Clarendon Press, 1921.

Scott, Peter T. "Captive Labour: The German Companies of the B.E.F., 1916–1920," *Army Quarterly and Defence Journal* 110, no. 3 (London, 1980).

Scudamore, Major T. M. *Lighter Episodes in the Life of a Prisoner of War.* Aldershot: Gale & Polden, 1933. From articles published in the *Canadian Defence Quarterly* 7, no. 3 (1930).

Sergeant, A. [pseud.] "A Year in German Military Hospitals," *Saturday Westminster Gazette*, 6 January 1917.

Smythe, Conn. *If You Can't Beat 'Em in the Alley.* Toronto: McClelland & Stewart, 1981.

Speed, Richard. *Prisoners, Diplomats and the Great War: A Study in the Diplomacy of Captivity.* New York, Greenwood [1990].

Strachan, Tony, ed. *In the Clutch of Circumstances: Reminiscences of Members of the Canadian National Prisoners of War Association.* Victoria: Cappis Press, 1985.

Thorn, Major J. C. *Three Years a Prisoner in Germany: The Story of Major J. C. Thorn, A First Canadian Contingent Officer who was Captured by the Germans at Ypres on April 24th, 1915, Relating His Many Attempts to Escape (Once Disguised as a Widow) and Life in

Various Camps and Fortresses with Illustrations. Vancouver: Cowan and Brockhouse, 1919.

Tippett, Maria. *Art in the Service of War: Canada, Art and the Great War.* Toronto: University of Toronto Press, 1984.

Williamson, Samuel R. and Peter Pastor, eds. *Essays on World War I: Origins and Prisoners of War.* Brooklyn, N.Y.: Brooklyn College Press, 1983.

Wilson, Trevor. *The Myriad Faces of War: Britain and the Great War, 1914–1918.* Cambridge: Polity Press, 1986.

Wise, S. F. *Canadian Airmen and the First World War: The Official History of the Royal Canadian Air Force,* Vol. I. Toronto: University of Toronto Press, 1980.

Unpublished Manuscripts and Documentary Collections

NATIONAL ARCHIVES OF CANADA:

Bennett, Richard Bedford. Papers. Manuscript Group 26 K.

Borden, Robert L. Papers. Manuscript Group 26 H.

Crosman, Capt. A. E. Papers. Manuscript Group 30 E 36.

Department of Militia and Defence. Record Group 9.

Department of National Defence. Record Group 24.

Gosford, Thomas William. Papers. Manuscript Group 30 E 475.

Howland, Harry. "Come March With Me." Manuscript Group 30 E 204.

Kemp, Edward Albert. Papers. Manuscript Group 27 III.

Maheux, Francis Xavier. Papers. Manuscript Group 30 E 297.

Newberry, F. W. Papers. Manuscript Group 30 E 525.

O'Brien, David Stephen. Papers. Manuscript Group 30 E 426.

Quinton, William. "Two Years in Germany." Manuscript Group 30 E 162.

Scott, George. "Three Years and Eight Months in a German Prison." Manuscript Group 30 E 28.

Ussher, Lt. Col. J. Papers. Manuscript Group 30 E 376.

Wilken, Major Gillies. Papers. Manuscript Group 30 E 33.

AUTHOR'S COLLECTION:

Chadwick, Arnold. Scrapbooks.

Chambers, W.F. and M. "The Unwilling Guest."

Ferguson, Alvin.

Williams, General Victor. Interrogation of. Hauptstadtarchiv Stuttgart, MI/LL BN500.

PUBLISHED REPORTS:

Reports of the Department of Pensions and National Health.

Reports of the Department of Soldiers' Civil Re-establishment.

Report of the Ministry of Overseas Military Forces of Canada, 1918. London: n.p., 1919.

Report on the Employment in Coal and Salt Mines of British Prisoners of War in Germany. (Justice Robert Younger) Comd. 9150, 2 November 1918. London: His Majesty's Stationery Office, 1918.

Report on the Treatment by the Enemy of British Prisoners of War Behind the Firing Lines in France and Belgium. Comd. 8988, 1918. London, HMSO, 1918.

Report on the Treatment by the Germans of Prisoners of War Taken During the Spring Offensives of 1918. (Justice Robert Younger) Comd. 9106 Misc. (7) 1918. London: HMSO, 1918.

Royal Commission . . . to investigate and report upon all claims which may be submitted to the Commission for the purpose of determining whether they are within the First Annex to Section 1 of Part VIII of the Treaty of Versailles and the fair amount of such claims, and the return of sequestrated property in necessitous cases. (James Friel, Commissioner) Report, 14 December 1927. Ottawa: King's Printer, 1928.

Royal Commission for the Investigation of Illegal Warfare Claims and for the Return of Sequestered Property in Necessitous Cases. (Errol M. McDougall, Commissioner) Interim Report. Ottawa: King's Printer, 1931. *Supplementary Report*. Ottawa: King's Printer, 1931. *Special Report upon Armenian Claims*. Ottawa: King's Printer, 1931. *Report of the Commission on Reparations, 1930–1931: Maltreatment of Prisoners of War*. Ottawa: King's Printer, 1932. *Reparations, 1932: Further Report*. Ottawa: King's Printer, 1933. *Reparations, 1932: Final Report*. Ottawa: King's Printer, 1933.

Statistics of the Military Effort of the British Empire. London: HMSO, 1923.

Index